Voices from Jutland

This book is dedicated to my wife, Anne, who has to tolerate my obsession with naval and military history.

Voices from Jutland

A Centenary Commemoration

Jim Crossley

Pen & Sword
MARITIME

First published in Great Britain in 2016 by
Pen & Sword Maritime
an imprint of
Pen & Sword Books Ltd
47 Church Street
Barnsley
South Yorkshire
S70 2AS

ISBN 978 1 47382 371 6

Typeset in Ehrhardt by
Mac Style Ltd, Bridlington, East Yorkshire
Printed and bound in the UK by CPI Group (UK) Ltd,
Croydon, CRO 4YY

Pen & Sword Books Ltd incorporates the imprints of Pen & Sword
Archaeology, Atlas, Aviation, Battleground, Discovery, Family
History, History, Maritime, Military, Naval, Politics, Railways, Select,
Transport, True Crime, and Fiction, Frontline Books, Leo Cooper,
Praetorian Press, Seaforth Publishing and Wharncliffe.

For a complete list of Pen & Sword titles please contact
PEN & SWORD BOOKS LIMITED
47 Church Street, Barnsley, South Yorkshire, S70 2AS, England
E-mail: enquiries@pen-and-sword.co.uk
Website: www.pen-and-sword.co.uk

Contents

Chapter One

The Rivals

There is one obvious question about the Battle of Jutland – 'Who won?' Looking back now, almost a hundred years after the battle, the answer is clear. The victors were the British. They achieved exactly what they needed from Jutland, although this was not apparent at the time. Their imperative was to maintain status quo in the North Sea. The Royal Navy's stranglehold on maritime traffic to and from northern Europe enabled Britain to tighten the distant blockade of Germany, denying her imports of strategic materials, food and fertiliser, eventually leading to starvation, the downfall of the Kaiser's regime and total victory for the Allies. Dominance of the North Sea also ensured that Britain's own maritime trade could continue with little serious interruption from enemy surface vessels. Declaring a British victory however does not imply that the British fought better than their opponents or that they did not make strategic and tactical blunders before and during the battle. Undeniably, the German High Seas Fleet showed itself superior to the British in tactics, training and in the durability of its ships. The men of the Kaiser's High Seas Fleet had much to be proud of; they were the heroes, but they were not the victors.

It has often been argued that British naval strategy in the First World War was mistaken and that the absence of any Trafalgar-like naval victory was due to incompetence and a woeful lack of enterprise on the part of the Admiralty. Supporters of this view point to failures in the Dardanelles, the North Sea and the stubborn refusal to introduce a convoy system until the country was on the brink of disaster. This is not a fair assessment. A dispassionate study of the Admiralty staff's activities and priorities from 1914 onwards shows a steady and logical development of policies that eventually resulted in the collapse of the Kaiser's regime. It is certainly possible to criticize the conduct of senior officers afloat and ashore, but any such criticism needs to take into account the quite amazing revolution in naval technology which had taken place during the course of their professional careers. Trained in the age when sail still dominated naval thinking and wooden ships with broadside muzzle-loading guns were still in first line service, they needed to take an enormous leap forward in their thinking to be ready for naval warfare in 1914. As we shall see, that leap proved impossible for many of them to achieve. Life in the Navy of the Victorian and Edwardian eras had done little to prepare them for it. Insofar as the Royal Navy failed to achieve the dramatic victory at sea which the nation expected in the Great War, the failure was not one of grand strategy, nor was it due to inadequate ship design; it was the result of poor execution by officers who never managed to achieve the skills or technical competence needed to command ships in a twentieth century battle environment. The underlying British strategy however, was sound and it was pursued consistently and purposefully. The dedicated officers and men in the small ships which enforced the blockade, laid and swept mines and protected merchant shipping, ultimately delivered total victory. Significantly, many of these were reserve officers or volunteer members of the Royal Naval Volunteer Reserve (RNVR) and the Royal Naval Minesweeping Reserve (RNMR) or of the Royal Naval Reserve (RNR), not naval professionals.

To understand the thinking of senior naval officers in 1914 we can follow the career of Ned Charlton, scion of an aristocratic but impecunious Roman Catholic family from Durham. Ned joined the Royal Navy in 1878 at the age of twelve. Entry into the service at that time, the time indeed when most of those who would be senior officers in 1916 joined the service, required a boy to pass a rather simple examination in mathematics (Ned prepared for this at a specialist school in Gosport) and much more importantly, to be recommended by a family friend with some influence in official circles. Through the Duchess of Norfolk, Ned's mother had engineered a recommendation for her son from Admiral Sir Hastings Yelverton. In addition to this recommendation the family had to undertake to fix a sum of £50 per year on young Ned to cover essential expenses during his cadetship. Fifty pounds was a considerable sum in those days; it would have been more, for example, than the Nelson family could have afforded a little over a hundred years earlier to get young Horatio into the Navy. The requirement meant, as Admiral Sir Jacky Fisher remarked a little later, that all the commissioned officers in the Navy were drawn from the 'top ten' of the nation; in his opinion an entirely unacceptable situation. He wanted officers selected by ability and not by social status.

Ned was sent to HMS *Britannia* at Dartmouth as a cadet to learn the basics of his chosen calling. The most remarkable event during his cadetship occurred when an officer entered a noisy classroom and Ned got blamed for the indiscipline. Considering himself innocent, he hurled an inkpot at the lad who had accused him, missed and hit Prince George, the future King George V, who as king, reminded him of the incident many years later.

From *Britannia*, Ned was sent as a midshipman to the Mediterranean aboard the new ironclad, HMS *Alexandria* in 1880. *Alexandria* (Captain Lord Walter Kerr) was a novel design of warship, fully rigged and fitted with an 8,500 horsepower engine giving her a speed under power of 14.5 knots. She had her two 11-inch and ten 10-inch guns mounted in a central battery protected by twelve inches of wrought iron armour. Her guns were muzzle loaders, firing projectiles which were made to spin by studs projecting into spiral grooves inside the stubby gun barrels. She represented a stage in the bewilderingly rapid evolution of warships from *Warrior* (1861), an ironclad with her heavy guns arranged for broadside bombardment, to the steel hulled turbine-engined dreadnoughts in service fifty years later.

Alexandria was based at Malta, where Ned was able to call on several aristocratic family connections, and cruised grandly around the Mediterranean eagerly challenging any ship she met in the speed at which she could hoist her yards and sails. Ned resolved to specialize not in gunnery, as was normal for an aspiring young officer, but in torpedoes, then in their infancy. His first taste of action however was to involve making use of *Alexandria's* heavy guns against the shore batteries around the port of Alexandria in 1882. This was the opening of a campaign to put down an Egyptian nationalist movement and secure the Suez Cannel. Egyptian resistance soon crumbled and parties of sailors went ashore to help to patrol the town. Heavy naval guns were landed to support the soldiers and marines. Ned enjoyed himself blowing up a railway line so as to deny its use to the defenders. Playing around with explosives was supposed to be a suitable occupation for a very young torpedo specialist.

This campaign was typical of the sort of skirmish on land that was to be the main operational experience of the Navy in the Victorian era, and it was carried out with daring and efficiency.

No sooner had the action been successfully concluded than Ned was transferred to HMS *Cruiser*, a pure sailing ship with no engine. He was delighted. Like most officers of his time he detested engines, the smoke dirtied the sails, the noise was horrible and the dirty coal spoilt the beauty of the ship. Maybe they might come in useful for driving the ship into action in a calm, but any captain who could not bring his ship into harbour, however narrow and difficult, under sail, was certainly no seaman. His stay in *Cruiser* seems to have been brief as in 1883 he served on another fully rigged barque, the *Neptune*, and in her returned to England for a brief spell of home leave, which he spent with his family, taking the opportunity to disport himself for the first time on the hunting field. In December, he passed his lieutenant's exam with flying colours and was promoted to Acting Sub Lieutenant. That led him on to a period of training on HMS *Vernon*, the Navy's torpedo school, which was to become the main conduit for introducing new weapons and technology into the service.

It was as a full lieutenant that he joined HMS *Rapid* at Cape Town in 1886. *Rapid* was a sloop with a full set of sails and a steam engine, armed with 6-inch guns arranged in the typical broadside fashion. She was designed to project a naval presence in distant outposts and colonies and was a powerful, seaworthy, ocean cruiser, using her engine only on rare occasions when the wind failed her. South Africa was peaceful at the time and *Rapid's* crew grew famous for their 'picnics' and parties ashore. These were punctuated with voyages up the coast to Nigeria and to the Gold Coast where the main and deadly enemies were malaria and various swamp fevers. Anchored off Sierra Leone, the ship had the distinction of being the destination of the first telegram ever sent to the colony. Surviving the local hazards, the sloop's crew were ordered to take her to Australia. Here they arrived on station after a boisterous and rapid passage. This was at the height of the Australian gold rush, which made it difficult for the officers to prevent members of the crew from slipping off to the diggings. At Sydney however, the ship resumed her social functions with hunting parties, balls and endless social engagements. The officers were furious when the formidable Admiral Tyron, on a visit to the Australia Station, prevented them from sailing to Melbourne for the races.

On a trip to the Northern Territories Ned was landed with the job of navigating his ship out of the shallow mouth of Moreton Bay, the regular navigating officer being sick. He was very pleased to have achieved it without mishap. On a visit to New Guinea, *Rapid's* company was ordered to sort out a problem caused by a Chinese fishing boat which had gone aground and whose crew were saved by some seeming friendly natives. They were well looked after and fed for a few days, then were coolly slaughtered for the table. Only the captain managed to escape, and being the holder of a British merchant ship master's ticket, felt free to call on the Royal Navy for help. Ned led a landing party which burnt huts, ring barked coconut trees and destroyed native catamarans, while *Rapid's* artillery bombarded likely patches of jungle. After several more such incidents the ship moved to New Zealand where the hospitality of the locals was overwhelming, then back to Sydney where Ned apparently broke a few hearts before making the long voyage back to England under sail in the *Thalia*.

Back home he was sent to the Royal Naval College at Greenwich, where he struggled with differential calculus, then to *Vernon* for further torpedo training before being given his first command, *Her Majesty's Torpedo Boat 82*, in July 1890. 1892 found him as torpedo officer on a new and revolutionary battleship, HMS *Colossus*. She was the first ship mounted with a new generation of breech loading rifled guns. Breech loading had been tried in the 1860s but had resulted in many fatal accidents due to the fast burning powder bursting the breech mechanism. Now, new slow burning powder allowed a combination of safe breech loading and long rifled barrels, giving the projectiles a higher velocity and better accuracy. *Colossus* was also the first major warship to be built mainly of steel in place of iron. Masts and yards were almost gone and only a token rig remained. Altogether she marked an important stage in the development of warships, but her rate of fire was only about one round in three minutes and maximum accurate range about 2,000 yards. Once again there was stately progress around the Mediterranean until, in 1893, Ned was transferred to HMS *Hood*. *Hood* was another new battleship and marked a further step forward in design. In place of a fortified citadel amidships, she had her 13.5-inch guns mounted in rotating turrets. These were extremely heavy however, making the ship very low in the water and liable to ship waves 'green' over the decks in rough weather. Ned was the ship's navigating officer, as well as being in charge of the torpedoes. He was thankful not to have been with Tyron's squadron, which experienced the disastrous collision between *Victoria*, the flagship, and *Camperdown* in which Tyron himself and 357 officers and men perished. *Victoria* was lost entirely because although the officers on the bridge knew that Tyron's orders placed her on a course which inevitably lead to a collision, because Tyron was the admiral, his orders could not be questioned. Thus blind discipline was the cause of mortal disaster. Ironically, one of the survivors of the wreck was a junior but promising Commander, John Jellicoe. He had not been on the bridge but was confined to bed with a fever. A strong swimmer, he survived and remarked later that the incident had entirely cured his ailment. Unfortunately, it did not cure the Royal Navy of the habit of blind, thoughtless, obedience.

There was more policing and partying, this time mainly in Greek waters. Next followed another spell in England until 1899, when the Boxer Rebellion shook the European community in the Far East, and Ned, now with the rank of Commander, sailed for Hong Kong as second in command of HMS *Orlando*.

Orlando was typical of the ships built in Britain at the time to secure command of even the most distant oceans, but utterly unsuitable for anything like twentieth century warfare. She landed her marines and most of her seamen to help an international force that was pushing its way up towards Peking (Beijing). To his disgust Ned was left behind in command of the ship with a skeleton crew remaining on board instead of marching off to fight on land. He witnessed the gallant action to take the Taku Forts, a very formidable fortification built for the Chinese by the German firm Krupp. Eventually the landing parties achieved their objectives and *Orlando* moved down to Shanghai. The ship had lost ten men killed ashore and fifty-three wounded, including Captain Halliday of the Royal Marines, who received the VC. While she was on station, in the autumn of 1900, *Orlando* was fitted with her first wireless set – a sign of things to come. After two and a half years in China, the latter part spent helping to clear up the mess and establish burial grounds for Britons killed in the fighting, Ned was ordered home via the Canadian Pacific Railway for another spell at *Vernon*, being promoted Captain in 1903. There were, as we shall see later, significant improvements being made to torpedoes at the time, so his choice of specialism put Ned in a good position for advancement. He took advantage of this spell in England to get married and start what was to become a large family.

In 1905 it was back to the Far East, commanding a small flotilla of torpedo boat destroyers (the name was later shortened to 'destroyers'). During his voyage to his new station he saw some of the Russian Baltic fleet on their way to their terrible destiny at Tsushima. The flotilla practised some torpedo tactics and also the highly dangerous technique of destroying enemy mines by 'counter-mining'; essentially bringing a small boat into a minefield and exploding a charge that would cause all the mines in the area to detonate in sympathy. A return to England in 1906 brought him command of a squadron of cruisers acting as depot ships for destroyers, promotion to Commodore and eventually a move to the Admiralty as Assistant Director of Torpedoes. In 1913 he was promoted Rear Admiral at the unusually young age of 48. The outbreak of war saw him as Admiral Commanding Minesweepers. This was a key job as mines were a major threat to shipping, especially in the North Sea. The only British (or German) dreadnought battleship lost during the war, *Audacious*, fell victim to a mine. Jacky Fisher, the First Sea Lord, did not think Ned up to the job, but he survived in it until October 1915, when he was appointed to command the South Africa station.

Charlton's subsequent career need not detain us as he was not at Jutland, however his life as a promising naval officer was typical of the Royal Navy of the time. He was courageous, an excellent leader, an experienced fighter and a superb seaman, but there is no indication that he had any experience of handling, or being part of, a fleet in a major battle practise, or of exercising ships in the sort of high speed fleet manoeuvres and night fighting which had made the victorious Japanese fleet at Tsushima so formidable. German senior officers, distracted by far fewer colonial policing engagements, spent month after month carrying out complex fleet exercises by day and by night in the Baltic. They had few colonial wars to detain them and were able to concentrate hard on gun drills and fleet manoeuvres and on getting the very best out of their ships and men. The Royal Navy, by contrast, spent most of its time showing the flag or landing men and guns to fight ashore. For the

British Army, colonial wars, especially the Boer Wars, were to a great extent
a preparation for the battlefields of France and Flanders and important
lessons were learnt and skills developed. These conflicts could however,
teach the Navy nothing at all about fighting a modern war at sea. True, there
were annual fleet exercises in which the Channel Fleet might be set against
the Mediterranean in an imaginary assault on the Scottish coast, but these
tested the cunning of the senior commanders, not the gunnery of the fleets.
Often they were little more than showpieces for the Press. The Navy was also
plagued by a numbing 'top down' system of management and operations.
Every move, every change of course, even the hanging out of the washing to
dry, had to be authorized by the senior officer present. The notorious Signal
Book contained instructions for every manoeuvre, every evolution which a
fleet might undertake. There was no scope for, or tolerance of, individual
initiative. Worst of all was the appalling standard of gunnery prevalent in
many formations in the Royal Navy. The Mediterranean Fleet for example,
was capable of the most precise station keeping and their ships were
immaculately smart, clean and well maintained, but they seldom attempted
to fire their guns at anything more than 5,000 yards away, and then it was
often a stationary or slow moving target. In the real world a target might
be moving at over thirty knots, twisting and turning and returning fire.
Opposing ships, when war came, would have to be ready to open accurate
fire at 20,000 yards.

All from the same social background, educated in the same schools and
instructed in the same skills, it is little wonder that most senior officers of
the Royal Navy adhered closely to a single, intensely conformist pattern of
behaviour and thinking.

There were of course exceptions. A revolutionary school of thought, led
by Jacky Fisher realized that a navy of heterogeneous battleships and of
cruisers 'too weak to fight and too slow to run away', designed for colonial
wars, would be quite incapable of modern warfare. Son of an obscure colonial
family, relentlessly ambitious and radical in his thinking, Fisher was a rare
maverick in the naval establishment. In command of the Mediterranean Fleet
he ruthlessly drove his ships at full speed and forced them to begin using
their great guns at longer ranges. Captains who did not like the new regime
soon found themselves on the boat home. His high-handed conduct made

him many enemies, and led to a bitter dispute with Admiral Lord Charles Beresford, leader of the traditionalist party. In the end, Fisher emerged victorious. He was able to revolutionize warship technology by commissioning HMS *Dreadnought*, he developed the submarine fleet, reduced the forces in the Mediterranean so as to concentrate his strength to face Germany in the North Sea and got rid of the vast majority of the obsolete cruisers, built for colonial wars. Fisher had some notable supporters, members of the 'fishpond' as they were called, and enjoyed excellent relationships with members of the royal family, but it was a bitter battle to get politicians and the Admiralty to understand that a sea war against Germany, which Fisher rightly predicted, would be a serious business demanding commanders who were professional exponents of twentieth century warfare, not just brave, competent, seamen. War with Germany, he knew, would require leaders who were quick thinking, innovative professionals who could outmanoeuvre, outshoot and out-think a cunning and superbly trained enemy.

Another exception to the general rule of conformity in the service was what became known as 'The Small Ship Navy.' This consisted of officers specializing in submarines, torpedo boats and destroyers. In these little ships there was no room for class divisions and little tolerance of strict rules. Quick thinking, clear decision taking and technical competence mattered much more than conformity. Being in a small ship for a long time was not generally a favoured career path in the Victorian or Edwardian Navy, but once war broke out it was the small ships which saw most of the action and it was from them that the great naval leaders of the future like Cunningham and Tovey were to spring.

As in Britain's wars of the nineteenth century, the strategy in 1914 was one of blockade. Not now close blockade as in the Napoleonic wars, but distant blockade that intercepted any ship, enemy or neutral, carrying goods that might aid Germany or her war effort. The invention of submarines and mines had rendered close blockade impossibly dangerous. To operate a distant blockade, Britain needed two critical assets; total superiority in the North Sea and the English Channel and a thorough understanding of the ways of merchant shipping. Command of the seas around northern Europe was vital so that the assortment of small ships used to enforce the blockade, mostly armed merchantmen, could do their business. This dominance could only be achieved by having a more powerful fleet than the enemy, ready to pounce on any hostile incursion into the critical sea lanes or interference with the blockading forces. Superiority at sea however, would be useless without a deep understanding of merchant shipping and of diplomacy, so that the blockading could be done without driving neutrals like Holland or the Scandinavian countries into the enemy camp. In this second, unglamorous, task the Admiralty was astonishingly successful, establishing treaties and agreements with neutrals which were effective and avoided unnecessary friction. Often the Admiralty found itself in conflict with the Foreign Office in determining how neutrals should be handled, but eventually sensible compromises were reached and the blockade was effective, creating no new enemies. As early as 1901, Fisher had set up an Intelligence Department which worked with shipping companies, Lloyds of London and with the overseas consular services, to gain a profound understanding of commercial shipping, the trade routes used and cargoes carried. This was to prove an invaluable tool in enforcing the blockade. All the diplomacy in the world however, would be useless if command of the seas was lost. Jutland was to prove that Britain had the ability to retain it.

The German Navy hardly existed until the very end of the nineteenth century. Before then it was nothing more than a coastal defence force with some experience in mine laying and sweeping, acquired during the wars with France and Denmark. Many in Germany thought things should stay that way. Bismarck, the great chancellor, scorned the idea of building a navy. 'All it will achieve' he said, 'is to make an enemy of the British.' The young Kaiser had other ideas. He had made frequent visits to England and knew how much his royal English relations loved their senior service. He had avidly read the works on Alfred Mahan, the American admiral, who argued convincingly that command of the oceans was the key to strategic dominance and world power. A vain man, he loved racing in his great yacht, the *Meteor*, and cruising in the *Hohenzollern*, his royal steam yacht. Bismarck or not, he was determined to have a navy and that it should follow the traditions of the greatest navy in the world – the British. William soon found the man who could deliver him such a navy – Alfred von Tirpitz.

Tirpitz's achievement was truly astonishing. He formed a 'Navy League' to raise funds, and propagating the idea of the new service, he worked with the great German shipyards and engineering companies to evolve ship design and most importantly of all he pressured the Reichstag into voting the necessary funds. The arguments he used were carefully trimmed to suit whoever he was talking to. To some audiences he stressed the number of new skilled jobs that would be created in the dockyards. Warship building was, he said, a tool the government could use to prevent unemployment and social unrest during a slump. To others he spoke eloquently of Germany's need for 'a place in the sun', a colonial empire such as that of Britain, France, Portugal and even little Belgium, to supply raw materials and become markets for German goods. Such an empire would need to have a strong navy to protect it. Another approach was to talk about the security of the realm. Germany might well find itself at odds with Russia, already building a powerful navy in the Baltic, with France, the world's second naval power, or even, who knew, with Britain. National security could only be assured by building a navy strong enough to face even the British, at least in the North Sea. His strongest argument with many politicians was that this was the Kaiser's desire. There would be honours for those who helped, problems for those who obstructed.

Tirpitz was successful; the building programme went ahead. There was also the issue of manning the ships. Germany had a tradition of sending the sons of noble and aristocratic families into the army, so much so that promotion was slow and uncertain. In trying to recruit potential officers for his new navy, Tirpitz was able to point out that promotion could be more rapid in a new, expanding force. He used the Navy League to help him to recruit the sons of upper class families into the service, setting up a selection process and a naval training school. Strangely, he reproduced many of the worst features of the British system in his selection process. Parents had to pay substantial sums for training, eliminating the chance of recruiting youths with seagoing experience from poor coastal communities. He also created rigid divisions between sea officers and engineers, consigning the latter to poorer messes, different uniforms and lower status. This was at the very time when such prejudices were beginning to be discouraged in the Royal Navy.

In the Royal Navy, other ranks and petty officers were almost all volunteers. In 1916 no less than seventy-five per cent of the lower deck seamen were either regulars or ex regulars re-enlisted for the duration of hostilities. By contrast the Germans were conscripts, serving three years active service and four in the reserve. Very few of their ratings were professionals. Promotion from the lower deck to commissioned status in the German service was unheard of, instead there was an intermediate rank of 'Deck Officer', a sort of senior petty officer, without a commission. In the Royal Navy, outstanding men could work their way to a commission and achieve high rank, although this was still rare. In general the German system worked far better than might have been expected and when they came to be tested in battle, officers and ratings showed initiative and skill that was sadly lacking in their opponents. However, the rigid class divisions and lack of empathy between officers and other ranks was to be a major cause of the total breakdown of German naval discipline in 1918. Britain with her long naval tradition and at least a degree of mutual respect between officers and men suffered no such problems during the course of the war.

The Imperial Navy had one critical advantage over the British. Moltke, who had made the nineteenth century Prussian Army the formidable machine that it was, was a confirmed believer in the dictum that 'No plan survives contact with the enemy.' It was drummed into officers and NCOs that they were responsible not just for carrying out orders blindly, but for using their brains to determine what they should do in the situation in which they found themselves in order to achieve the objectives set. The modern expression would be 'mission focus'. They must learn to think and act quickly, not wait to be told what to do or how to do it. Moltke's doctrine was adopted enthusiastically by Tirpitz's navy. Captains particularly had to think of what course of action they should take to achieve the fleet's aims and not wait for the admiral to do the thinking for them. They, the captains, were on the spot and best placed to make judgements and take rapid, determined action. This was the sort of conduct which had led the Royal Navy to victory at the battles of St Vincent and Copenhagen and which characterized Nelson's 'band of brothers', but it was miles apart from the training and disciplines which pervaded the Royal Navy in 1914.

It is appropriate at this stage of our narrative to introduce the most important personalities on both sides.

Jacky Fisher, who we have already encountered, had retired from the Admiralty in disgust at the Gallipoli Campaign, so he played no part in the

Jutland battle. His influence in the choice of commanders, the design of the ships and the tactics involved was however, profound. Convinced that Britain would have to eventually fight Germany, he had effectively concentrated the bulk of the Royal Navy into the Grand Fleet, based at Scapa Flow. The Mediterranean was left principally to the French.

Alfred von Tirpitz was also out of the direct line of command of the force which he had created, and was rapidly falling out of favour with the Kaiser. He had no direct involvement in the planning or conduct of the Battle of Jutland.

Admiral Sir John Jellicoe was Fisher's choice to command the Grand Fleet. Born in 1859 into a Merchant Navy family, he had joined the Royal Navy in 1872, and like Ned Charleton, had lived through the golden age of the Mediterranean Fleet. He had his first taste of active service in China where at one stage he had a formation of German marine infantry under his command (See letter 2). On several occasions he displayed great personal bravery, once diving overboard from the battleship *Colossus* in a gale to save a drowning man. He was a gunnery specialist and caught the eye of Fisher, becoming a prominent member of the 'fish pond.' Fisher insisted that he was appointed Commander of the Grand Fleet in 1914. He was clear thinking, cautious and determined, proving quite adept at dealing with the Admiralty. If he had a fault it was that he took too much on himself and delegated too little, so that sometimes even his formidable capacity for work was overwhelmed. He had a profound and detailed understanding of every aspect of his profession, and had made a special study of the contrast between German and British training methods and ship design. He was thus well aware of the relative weakness of British defensive armour, especially in respect of underwater protection from mines and torpedoes and of German prowess in fleet manoeuvres, especially at night. Jellicoe comes across as an extremely pleasant man, personally very considerate, loyal and kind to his subordinates, who liked and admired him, and popular on the lower deck where he used to walk around chatting in a friendly way to all ranks. He was devoted to his wife and family, as is illustrated by the letter to his daughters written slightly before Jutland (Letter 1). His determination not to seek for personal glory by hazarding his fleet in unfavourable circumstances demonstrated the highest form of courage. Significantly he wrote to the Admiralty on taking command:

> *'If, for instance, the enemy battle fleet were to turn away from our advancing fleet I should assume the intention was to lead us over mines and submarines and decline to be so drawn. I desire particularly to draw the attention of their Lordships to this point, since it may be deemed a refusal of battle and might possibly result in failure to bring the enemy to action as soon as it is expected. Such a result would be absolutely repugnant to the feelings of all British naval officers and men but with the new untried methods of warfare new tactics must be devised. These, if not understood, may bring odium upon me, but so long as I have the confidence of their Lordships I intend to pursue the proper course to defeat and annihilate the enemy's battle fleet without regard to uninstructed opinion or criticism.*
>
> *The situation is a difficult one it is quite possible that half of our battle fleet might be disabled by underwater attack before our guns opened fire at all ...'*

Jellocoe's opposite number, Vice Admiral Reinhard Scheer, was a protégé of Tirpitz. A fire breathing German nationalist, he had at first been prevented from becoming commander of the High Seas Fleet by the Kaiser who thought him too likely to take unacceptable risks with his precious warships. Scheer was highly critical of von Ingenohl and von Pohl, his two predecessors in command of the High Seas Fleet, pouring scorn on their, in his opinion, over cautious conduct. In January 1916 however, he got the command he had longed for and began to plan a more aggressive stance. An expert strategist and highly professional in every aspect of his activities, he was to prove a formidable opponent. Like Tirpitz, he had specialized in torpedo tactics, and had high hopes for planned attacks on the enemy battle fleet by fast torpedo boats. Immensely tough and determined, he was able to take and stick to his tactical decisions even when they seemed to be going wrong. He was popular with his subordinates, displaying the highest qualities of leadership and the ability to get the very best out each man in his team.

Vice Admiral Sir David Beatty, commander of the Battle Cruiser Fleet (*Note:* This was called the 'Battle Cruiser Force' until February 1915) was a tough, ruthless leader whose aggressive spirit often overrode any sober tactical judgement. Of Irish extraction, he was extremely loyal to his chosen band of subordinates, but made himself very unpopular elsewhere by his haughty manner and his enthusiasm for self-publicity. He had made his name in the Egyptian campaign of 1896-8 when he commanded gunboats operating on the Nile in support of the army. He displayed a degree of skill and courage that impressed the soldiers on land, and especially the young Winston Churchill who became a powerful friend. After a spell alongside Charleton and Jellicoe, putting down the Boxer rebellion in China, he returned to England and married an American divorcee heiress. The marriage was tempestuous and put a great emotional strain on Beatty. He was nearly dismissed from the service for refusing, at his wife's insistence, the offer of command of the Atlantic Fleet, but was reprieved by Churchill to take up the leadership of the glamorous Battle Cruiser Fleet, in which role he reported directly to Jellicoe. He proved a charismatic and enterprising leader of his command and won the loyalty, even devotion, of many of his close-knit band of officers; however there were severe weaknesses in his leadership style. He seems to have had little interest in the detail of the operation of his ships, allowing for example, slack and dangerous practices to develop in the way in which ammunition was fed to the gun turrets. Gunnery in the Battle Cruiser Fleet was notoriously poor when he was in command. He tolerated woeful incompetence in his signals officer, Ralph Seymour, who remained in post in spite of making a series of disastrous errors. Not even a fully qualified signals specialist, Seymour held onto his post simply because Beatty liked 'His little round flag lieutenant' and found him amusing. He was also a poor communicator and failed to brief his subordinates properly, leading to mistakes being made in action and too many signals being made to try to correct them, causing further confusion.

Beatty's opposite number was Vice Admiral Franz von Hipper, commander of the 1st Scouting Group, comprising the German battle cruiser fleet and its associated destroyers and light cruisers. He was a Bavarian from Oberbayern near Munich. His military career started with a brief spell in the army, but he rapidly transferred to the navy in 1881, at the age of eighteen. He specialized in torpedoes and torpedo boats. Eventually he was appointed to the royal yacht *Hohenzollern*. A spell taking the Kaiser about the world did his career no harm at all, leading to the command of a number of cruisers in which he further distinguished himself. Here surely, was a future leader for the new Imperial Navy. In 1911 he was in command of the heavy cruiser *Yorck*, and soon found himself promoted Rear Admiral. In 1913 he took command of the newly formed 1st Scouting Group, then consisting of Germany's new generation of battle cruisers plus a handful of older heavy cruisers. His subsequent career certainly justified the confidence placed in him by his superiors.

Rear Admiral Hugh Evan-Thomas also features in any history of Jutland. He commanded the 5th Battle Squadron (5BS) consisting of the most formidable warships in the world at the time, the *Queen Elizabeth* class fast battleships armed with 15-inch guns. 5BS was normally under direct command of Jellicoe, but transferred to Beatty's force at the time of the battle in order to compensate for the temporary removal from the Battle Cruiser Force of three battle cruisers, the elderly *Invincibles*, which had been ordered to Scapa for gunnery practise. Actually Beatty had been trying to get 5BS transferred to his command for some months before the battle. Jellicoe had refused. Joining the Navy in 1877, Evan-Thomas quickly distinguished himself as a vigorous and capable officer and was selected to take care of the two young royal princes, Albert and George ('Sprat and Herring'), serving aboard the training ship *Baccante*. With them he struck up lasting and valuable friendships. He served on the ill-fated *Victoria* in the Mediterranean, then on the royal yacht *Osborne*, with a spell 'nannying' Prince George, who was nominally captain of the small warship *Melampus*, a post in which the prince was far out of his depth. Evan-Thomas next became flag lieutenant to Admiral Culme-Seymour, commanding the Mediterranean Fleet, in which role he became much involved with revisions to the Navy's Signal Book, virtually the bible of all fleet manoeuvres and in effect a stultifying destroyer of initiative which was to cost the Navy dearly. Evan-Thomas's work in this field continued on his return to England and was enlarged by involvement in the early days of wireless. In all his postings he received the highest praise from his seniors including Culme-Seymore, Fisher and Lord Charles Beresford. Next came a spell as a captain of one of the first dreadnought battleships, then briefly command of the training college *Britannia* at Dartmouth. In October 1915 he was appointed to command

5BS, consisting eventually of the five 'Queen Elizabeths'. These ships were to prove their toughness and worth convincingly during the battle.

One other character in the Royal Navy played a significant part in the action, Commodore William Goodenough. Goodenough was descended from a distinguished Oxfordshire family that had produced famous churchmen, soldiers and sailors. His father, James, was the last man in the Royal Navy to be killed by a poisoned arrow. His uncle, also William, was a distinguished general. His naval career followed conventional lines, with service in the Mediterranean Fleet and on the China station. He became a close friend of Jellicoe, acting for a time as his flag captain in the battleship *Colossus*. The two of them worked together to practise long-range gunnery in the early dreadnought battleships. In 1914 Goodenough was with a squadron visiting the Imperial Navy at Kiel where he was able to meet not only the Kaiser, who he found stiff and awkward, but also Hipper and Scheer, both of whom he admired professionally. He seems to have made a particular friend of Prince Henry, the Kaiser's younger brother, who was himself a naval officer. At the time of the battle he was in command of the 2nd Light Cruiser Squadron (2LCS) coming under command of David Beatty. Goodenough wrote generously of Beatty, but history suggests that their relationship was sometimes stormy. The light cruiser squadron was in the thick of the fighting at Jutland and Goodenough distinguished himself as an intelligent and effective leader, using his ships to the best advantage throughout the battle, and in particular making proper use of radio communication, in contrast to many more senior officers.

Chapter Two

Ships, Weapons and Tactics

An astonishing fact about naval warfare in the early part of the twentieth century is the extent to which the power of naval armament had moved ahead of the means of directing it. Guns in Nelson's navy had a range of a few hundred yards and fired a maximum weight of slightly over sixty pounds; a battleship in 1916 might fire a missile weighing almost a ton nearly fifteen miles, yet both depended on the same 'Mark 1 Eyeball' assisted by a telescope to see the enemy and aim the gun. How often is visibility fifteen miles at sea? How can normal eyesight penetrate the smoke of gunfire or of a smokestack? It is possible to visualize the dreadnought battleship as a monster, with massive limbs and terrible claws, blundering about a darkened field trying to come to grips with another, similarly blind creature.

Electronics which could penetrate the darkness and murk and allow the guns to operate at their full potential were far away in the future.

Nevertheless, the development of naval technology in the latter part of the nineteenth century had been astonishingly rapid. Ships like *Colossus*, on which Charlton had sailed in the 1890s, were at least as out dated by 1910, as a First World War fighter plane would have been in 1945. In particular, the effective range of Colossus's guns was 2,000 yards, as against 18,000 to 20,000 in 1914. Such revolutionary developments called for entirely new fighting tactics for which there could be no effective rehearsal. The only relevant experience was the Battle of Tsushima in 1905. At Tsushima the Japanese Navy almost completely destroyed a fleet of Russian heavy ships that had steamed round from the Baltic. Although prior to the age of the dreadnought proper, Tsushima did provide a good example of how well practised communication, determined leadership and rigorous training might enable a force of modern, fast, warships to achieve a victory even more complete than Trafalgar. A small British party on board the Japanese flagship at Tsushima learnt a lot from what they saw, but the Royal Navy was too set in its ways to be prepared to copy the training methods and ruthless search for efficiency which had made the Japanese fleet (much of it actually built in Britain), so formidable.

An aspect of sea warfare that no one foresaw, even after Tsushima, was the very long ranges at which sea fighting would actually take place. The Japanese had opened fire on the Russians at about 8,000 yards in poor visibility and their destroyers had been able to get very close to their prey under cover of darkness and fog. At the battles of the Dogger Bank and Jutland, effective fire was exchanged between heavy ships at more than twice this range. In reasonable visibility it was difficult for destroyers to get close enough to the enemy to use their torpedoes effectively, because the opposing battle fleets were so far apart that the quick-firing secondary armament of battleships had plenty of opportunity to drive them off. Another effect of this surprisingly long-range fighting concerned the effectiveness of shellfire and armour. Fired at long ranges, naval heavy guns would be elevated to twenty degrees or more, meaning that the shells would be plunging downwards when they struck the enemy ship, so they would not strike the heavily armoured sides of the victim, but its much more lightly armoured deck and turret tops. This was not anticipated by either British or German ship designers. A further unexpected effect of long-range engagements was that the percentage of hits was inevitably much lower than expected, never more than five per cent. As a result, ammunition expenditure was much higher than expected and battle experience led to large increases in the number of shells and propellant charges carried on capital ships.

Appendices II and III show clearly how dreadnought battleships and battle cruisers had developed during the first years of the twentieth century and the contrast between British and German ships. *Dreadnought* herself was a ship of 22,000 tons war displacement with ten 12-inch guns mounted in five turrets. The turrets were protected with eleven to twelve inches of armour on the sides and three inches on the top. She had Parsons turbine engines of 23,000 horsepower burning coal, with the ability to inject oil for maximum performance. Maximum speed was 21.6 knots. Turbine engines were a revolutionary innovation for large warships, being far more efficient, quieter and much more reliable than piston engines, but they were untried and unfamiliar to ship's engineers. They also gave problems when manoeuvring, being inefficient at low speeds and requiring separate engines for going astern. Adopting them wholesale, as the Royal Navy did, was indeed a bold move. Unlike her German counterparts, *Dreadnought* was designed for service worldwide, and the crew lived on board. German crews lived in barracks except when the ship was at sea. The hulls of the German ships were generally more heavily protected than their British counterparts, as the appendices show clearly, partly because of less need for accommodation space and partly because Tirpitz, who always took the closest interest in warship design, insisted that the main task of a ship was to keep afloat. This thinking was fundamental to all German heavy ship development. The British and especially Fisher himself, the originator of the Dreadnought project, were more interested in speed and hitting power. German ships were also generally more 'beamy' than British, which enabled them to accommodate extremely good underwater protection against mines or torpedoes. *Nassau* for example, the first German dreadnought, had a length to beam ratio of 5.4:1 compared to 6.4:1 for *Dreadnought* herself. This was possible because the Germans built building docks wide enough to accommodate their ship designs. British warships had to be fitted into existing building docks. Tirpitz was also quite conservative as regards technology and was a stickler for getting things done properly. No ship sailed with the fleet unless it had been meticulously worked up and the crew trained in the safety of the Baltic.

Although German shells were generally lighter than British, their armour piercing capability seems to have been as good or better. This was mainly because the standard British AP shell was inclined to break up on impact. This fault was not corrected until late in 1917, and was to have a severely damaging effect on the fighting effectiveness of British ships. Although German guns were mostly smaller, they had similar or in some cases higher muzzle velocity than British (typically 2,805 feet/sec), so effective range was similar. Both sides thought that torpedoes would be a useful addition to a battleship's weaponry, which is surprising considering a torpedo's limited range compared to that of a heavy gun. There is only one recorded incident in history of one modern battleship torpedoing another – *Rodney* on the already helpless *Bismarck* in 1941. At Jutland, torpedoes were fired by capital ships on both sides, but not one found its mark.

The greatest challenge for a warship's gunners is to hit the enemy ship. This sounds simple but a little thought will illustrate how difficult it is. A shell must be aimed to hit the target where it will be at the moment of impact, not where it is when the shell is fired. At a range of twelve miles a shell will take about forty seconds to reach its target; during this time the ship will have travelled about 1,500 feet or almost three times its length. The gun aimer thus has to know the course and speed of the enemy ship as well as of his own if he is to have any chance of making a hit. Many other factors also come into play including wind, humidity, condition of the gun barrels and atmospheric conditions. The ship will probably be rolling and pitching which will also affect aim. By 1916, capital ships on both sides were fitted with centralized fire control, known as director control, with the principle responsibility for aiming the massive weapons in the hands of a single gunnery officer. The two sides applied their director control systems in slightly different ways. The British used a Barr and Stroud coincidence rangefinder, which was mounted in the director tower on the foremast. This produced an image of the target and the operator had to find a vertical line, such as a mast, on the target and adjust the rangefinder until it appeared to be unbroken. This data was then fed into a Dreyer fire control computer. The Dreyer was an immensely complex analogue computer. Its inputs were derived from observation of the enemy course and speed, data from the rangefinder, the weather conditions and the bearing of the enemy ship. The speed and heading of one's own ship was fed in automatically. All this data, much of it still depending on the operator's judgement, was fed into the Dryer, which would then determine the correct azimuth and elevation of the guns. In case this system was not complex enough, another analogue computer, the Dumaresq, was used to calculate range rate, that is to say how the bearing and range of the target would change between the firing of the gun and the moment of impact.

The delicate and complex Dreyer table was housed deep in an underwater plotting room. Up to sixteen men were involved in operating it. From the plotting room, signals were sent electrically to the turrets where they activated dials that showed the calculated direction and elevation for the gun barrels. The turret crews pointed the guns exactly in accordance with instructions sent from the plotting room and when they reported, 'Ready' the great guns were fired electrically from the foretop where the gunnery officer was normally situated. On British ships the guns were elevated and rotated hydraulically; German ships used hydraulic elevation and electric rotation of the turret. A good ship might achieve three salvoes a minute in practice, although in battle conditions the rate was normally slower. An observer in the foretop would watch for the splash of the shell in the water near the enemy ship and signal adjustments to be made. This was not as easy as it sounds. The target, even viewed through powerful glasses, might be little more than a speck on the horizon, and quite possibly another ship would be firing at it also, so that it was difficult to tell which splash was generated by whose salvo. Also, the foretop itself was often close to a funnel, so that it was liable be shrouded in smoke. Smoke was indeed the worst enemy of good gun laying, as when guns were being fired, great clouds of cordite smoke would obscure the view from the rangefinder and from the foretop, making correct adjustments to aim impossible to achieve.

It is not surprising that this did not prove to be a very robust or satisfactory system in service. Often in cases where ships made frequent alteration of course and speed, the whole system would fail to cope with the situation. Some gunnery officers actually preferred shooting 'by eye' rather than relying on the Dryer and Dumaresq systems. When ships were moving fast and frequently changing course they had no option but to ignore the systems as the computers could not keep up with what was going on. Both British and German warships had secondary rangefinders mounted on top of the turrets so that in an emergency the turret could operate independently. An alternative system to the Dryer, known as the 'Argo Table' had been developed and, according to most reports, was markedly better. It was rejected by the Admiralty for reasons that remain obscure, but was fitted for trial purposes to a few ships, including the battle cruiser, *Queen Mary*, a particularly good gunnery ship.

German dreadnoughts had a simpler version of the Dryer/Dumaresq system in which the gunnery officer had to estimate the range rate by experience. He had the advantage of a Zeiss stereoscopic rangefinder that was more accurate and easier to use than the Barr and Stroud. Unlike the British, the German guns were fired from within the turret. In battle, German ships seem to have found the range more quickly and opened fire more accurately than British, although after the first few salvoes there was little difference between the two.

The turrets themselves were incredibly complicated and expensive pieces of engineering. Britain had three suppliers, Vickers, Elswick and the Admiralty's own factory in Coventry (See Drawing 1). The gun barrels themselves were made of nickel steel with a carbon steel jacket and breech ring. Around each nickel steel inner barrel was wound 200 miles of steel wire, pulled tightly. This gave the structure a degree of elasticity. Guns and turrets were not scrapped when ships were taken out of service. They were stored and used on another generation of warship. Shells for the main armament of capital ships were separate from the cordite charges used as a propellant; both were stowed separately, well below the water line. On British ships, four silk bags of cordite were used together for each firing. The cordite charges themselves were detonated by gunpowder, a small bag of which was enclosed in each of the silk cordite bags. To load the guns, a shell and the cordite bags would be placed on separate trays on the main ammunition hoist and carried up to the working chamber below the turret itself. Here they were prepared and transferred to waiting trays, ready to be placed in a further hoist which took them up to the gun itself. The hoists in the working chambers were fitted with flash guards to prevent flames from an explosion getting back down the main ammunition hoist and into the magazine. German ships used a slightly different method of handling the cordite. A small amount was contained, with a detonation charge, in a silk bag, but the bulk of it was in brass cartridges, which provided a much safer means of handling.

As well as their great guns, dreadnoughts all required secondary armament, mainly to drive off attacks from destroyers or light cruisers which might get close enough to fire a torpedo. The British used a variety of weapons for this. *Dreadnought* herself had twenty-seven 3-inch quick firers as secondary armament plus a range of lighter weapons; the next generation of dreadnoughts had sixteen 4-inch, and the later ships, twelve 6-inch weapons. German ships placed much more emphasis on secondary armament. They kept it all fully manned in battle (the British used men from the main turrets who were moved to the smaller guns only when a torpedo attack was expected) and the Germans invariably used twelve or fourteen 5.9-inch weapons. All ships on both sides gradually increased their complement of anti-aircraft armament as the war progressed.

A significant initial difference between the first German and the British dreadnought battleships was in their propulsion machinery. Tirpitz did not like the fact that turbines were untried and stuck to piston engines until it came to the later series of dreadnoughts built before the war. He may well have been under some pressure from German shipbuilders who had no experience in building big turbine driven warships and who also made good profits building large piston engines in their own workshops. Turbines had to be purchased from elsewhere. Turbines did have the disadvantage of being very inefficient at low speeds, especially as at that time they were arranged to drive the propellers directly with no reduction gearing. To get over this difficulty both sides contemplated using diesels to drive ships at cruising speeds. Fisher was particularly keen on them, but neither Britain nor Germany had enough confidence in the reliability of large diesels to take the plunge (experience with early marine diesels in British monitors justified their caution). The result of sticking to piston engines in battleships was a distinct loss of speed, poor reliability and less comfortable cruising. The engine room of a piston-engined warship at speed was described as being 'like a snipe bog.' Water, oil and grease were everywhere. Terrible vibrations, especially when the pistons of two of the engines came into sync, shook the whole ship. They were also almost certain to give mechanical trouble after more than a few hours running at full speed.

The Germans were also more cautious than the British in respect of the fuel used for the boilers. German ships were coal burners with the associated filth and hard labour moving coal from bunkers to the furnaces. Only the last two series of battleships, the *Konigs* and the *Bayerns* had the possibility of oil injection. British dreadnoughts had oil injection from the start. Fisher wanted an all oil-burning navy and the later battleships burnt oil only. Coal did have one big advantage. Stacked against the sides of the ship it proved useful as torpedo protection. Oil however, meant a smaller crew, a cleaner ship, less funnel smoke, and was lighter and took up far less space. The Battle of Jutland in one respect vindicated the German choice of fuel. British oil burning destroyers proved to have a significantly greater tendency to catch fire and explode when hit than their German counterparts.

German battle cruisers, unlike their battleships, were turbine powered, the engines mostly being imported from Parsons, because it would have been impossible to generate the power required for their high speeds using a piston engine within the weight and space restrictions imposed. Here again the early ships were coal burners; the last two built only had oil injection. The turbines proved themselves astonishingly efficient. The first battle cruiser, *Von der Tann* achieved twenty-eight knots on her trials, and crossed the Atlantic at an average speed of over twenty-four knots, running her turbines constantly at high speed. Any steam piston engine would have broken down after a few hours of such harsh treatment.

An area of distinct German superiority was protection of the hull and deck. German Krupp cemented armour was considered the optimum material for this and German ship designers used it generously at the sacrifice of speed and main armament. Appendices II and III illustrate this. It is very clear that German ships had a far larger proportion of their total weight in the form of armour – following Tirpitz's dictum about the need to stay afloat. The appendices also show the usual pattern of ships getting gradually bigger and more heavily armed over time. Standing out from all the other ships involved at Jutland are the fast battleships of the *Queen Elizabeth* class. These were magnificent ships, proving their value in two world wars, all but one of them, *Barham*, surviving until 1946.

Both Britain and Germany still had fleets of 'pre-dreadnought' battleships throughout the war. The British ones were used mainly for shore bombardment and as guard ships. They also had extensive use in the Dardanelles campaign, but were not used at Jutland as they were too slow to operate with the Grand Fleet. Germany, with her much smaller inventory of dreadnoughts, elected to use her old battleships with the High Seas Fleet. They were in the event more of a hindrance than a help as they reduced the fleet's speed. Christened 'Five Minute Ships', that being the length of time they would survive a battle with a dreadnought, they did little to increase the German's effective firepower.

Battle cruisers were a prominent feature in both navies, experiencing the lion's share of the fighting and of many of the casualties on both sides. The evolution of the battle cruiser concept is interesting. Fisher had it firmly fixed in his mind that 'Speed is armour', a theory which makes good sense when you are running away, but is not much good when you are fighting head to head with a powerful armoured ship. He had long held the opinion that a very fast, well armed, cruiser would be the perfect tool for establishing worldwide superiority at sea. He also, when studying the project, discovered that an all big gun dreadnought battle cruiser could be cheaper to build that a battleship, even though it would be as large, impressive looking and faster, pleasing his colleagues in the Treasury, and of course, the Press. The keels of the first three of this new type of ship, the '*Invincibles*,' were laid down in 1906, before *Dreadnought* had been launched. The three were almost identical, all having big guns, high speed and relatively light protective armour. Britain would learn the hard way that although such ships were useful in many situations, exposed to the fire of heavy guns they were death traps. Appendix III lists the characteristic of British and German battle cruisers. The great difference in weight of armour partly reflects the different roles envisaged by the two sides for battle cruisers. The British saw them as a weapon to establish worldwide superiority at sea, able to make far ranging forays into the South Atlantic and the Pacific to handle any situation that might arise. As we shall see, they achieved an excellent demonstration of this in the Battle of the Falkland Islands. Scouting for the battle fleet was their alternative role. The Royal Navy also envisaged their only having to handle opponents at relatively short ranges, up to about 10,000 yards. At this range the trajectory of a shell is relatively flat and will strike the sides and upperworks of the ship. Nobody envisaged their having to absorb long-range fire in which a plunging missile will tend to crash downwards through the deck. Hence their quite thin deck armour. The Germans by contrast, built their navy primarily to fight in the North Sea as an adjunct to the main battle fleet. Designed for this more limited purpose, they were much more suitable to partake in a fleet action than their British opponents. As the appendices show, the German battle cruisers had roughly the same proportion of their weight as armour as British battleships. They also had excellent underwater torpedo protection. Drawing 2 shows the difference in underwater armour between *Invincible* and *Von der Tann*, the first German battle cruiser. The German battle cruisers were to put up a heroic fight when faced by a larger number of British opponents. Surprisingly, Tirpitz himself had never envisaged this role for his battle cruisers, insisting that they were suitable only for fighting other cruisers. He was overruled however by the younger bloods in the Imperial Navy.

In spite of Fisher's ruthless culling of obsolete cruisers, a few 'armoured cruisers' remained with the Grand Fleet. Known as the *Duke of Edinburgh* class they were indeed the British 'five minute ships', with light armour and a mixture of 9.2 and 6-inch casement guns. They were also slow, with a maximum speed of twenty-three knots; they could barely keep up with the fast battleships, although their role was to scout for the fleet. Coal burners, they were famous for the terrific volumes of smoke which poured from their funnels. The Germans used no such ships at Jutland.

Much more useful in the scouting role were the light cruisers which were used extensively by both fleets. These were fast (twenty-three to twenty-eight knot) vessels of about 5,000 tons, typically armed with four 6-inch guns. They also had torpedo armament and could be fitted to lay mines. Highly manoeuvrable, they proved able to avoid enemy shellfire while scouting close to enemy ships, and their mines and torpedoes were a constant threat in a night action or in thick weather. Light cruisers would sometimes act as lead ship for a flotilla of destroyers, although by 1916 this job was more often performed for the Royal Navy by more specialized, even faster ships. The older German light cruisers were generally smaller and not so fast as the British and instead of 6-inch guns had a larger number of smaller calibre weapons, designed for fighting at close quarters. More recent German designs closely resembled their British counterparts.

Fleet destroyers brought into play an entirely new strand of naval tactical thinking. Until the dawn of the twentieth century there had never been any question of a small ship being a danger to a much larger one. Frigates for example, did not fight with battleships. In a fleet action they would withdraw and concentrate on picking up casualties or damaged stragglers. The development of the Whitehead torpedo completely changed this situation. Suddenly, small torpedo-armed boats could constitute a real danger to a fleet at anchor by sneaking up under cover of darkness or in thick weather and launching a devastating weapon. To guard against this horrific possibility, the Royal Navy developed the 'torpedo boat destroyer' (TBD) which was designed to run down and destroy enemy torpedo boats with gunfire. While they were about it, designers armed the TBD's themselves with torpedoes.

By the early 1900s the torpedoes had improved enormously. Gyroscopes enabled them to hold their course accurately and the new generation of the Peter Brotherhood engine, in which the compressed air driving the torpedo was heated so as to give it more energy, transformed them from very short-range weapons, suitable only for attacking ships anchored in harbour, into fast, powerful missiles which could be used at sea in a fleet action. Range was typically 3,800 yards at forty-five knots or 10,000 yards at twenty-eight knots, although as we shall see, it was almost impossible to hit a moving enemy ship at anything like these ranges in battle conditions. The explosive charge was in most cases 300lbs. As the explosive charge of a torpedo was detonated under water, it was far more damaging than a similar weight of explosive delivered by a shell strike above water.

Equipped with such a weapon, TBDs could take their place as a formidable part of the order of battle. British destroyers were by 1916 mostly armed with 21-inch torpedoes. They consisted of a number of different classes; the 1000-ton 'M' class, which was the most numerous, could make thirty-four to thirty-six knots in calm water. Besides their torpedoes, they were armed with three 4-inch guns. German destroyers were generally smaller than British and less well armed, although their torpedo armament was very similar, using 19.7-inch weapons. By 1916 new classes of larger German destroyer were coming into service. These were quite similar to their British counterparts.

Both sides had expected their destroyers to play a major part in any fleet action. We shall see, in the following chapters, what they actually achieved. It is clear that British and German commanders greatly underestimated the difficulty of firing a torpedo with any accuracy at a moving target when under effective enemy fire. Because the torpedo moves so slowly compared to a shell, the enemy may well see it coming by the line of bubbles left by the compressed air motor astern, and be able to take avoiding action. The torpedo aimer has to anticipate the movement of the enemy ship very accurately, and the torpedo itself is very likely to be disrupted by enemy fire, rough seas, or a host of other factors. Both British and German pre-war estimates suggested that thirty per cent of torpedoes fired would score hits. In reality, the Germans fired 105 torpedoes and scored two, or possibly three hits, the British 96 for five or six hits. It is possible that the German torpedoes used at Jutland had a fault in their depth control mechanism, which would account for their poor performance.

Capital ships threatened by torpedoes would generally turn away, so that the torpedo might well run out of energy before it reached them. A keen-eyed lookout could spot their approach and help the helmsman to take avoiding action. Approach speed might only be about ten knots as the target might be moving away at twenty to thirty knots. Even if the torpedo did catch a big warship from astern, the propeller wash of a ship at speed might easily force the weapon off course.

As well as fleet destroyers, Britain had ships known as 'destroyer leaders.' These had similar performance and armament to conventional destroyers but were larger and had accommodation for the flotilla commander and his staff. Typical of these was the 'Marksman' class of 1,600 tons, capable of thirty-four knots. To attack an enemy ship, a destroyer or more likely, a group of destroyers, would approach as closely as it could without falling victim to the hail of shells fired at it by the enemy's secondary armament. It would then turn broadside on to the target, a little ahead, and steam at as near the same speed and course as possible so as to make aiming the torpedo less difficult. As soon as the weapon was fired the destroyer would dash off, probably making smoke to cover its retreat. This was all a risky and skilful business, requiring judgement and cool nerves. In practice, a hit was unlikely if the range was much over 2000 yards, even in daylight. At night it was expected that destroyers might be able to use the cover of darkness to get much closer to enemy ships without being seen and get off torpedoes accurately at close range. This tactic had been used with devastating success by the Japanese against the Russians at Tsushima, and the German destroyer flotillas trained hard to use it to compensate for the relative weakness of their High Seas Fleet. We shall see what success they achieved.

One further threat posed by destroyers was mine laying. Some of the large British destroyers were converted into specialist minelayers and most German destroyers were able to lay mines. A fleeing fleet might sow a minefield as it went, making it fatal for its enemy to follow in its wake. Also, to cover a retreat, the Germans developed extremely effective smoke floats which destroyers would carry into battle. These could screen a retreating fleet or cover a damaged heavy ship while repairs were made.

Destroyers and light cruisers, having no effective protection from enemy shellfire, would have to use their agility to avoid being hit. One tactic was to steer for the last shell burst, on the theory that the next shell would never land on the same spot. Another would be to watch for the enemy gun flashes and turn violently as soon as they were seen, so that the little ship would not be in the position predicted by the gun aimer when the shell arrived.

Note: More detailed technical information about ships in both navies is given in Appendices II, III and IV.

Submarines played very little part in the Jutland battle in spite of both side's efforts to deploy them. They were in theory a very serious threat to surface ships; they could fire torpedoes and lay mines without being seen and there was no effective way of detecting them once they had dived. The hydrophones then in use could sometimes detect motor sounds if the sub tried to move, but if it stayed still it was impossible to locate and the vessel using the hydrophone had to remain stationary or its own propeller noise would drown any sound made by its quarry. Subs were, however extremely difficult to integrate into any fleet action. They were too slow and their communications too uncertain to enable them to appear in the right place at the right time. Even when they were in place, visibility was so poor from the low conning tower or periscope that they often failed to see the enemy. Both British and German submarines had very low power radio sets, so they were unable to contact their base reliably at any range over thirty miles, although they could receive signals from a longer range. This made them virtually useless for spotting for the main fleets. The fear of submarines however, was a major factor in both fleet's tactical manoeuvres and 'sightings' of imaginary torpedoes and conning towers caused frequent disruptions.

Aircraft were also of only marginal importance at Jutland. The British had two seaplane carriers attached to the Grand Fleet, only one of which (*Engardine*), actually put to sea at Jutland, but signalling problems rendered her observation reports useless. The Germans used Zeppelins extensively for reconnaissance and for bombing activities, but in practice they achieved very little. Poor visibility was a constant problem for them, and they had great difficulty in identifying ships from a height at which they were safe from gunfire. In strong headwinds they could make no progress at all and they could not operate in thick weather. Because they were so slow and because wind speed and direction were difficult to estimate, they seldom knew exactly where they were when over water, except when they could see a recognisable feature on land. Consequently their reports of enemy ship movements were often misleading. Attempts to bomb ships from the air were very seldom effective.

Wireless began to appear on large ships in the early 1900s and was in place on all major warships before 1914. It had been given great impetus as a result of the successful use of radio by the Japanese at the Battle of Tsushima. The sets in use could only transmit morse or similar codes; voice communication was still years away. Sets were installed deep in the bowels of the ships, with most having only one set and one signaller on duty with the result that communications could easily be delayed or confused. At best, it would be ten to fifteen minutes before a signal received by a ship's radio found its way to the bridge. From the first, radio was a two-edged weapon, essential for controlling a battle fleet at sea, but also potentially a valuable source of intelligence to the enemy. Thus from the beginning of naval radio there was jamming, encryption and deception of many kinds. Both sides also had direction finding radio stations which could accurately locate the source of any radio transmission, the British DF stations being much more numerous and effective than the Germans, especially at long ranges. Signalling by flags or by lamp was much preferred to radio. Such signals were more secure, could be read instantly by officers on the bridge, were not subject to jamming and were more reliable. Almost all communications between ships within a formation were made by these visual means, which had developed little since the days of Trafalgar. Both British and German fleets had expert signallers although, as we shall see, British signals officers were guilty of some horrific blunders.

Early in the war, the British had set up a signals intelligence branch under Sir Alfred Ewing which was able to receive radio signals on the 400 metre band, used by the German High Seas Fleet. At almost the same time three incredible pieces of luck blessed Room 40, as the new intelligence branch was called. Firstly, the German cypher book for the code used by merchant ships, Zeppelins and auxiliaries, was seized by the Royal Australian Navy from a merchant ship. Secondly, the regular naval code book was taken from the body of a German petty officer, who had tried to swim ashore from the grounded cruiser *Magdeburg* in the Baltic, and the Russian captors gave Room 40 a copy. Thirdly, a copy of the high level code book for inter service and diplomatic communications was ditched by a German TBD which was being sunk by a British patrol off Texel, then was by chance recovered by a British trawler and handed over to the Admiralty. Once they had mastered how these jewels could be used, Room 40 staff had the key to a huge volume of German signal traffic. They called it 'The miraculous draft of fishes.' New listening stations were established around the British Isles, keeping a constant radio watch. In October 1914, responsibility for naval intelligence and for Room 40 was assumed by Captain 'Blinker' Hall who was perhaps to contribute more to the victory of the Allies than any other single individual. One of his first acts was to commission a chain of direction finding radio stations along the east coast of England. These used a new technology, developed by the Marconi company, which used thermionic valves instead of crystals to pick up even the weakest signals and pinpoint the source. Any ship using a radio transmitter was thus giving Hall its exact position, and his team of cypher experts could read the signal.

Germany was also active in radio intelligence and was able to break at least some of the British naval codes. A central station at Neumunster was set up to coordinate activities and pass information to ships at sea. German technology was similar to British, but the intelligence operation was on a smaller scale and was generally less effective. The British high level naval codes were never broken. Both sides were aware of the other's snooping on their radio messages and imposed strict radio discipline on ships and shore stations. Ship's radios were given special low power settings so that the reduced range would prevent them being picked up except by nearby vessels, and whenever possible old fashioned flag and light signals were used. Nevertheless, the Germans particularly, gave away vast amounts of valuable information to the Allies and were never able to understand why their system was so leaky. They often blamed 'spy trawlers' for warning the British of their movements, and also looked diligently within their signals staff to find out if a traitor was at work. Needless to say they found nothing. The Grand Fleet also became adept at bluffing the Germans by putting to sea when they had no radio intelligence at all of an enemy sortie and making sure Neumunster knew about it, thus adding to the German confusion.

Neumunster did however make some very valuable interceptions of British radio traffic at Jutland, with devastating effect to some British ships during the night-time action, as we shall see.

It is impossible to understand the battle without some basic comprehension of naval tactics and fleet handling. Fleets would normally fight in column, with ships steaming about two ship's lengths apart. Columns of ships would always try to get into a position to allow the full broadside of all the ships in the fleet to bear on the enemy. Column was not however a suitable formation for cruising. A column of twenty-four Dreadnoughts would be about six miles long, a very difficult 'snake' to control, and a wonderful target for a submarine on its flank. A torpedo fired at random at the column would have a 3:1 chance of scoring a hit. Normally therefore, a fleet would cruise in a box formation consisting typically of five or six columns of four ships each, each column being led by a flag officer. The columns would be spaced about one mile apart. On all four sides of the box, destroyers and light cruisers would patrol, making it impossible for a submarine to approach on the surface. When the enemy was sighted the ships in the nearest column would hold their course while the other five columns would turn so as to fall in behind, keeping their two ship's length spacing. They could form up on either the port, starboard, or central column of the box. Once it was formed, the column could be sidled in either direction by all the ships turning through about thirty degrees simultaneously, holding this course for a set time then resuming their original heading. Sometimes when the enemy was sighted the fleet might want to get away. This could be achieved either by turning together so that the column simply reverses, or by turning in succession in which case each ship turns on the same spot as the leader of its column. The German fleet practised another technique, the 'Battle Turn Away' in which the rear ship in a column turns first and the ships ahead follow in quick succession. For a long column of ships this is safer, especially under battle conditions, than a simultaneous reversal of course where a single ship missing a signal might easily lead to a collision. It also ensures that the rear ships in the column, normally the most vulnerable, remain undamaged by enemy fire, leaving the powerful battleships in the van to do most of the fighting.

Ideally an admiral would try to 'cross the tee' of the enemy, in such a way that all the ships in his column can fire on the leading ships of the enemy column, and are relatively safe from any of the enemy's guns except those of his leading ship which can be trained right ahead. If this happens the enemy either has to turn and run, or turn onto a course parallel to his opponent so that he can bring his own broadsides to bear, but this is a very difficult manoeuvre to perform. One of the most favourable situations for a fleet occurs when its scouting forces are able to let the admiral know the position and course of an approaching enemy. The admiral can then keep his fleet in box formation while positioning it to cross the enemy tee. As soon as the enemy is sighted the admiral can deploy into column and bring all his big guns to bear.

Chasing a fleeing enemy was an operation fraught with danger. Jellicoe as we have seen, went so far as to inform the Admiralty that he would not risk the fleet by doing this, although he knew that giving up a chase would make him an object of criticism for armchair admirals, politicians and journalists. It would be too easy for a fleeing fleet to sow a minefield as it retreated or to draw its opponent onto a submarine trap. In a situation like that which faced the Grand Fleet in 1916, chasing a fleeing enemy would have been the height of folly.

Chapter Three

The War at Sea Before Jutland

Britain and France had divided responsibility for controlling the seas, with France taking the lead in the Mediterranean, and Britain with her much bigger navy, elsewhere. The policy of distant blockade had been decided before the war and the dreadnoughts and battle cruisers of the Royal Navy were concentrated into the Grand Fleet. This sound strategy of concentration of forces was the culmination of Fisher's cleaning of the Augean Stables during his period as First Sea Lord. The Grand Fleet was intended to be based at Scapa Flow, but the danger from submarines made the anchorage there unsafe until proper defences were built, so the fleet moved to sea lochs on the west coast of Scotland and Northern Ireland. This evacuation hardly looked Nelsonian, but it was the correct strategy. Britain only had a single ship lead over Germany in dreadnoughts in the winter of 1914/15 (18 British and 17 German). *Audacious* had been lost due to a mine strike, *Monarch* and *Conqueror* had been damaged in a collision, and other dreadnoughts were undergoing routine maintenance. To lose the upper hand at any stage could mean loss of the whole war. Jellicoe, far-sighted and cautious as ever, saw this and made sure of the safety of his fleet. He was, as Churchill remarked, 'The one man who could lose the war in an afternoon.' He well understood the heavy responsibility which rested on him and did not intend to demonstrate the truth of Churchill's dictum.

The Battle Cruiser Force, under Beatty, was deployed separately from the Grand Fleet, although it was part of Jellicoe's command. In order to protect the east coast of Britain from surprise attack, it was based further south than the main battle fleet, first on the Cromarty Firth, then on the Firth of Forth.

While the Grand Fleet was lurking in northern waters, the small ship navy and the battle cruisers had plenty to do. The Channel had to be kept safe for troop carriers and supply ships going to France, German fishing fleets had to be rounded up and destroyed and a start made on protective mining of British seaports. The German mine menace also had to be dealt with. Undersea cables linking Germany and her allies with the rest of the world had to be dredged up and either cut or tapped. Most important of all, the German merchant marine had to be sought out and destroyed or immobilized, and neutral ships bringing materials to Germany had to be stopped and searched. In this task the naval intelligence service played an invaluable role, knowing as they did, all about the movements of merchant ships, what cargoes were loaded and where and how the communications links between Europe and the rest of the world operated.

There was scope for offensive operations as well. Germany had a number of cruisers operating across the oceans trying to interrupt Allied trade links. These had to be hunted down and sunk. Also, troop convoys from Australia, New Zealand and Canada had to be strongly protected, requiring the attention of powerful escorts, including sometimes one or two of the fast battle cruisers. The marauding enemy cruisers, including the phenomenally successful *Emden* were rapidly dealt with; the last one, *Konigsberg,* being run to earth in the Rufigi River in East Africa and destroyed by a pair of monitors. Troop convoys moved safely across sea routes patrolled by the Royal Navy. The enemy's merchant marine was confined to port, many ships being immobilized in far-away foreign anchorages. After a shaky start, procedures for dealing with German offensive minefields were deployed and swept channels established for friendly and neutral ships.

While all this was going on the Germans concentrated their heavy ships in the Jade estuary, and used their small craft and a fleet of converted merchant ships and ferries to lay extensive minefields. The British policy of distant blockade in fact took them somewhat by surprise. They had confidently expected a close blockade of their coasts and possibly a raid by British heavy ships on the High Seas Fleet in its anchorage. Had the British attempted this, the results would have been almost certain disaster. The Germans had their strategy well worked out, using mines, submarines and light forces to damage the enemy fleet, then employing their dreadnoughts to cut off the retreating British as they staggered home across the North Sea. German preoccupation with this strategy however, meant that the English Channel could be used in relative safety by British and French forces, the distant blockade went almost unchallenged, and there was no protection for

German merchantmen in overseas ports, allowing their immobilization to proceed unmolested.

There was actually no shortage of people in Britain calling for the Royal Navy to adopt a more aggressive stance. Fisher and Churchill both had plans to land Allied troops on the Frisian Islands or in Pomerania so as to threaten the northern German flank. There was much talk of ferrying a Russian army to a point from which it could march to Berlin. Luckily these hare-brained schemes were scotched. Instead, the almost equally ill-considered Gallipoli expedition was mounted. Fortunately, this did not materially weaken the Grand Fleet as all but one of the battleships used, (*Queen Elizabeth)*, were obsolete pre-dreadnoughts.

At a lower level however, there were naval officers who advocated a more aggressive tactical stance. Based in Harwich were Commodore Tyrwhitt's force of destroyers and light cruisers and the submarine fleet under Commodore Roger Keyes. These two were both fire breathers and were to prove their worth as the war developed. Bored by defensive patrolling, they made a plea to the Admiralty for permission to carry out a scheme which they had hatched together.

Keyes, whose submarines had been regularly patrolling deep into the Helgoland Bight, had noticed a regular pattern of enemy patrols. At dawn and dusk every day German light cruisers escorted destroyers (still called 'torpedo boats' by the Germans throughout the war) to a point about twenty miles from Helgoland, from which the destroyers would fan out and patrol the Bight on the lookout for British submarines or minelayers. Tyrwhitt thought that he might be able to get his destroyers in between the German destroyers and their base and use the superior speed and firepower of British destroyers to annihilate them. The German boats would be lured away from their normal route home by some of Keyes's submarines, which would show themselves on the surface then dive to safety. While the enemy searched for the submarines, Tyrwhitt's force would have time to cut the enemy ships off from their base. Goodenough's light cruiser squadron would be standing by outside the Bight to deal with any of the German light cruisers which might emerge. It was a risky plan, involving using small ships within an hour's steaming from the enemy fleet base, but it appealed to Churchill, First Lord of the Admiralty, who suggested that Vice Admiral Sir Doveton Sturdee, the

Chief of Staff, should look seriously at it. Sturdee made some minor changes to the plan, mainly consisting of placing two battle cruisers to the west of the Bight, so that they could intervene in case of trouble. Goodenough's light cruisers were not to be involved.

The concept of this operation was fine, but the supporting staff work was appalling. The scheme, hatched in the Admiralty, was not communicated to Jellicoe at Scapa until the very last minute and even then no detail was given. Jellicoe, afraid of the dangers of operating so close to the enemy coast, immediately and on his own authority countermanded the Admiralty's orders and sent Goodenough's light cruiser squadron, which was based with the Battle Cruiser Force on the east coast of Scotland, to the Bight; ordered Beatty with three powerful battle cruisers, *Lion*, *Queen Mary* and *Princess Royal*, to stand by in close support and took the Grand Fleet itself to sea in case the enemy should come out in force. He did this on his own initiative, in the absence of any detailed information about the operation. He informed the Admiralty only when his supporting operation was in full swing so as to make sure that they could do nothing to prevent it. This was ultimately to save the day for the British. However the Admiralty, even when informed of Jellicoe's movements, did not communicate them to Tyrwhitt, by now at sea, or to Keyes's submarines, then cruising the Bight and only in sporadic contact with Keyes, who was himself at sea in the destroyer *Lurcher*, trying to co-ordinate the activities of his submarine force. Such communication was difficult as there was no reliable means of contacting the subs once they were on station. Everything was in place for a horrific 'blue on blue' disaster. In particular the submarines, which were not aware that Goodenough's light cruisers were to be involved, would naturally assume that any light cruisers they saw were enemies and attack them.

Luck, however was on the British side. The actual fight was complicated and doubly confused by poor visibility. The British light cruiser's heavier guns initially gave them a decided advantage and the German's planned refuge, under the protection of the heavy artillery on Helgoland itself, was denied by thick haze around the island which prevented the heavy coastal guns from seeing their targets. Most important of all was a factor that seems to have been totally overlooked by the British planners. The British action had begun at 7 am. On that day the tide in the Jade would not rise high enough to let any of the heavy German ships get to sea until about midday. Until afternoon, therefore the British forces would have to deal with nothing heavier than light cruisers. Of these however, there was no shortage. One by one they joined the foray during the morning and Tyrwhitt's force became hard pressed. As was to be the case in most encounters during the war, the Germans found the range quicker than their opponents, and since all the action took place at close range in poor visibility, German multiple 4-inch guns eventually proved more effective than the 6-inch main armament of the larger British cruisers. Even when Goodenough's modern light cruisers intervened, the British situation was critical, especially when *Arethusa*, Tyrwhitt's flagship, a brand new ship not yet over her teething problems, decided to break down and lose the use of her main armament. British submarines, unaware that Goodenough's four funnel light cruisers were in the area, took them to be the enemy and tried, unsuccessfully, to torpedo them. Shortly before midday, when German heavy ships might soon be in a position to emerge and finish off the intruders, Goodenough was able to get a wireless message to Beatty, still an hour's steaming away, informing him that the situation was serious. Beatty decided to ignore the threat of enemy mines and submarines and steamed at high speed towards the action. His intervention was decisive. Charging onto the battlefield, regardless of the threats posed by underwater weapons, the battle cruisers made short work of four light cruisers, then turned quickly for home. *Arethusa* was taken in tow and brought safely into port.

The battle represented a welcome victory for British sea power. The enemy had lost four light cruisers and one destroyer sunk, three light cruisers damaged and suffered 1,232 casualties and 336 prisoners of war. There were 75 British casualties and one cruiser and three destroyers damaged, but all four damaged ships were able to reach home. In effect, hopeless British staff work had been offset by an equally incompetent response on the part of the Germans. Their light cruisers had come on the scene one by one, not in any sort of co-ordinated formation, and although they had individually fought with skill and great courage they had been overwhelmed by the Royal Navy in spite of being only an hour's steaming from their own fleet base. Morale in the Imperial Navy suffered a crushing blow and the Kaiser, ever protective of his precious ships, ordered that they should never stray far from the German coast without his specific permission. Tirpitz, now sidelined by the regime, was furious, accusing the Kaiser of meddling, and Admiral von Ingenohl (Commander of the High Seas Fleet), of indecision and incompetence. There was justice in both accusations. Neither the British nor the Germans however, properly learnt the lessons of this encounter. British staff work remained poor and communication between the Admiralty and the Grand Fleet shaky, with no proper protocol for decision taking. The Germans lost their aggressive spirit, at least temporally, and let Tirpitz, who might have driven the Imperial Navy to seize the initiative, slide into disgruntled oblivion.

Far away in the in the southern oceans, the battles of Coronel and the Falkland Islands provided a perfect example of how the Royal Navy was able dominate the seas in 1914, and of how battle cruisers could be a decisive weapon in enforcing this.

The outbreak of the war had found Admiral von Spee in command of a squadron whose mission was to protect the German settlement in Tianjin and assert a German military presence in the Far East. As soon as hostilities commenced, Von Spee was ordered to abandon his mission and return as quickly as possible to join the High Seas Fleet in home waters, doing what damage he could to enemy shipping on his way. Such a long voyage was no easy task as Germany had very few colliers at large to refuel ships at sea and unlike Britain did not have a global network of coaling stations. Coal would have to be captured from enemy ships or shore installations. Von Spee's first move was to detach from his squadron the brilliantly successful 'freelance' commerce raiding light cruiser *Emden*, which spread havoc among Allied shipping in the Indian Ocean and beyond, thus effectively distracting the British ships of the Australia Squadron, which would otherwise have been able to join the hunt for the escaping German cruisers.

Von Spee had with him six ships; the armoured cruisers *Scharnhorst* and *Gneisenau* (11,400 tonnes 23 knots speed, 8.2-inch main armament), and the light cruisers *Dresden*, *Leipzig*, and *Nurnberg* (all 4.1-inch armament, speed 23–29 knots), together with attendant colliers and supply ships. The two armoured ships were built in 1906 and were powerful vessels, with heavy defensive armour and with their main armament in turrets enabling the heavy guns to be used in rough seas. This was not possible with the low down casement-mounted guns in older ships. Von Spee himself was an example of the best type of German officer, skilled, energetic and resourceful. He took a realistic view of his chances of getting home, which he believed were poor, but was also aware of the embarrassment he could cause if he was able to inflict substantial damage on the British in the attempt.

Facing this force, the Royal Navy was sadly disorganised. With the Australia Squadron engaged in searching for the *Emden* and in escorting troop convoys, the task of hunting the Germans fell to the West Indies based ships under command of Admiral Craddock. Craddock was a typical naval officer of his time, with little idea of grand strategy. To make matters worse he was beset by a continual stream of orders from the Admiralty which was as unschooled in the facts of twentieth century warfare as Craddock himself. Churchill, the First Lord, who persisted in considering himself an ace naval strategist, was as usual giving free reign to his ideas of himself as a commander of forces at sea, adding a degree of amateurism to proceedings which was unmatched even by his admirals.

Craddock had under his command a poorly matched group of vessels. *Canopus* (12,950 tonnes) was a pre-dreadnought battleship. Poor old *Canopus* was built in 1879 and had reciprocating coal-fired steam engines. She burnt nine tonnes of coal per hour and had a top speed of nineteen knots when all was going well. More commonly, twelve knots was the best she could do. She was heavily armoured and carried four 12-inch guns. Churchill referred to her as 'A citadel which the Germans would not dare to approach.' This was probably true, but as she was normally hundreds of miles astern of the cruisers, 'approaching' never came into the picture. *Good Hope* (14,100 tonnes) was an old type armoured cruiser launched in 1901. Her top speed was twenty-three knots, main armament was two 9.2-inch guns, each mounted in a turret and she had sixteen 6-inch casement guns that could not be operated in a seaway. She was, at least by German standards, extremely lightly armoured. *Monmouth* (9,800 tonnes) was a smaller armoured cruiser with only fourteen 6-inch guns, and the squadron was completed by the light cruiser *Glasgow* (25 knots, two 6-inch guns) and the armed merchantman *Otranto* (eight 4.7-inch guns). Craddock was promised reinforcement from *Defence*, another, more modern, armoured cruiser, but she did not materialize. The weight of the British guns should not be taken as an indication of their effectiveness. The German 8.2s had much higher velocity and longer range than *Canopus's* 12s or the 9.2s on *Good Hope*.

With this force, Craddock was instructed to proceed to the west coast of South America, where intelligence reported the Germans to be headed, to disrupt German trade there, and destroy von Spee's powerful squadron. He did not even reach the Pacific without incident. *Canopus* broke down in the Magellan Straight and remained there throughout the following action.

Craddock was coaling at Port Stanley when the order came by telegraph from the Admiralty to concentrate his force on the coast of Chile and 'bring the enemy to battle.' How to do this when Canopus was immobile was not explained. Even Craddock's sturdy optimism was deflated at this point and his telegrams to their lordships indicated his reluctance to face an enemy so superior in every respect to his own ancient little fleet. However, on 30 October his squadron, with the exception of *Canopus*, still repairing her engines near Cape Horn, was concentrated eighty miles west of Coronel and he bravely set out to search for the enemy. *Monmouth* had already picked up radio intercepts from *Leipzig*, which cleverly indicated that she was steaming south alone, so the British hoped to catch her unsupported. However, by 4.20 pm, two enemy armoured cruisers and three smaller ships had been sighted sailing in line astern approaching Craddock's force from the north east. *Glasgow*, which had been the first ship to sight them, closed on the flagship to her west, and Craddock's squadron turned to form a line of battle. As the Germans worked up to full speed, Craddock attempted to cross their tee by turning eastwards, but *Otranto* had a top speed of only fifteen knots, thus preventing any effective deployment, and von Spee easily avoided this danger. Both squadrons were now steaming south on roughly parallel courses, the British ahead and to the westward, about 15,000 yards apart; just out of effective range. The Germans gradually edged away eastwards towards the coast to avoid engaging with the setting sun in their eyes. Craddock now had a choice. Should he run south towards where his 'citadel', *Canopus'* was now getting up steam and so hope to engage the enemy on favourable terms, or should he close the range and attack at once, thus avoiding the risk of von Spee outrunning his slow ships and escaping round Cape Horn and towards Europe? Mindful of his orders from London he chose to fight. Neither *Good Hope* or *Monmouth* could use their casement guns in the heavy seas, but

Craddock gradually closed the range and at 7 pm, *Scharnhorst* and *Gneisenau* opened fire at 11,000 yards, while *Good Hope's* 9.2-inch turret guns replied. It was an unequal contest. Within a few minutes both the large British ships had been heavily hit and *Good Hope's* turrets were put out of action. Although hits had been scored on the German heavy armour they did virtually no damage. By 7.50 pm, *Good Hope* blew up and was left a darkened, helpless, hulk on the water. *Monmouth* and *Glasgow* tried to escape to the west, both had been hit, *Monmouth* heavily and *Glasgow* by one shell, which probably did not explode, on her port quarter. *Monmouth* was making water rapidly and barely under control. She tried to get stern to sea to prevent flooding from damage forward. Wallowing in the big seas she was closed by *Nurnberg*, who tried to finish her off with a torpedo. This failed and she imagined that the helpless *Monmouth* turned towards her as if to ram. *Nurnberg* now opened fire at close range and smashed her victim to pieces, in a merciless action that gave rise to controversy later. *Glasgow* limped off into the dark towards Cape Horn where she hoped to meet with *Canopus* and a degree of safety. *Otranto* had realized that her contribution to the British line was worse than useless and retired to the westward. So ended the Battle of Coronel. Lost were two heavy British cruisers and with them a large helping of British prestige, along with almost one thousand seamen.

Britain had to respond. Jacky Fisher was recalled to the Admiralty to replace Battenberg as First Sea Lord. Churchill over-rode objections from Jellicoe and ordered not only the cruisers from the West Indies Station, but also two of the most powerful ships in the world, the battle cruisers *Invincible* and *Inflexible* to the South Atlantic (actually Churchill asked for one only, Fisher insisted on two ships). As well as the battle cruisers the armoured cruiser *Defence*, and the light cruisers *Carnarvon*, *Cornwall*, *Bristol*, *Glasgow*, (hastily patched up at sea) and *Kent* formed a powerful British task force. *Canopus*, her engines now partly repaired, limped towards the Falklands to join them. The force was under command of Vice Admiral Sturdee. Sturdee was no friend of Fisher, and was in some degree of disgrace due to the chaotic organisation of the Helgoland Bight action, for which he had been responsible.

Von Spee, although he had no knowledge of British plans, was certain that retribution would come sooner or later. He suggested that one of the powerful German dreadnought battle cruisers should be sent to accompany him on his journey across the Atlantic, but the High Seas Fleet could not spare one of these most valuable ships for such a risky venture. Von Spee had fortunately been able to refuel from a captured British collier and this enabled him to round the Horn, but he still required more coal for the Atlantic crossing. He knew that the British had a coaling station on the Falklands and expected it to be only lightly protected, so he resolved to make a lightening raid on Port Stanley, coal his ships, then destroy the little town, set fire to its supplies, and proceed on his way.

Meanwhile Sturdee, still unaware that his opponent had rounded the Horn, also made for Port Stanley to coal and collect together his fleet. He meant to stay long enough only for coaling and to organize some local defence for the islands in the way of minefields and light forces. When he found *Canopus* in harbour, he had her beached to form a sort of shore battery protecting the bay, with her guns sighted from watchtowers on shore.

Von Spee arrived off Port Stanley early in the morning of 7 December 1914. At first, no ships were visible in harbour, then came a report of a few light cruisers, and some masts belonging to larger ships. Thinking these must be superannuated battleships, he continued to close on the island.

In Port Stanley some confusion reigned as soon as the Germans were sighted. The battle cruisers were coaling from lighters. *Kent* and *Cornwall* had not refuelled and only *Carnarvon*, *Bristol* and *Glasgow* had steam up. The considerable fleet was thus constricted and immobile at the moment when it was faced by a determined and skilful enemy. It would take at least two hours to raise steam in the battle cruisers that had lighters alongside and were busily coaling. Help however, appeared from an unexpected quarter. *Canopus*, sitting on her mud berth, was able to bring her four 12-inch guns to bear at 13,500 yards. By chance she had been preparing for gunnery practise that morning. The crew of the after turret were in deadly competition with the fore turret and had by night secretly loaded their guns with practise rounds so as to get a flying start in the competition scheduled to take place next day. It was impossible to unload the after turret and replace the practice rounds with live ones when suddenly a real target unexpectedly appeared, so the practice rounds had to be fired at the enemy ships. The first salvo from the fore turret fell well short and burst on contact with the water, but the solid practice rounds fired by the after turret hit the water just short of the target, bounced up and struck *Gneisenau's* funnel. Astonished, von Spee turned away to the north-east. He was confident that he could outpace any heavy British ships in the area, but could not risk damage from an encounter with even the oldest pre-dreadnought.

Frantic efforts were made in the harbour to cast off the lighters and make the battle cruisers ready for sea. Just after 10 am, the fleet left harbour and spread out in formation with the fast cruiser *Kent* ahead, maintaining visual contact with the enemy, just out of range of his guns. It was a calm clear day and at first the British were unable to get close enough to open fire due to the low speed of the armoured cruisers. Then Sturdee ordered the battle cruisers to forge ahead on full power and commence the battle by themselves. These ships could be put into emergency full speed mode for short periods by injecting oil as well as coal into the furnaces and they worked up to over twenty-six knots, well above their design maximum. At 12.47 pm, *Inflexible* opened fire at 16,500 yards on the slowest of the enemy cruisers, *Leipzig*. Realizing now that he was dealing with a superior force which was also faster than his own, von Spee ordered his light cruisers to try to escape southwards and brought his heavy ships into action. Sturdee replied by sending *Kent, Glasgow* and *Cornwall* after the light cruisers and concentrating the fire of the 'Invincibles' on *Scharnhorst* and *Gneisenau*. The Germans fought bravely and well, and had the advantage of the lee position, which meant that smoke prevented the British gunners from seeing the fall of their shot. The British guns however, had longer range and much greater hitting power, so the battle could only end in one way. Sturdee tried to keep out of range of the enemy guns so as to avoid the chance of damage from a lucky German shot, while remaining close enough to enable his own broadsides to smash into the unfortunate enemy ships. To achieve this he kept changing course, swerving to port or starboard whenever the enemy tried to close the range by turning towards him. This violent manoeuvring completely defeated the fire control systems of both battle cruisers, so that the guns had to be aimed visually. Nevertheless, the British fire soon began to tell. By 4.45 pm, *Scharnhorst*, which had been glowing like a torch from within but still firing her guns, suddenly listed to port and disappeared, taking von Spee and all his crew with her. An hour later *Gneisneau* was a wreck and hauled down her colours, sinking a few minutes later. Some 200 of her men were picked up. Only one seaman on the two 'Invincibles' was killed and two injured. Both British ships had superficial damage only.

In the meantime *Kent, Cornwall* and *Glasgow* were trying to catch the fleeing German light cruisers. *Leipzig* was the slowest, and by 3.40 pm *Glasgow* had caught her and a fierce fight took place between the two light cruisers. *Leipzig* was already badly damaged when *Cornwall* joined the battle. With all of her guns out of action, *Leipzig* tried to fire torpedoes, but the British kept out of range, and by 7.55 pm she sank with her colours flying. There were only twenty survivors. One British sailor was killed on *Glasgow*.

Kent, a twenty-four knot armoured cruiser had been left to chase *Nurnberg* by herself. By 5 pm she too was exceeding her design speed, the engines reported to be producing 5,000 more horsepower than normal. *Kent* had 6-inch guns, the same calibre as the German light cruisers but had better protection. She engaged *Nurnberg* at very close range, and soon had her opponent virtually knocked to pieces. At about 6.35 pm, *Nurnberg* sank. Only twelve survivors were picked up, and five of these died soon after. *Kent* lost two seamen.

Dresden survived, to Fisher's disgust, hiding in various neutral ports and anchorages searching desperately for coal until March, when she was caught by *Kent* and *Glasgow* in a Chilean harbour and destroyed, her crew escaping ashore to internment. Interestingly, her navigating officer, Wilhelm Canaris, who engineered the escape of the crew, was to become chief of German intelligence in the Second World War.

Hardly had the dreadful news about Coronel been received in Britain than the Imperial Navy conducted their first aggressive act in the North Sea. The German's North Sea coast is less than a hundred miles long, protected by fortified islands and in 1914, by extensive minefields. The British east coast by contrast, is over seven hundred miles long and was only very lightly defended. British defensive mine laying was extremely limited, partly because Britain entered the war with a stock of only about 4,000 mines and partly because the Admiralty considered that mining would unduly restrict the movement of Royal Navy ships and British commerce. This situation obviously gave Germany an opportunity to carry out hit and run raids on the British east coast. Admiral von Ingenohl, commander of the High Seas

Fleet, gained authorization for the first such raid in late October and on November 2, three of Hipper's battle cruisers, *Seydlitz*, *von der Tann* and *Moltke* accompanied by the heavy pre-dreadnought heavy cruiser *Blucher*, set off together with four light cruisers. Von Ingenohl himself put to sea with the High Seas Fleet, remaining within the Helgoland Bight, to give cover to Hipper on his return. The object of the raid was for the battle cruisers to create a diversion while the light cruisers would lay a minefield off Yarmouth. Von Ingenohl knew that there was little chance of interference from heavy British ships. The Grand Fleet was still based in Loch Swilly and Beatty's battle cruisers were in the Cromarty Firth and would take over a day to reach Yarmouth. Old pre-dreadnought battleships at the Nore were no threat to the fast, modern, German attackers.

The raid was not a success. Fire was exchanged with British light forces but no serious damage was done to either side. The battle cruisers let fly at Yarmouth but their shells fell harmlessly on the beach. The minefield was successfully laid off the Smith's Knoll and a British submarine, attempting to intervene, ran onto a mine and was lost, but the rest of the field was quite quickly marked and dealt with. Hipper turned around and made it back to the Jade without loss or damage. A heavy cruiser of the High Seas Fleet, standing by to the east, was not so lucky. *Yorck*, returning to port in thick weather, lost her way and failed to spot a minesweeper that was marking the end of a German defensive minefield. She was lost together with 235 men.

The 'Yarmouth Raid' as this exploit was called, brought little satisfaction to either side. In Britain the Admiralty was puzzled as to why the enemy should have sent such a powerful force to achieve so little, but the British public was affronted that their vaunted navy could have allowed large German ships to sail right up to their coast with impunity. The Germans on the other hand were disappointed in their own performance and shocked by the loss of *Yorck*. Hipper personally refused to wear the iron cross awarded to him for the raid by the Kaiser. Von Ingenohl realized however, that such attacks did have the potential to annoy the enemy and perhaps with luck, to lure out the battle cruisers and draw them towards the waiting High Seas Fleet, where they could be severely handled. Thus he could perhaps reduce the numerical superiority of the British Grand Fleet. Indeed, it was to be an elaboration of such an enterprise that eventually led to the Battle of Jutland itself.

On December 16, a far heavier blow fell on the English coast. Determined to avenge the defeat in the Falklands and to put up a better showing than it had achieved off Yarmouth, the High Seas Fleet had hatched a plan which, had it succeeded, might have wiped out British naval superiority completely. Aware that there would be pressure on the Royal Navy to prevent any repetition of the bombardment of Yarmouth, von Ingenohl guessed correctly that the British battle cruisers would be held ready to intervene if another attack began to materialize. He would therefore reconnoitre the north-east coast of England by submarine to determine the best spots to attack, then order Hipper to bombard them at close range for an extended period, at the same time using a light cruiser to put down a minefield. This would give the British time to set out to intercept the raiders on their way home. He himself would be at sea with the High Seas Fleet just east of the Dogger Bank and thus Hipper, seeming to flee Beatty's avenging battle cruisers, would actually be leading them onto the heavy guns of the German battleships. This was quite a high risk strategy for the German admiral to pursue because he would be flagrantly disobeying the Kaiser's instruction not to take the High Seas Fleet beyond the Helgoland Bight. However, pressure from his impatient subordinates, Scheer and Hipper, persuaded him to ignore orders. What the admiral did not know was that by this time Room 40 at the Admiralty was listening in to his signals traffic. The Royal Navy was therefore aware of the timing and the general nature of the battle cruiser attack well in advance. Room 40 did not however know that the High Seas Fleet was going to put to sea as well as the battle cruisers. The stage was set for Beatty to run at full speed into a most dangerous trap.

The Admiralty sent Beatty to sea before the raiders had reached their destination, instructing him to wait for Hipper to the east of the minefields off the English coast so as to be between the returning raiders and their home port. To make assurance double sure, six battleships under Admiral Warrender were detached from the Grand Fleet to join him in the attempt to ambush the returning enemy battle cruisers. Jellicoe strongly objected to this deployment of a section of the Grand Fleet, pointing out correctly, that if Warrender's squadron was led over a minefield or a submarine trap,

Britain's ability to dominate the North Sea would be lost, and quite possibly the war with it. He was overruled. Soon however, the weather took a hand. Hipper, steaming westwards across the North Sea encountered rough seas and a stiff headwind, which made it impossible for the accompanying destroyers to keep up with his great ships. He therefore detached most of his light forces, keeping with him only a few light cruisers, including *Kolberg*, which was to act as the minelayer. Early in the morning his main force arrived off the coast, fixed its position and started a heavy bombardment of Whitby, Scarborough and the industrial town of Hartlepool. The first two towns were of no major military or economic importance, but Hartlepool and its steelworks was defended by a small squadron of ancient cruisers and destroyers, and a single submarine. There were also three 6-inch coastal guns manned by men of the Durham Light Infantry. Inexcusably, the naval forces were not ready for action, and played only a futile part in the defence of the town. The submarine, had it been at sea, could have had a superb target in the slow moving ships, without their customary destroyer escorts, as they bombarded the sea front and factories. The Admiralty had actually warned the admiral commanding the east coast of the likelihood of a raid, but he had neglected to order any ships to sea. The army gunners put up a sturdy resistance and scored many hits, but the well-defended hulls of the battle cruisers were proof against 6-inch projectiles and only superficial damage was done. The bombarding ships did substantial damage to property and industrial plant, killing 105 civilians and wounding a further 525. *Kolberg* laid her mines as planned, and these were to do serious damage to coastal shipping and proved especially difficult to sweep in the bitter December weather.

This achieved, Hipper's force turned for home expecting to meet the High Seas Fleet on their way and possibly to become embroiled in a running fight with Beatty so as to lead him onto the guns of von Ingenohl's battleships. Hipper was however, unaware of events that had taken place 150 miles to the east, a few miles from where The High Seas Fleet was supposed to wait for him. Here, the light forces that had been detached due to the weather, clashed with Beatty's escorting destroyers and there was a brisk exchange of fire in which the Germans inflicted some damage on their opponents. The sound of gunfire however and the threat of a torpedo attack by destroyers seems to have been too much for the German admiral. Giving up his plan to ambush Beatty, von Ingenohl abandoned Hipper's battle cruisers to their fate, turned tail and made for harbour. Now, instead of the British steaming into a German trap, the German battle cruisers, unsupported as they now were, were about to enter the jaws of a British one.

In the event, success was to elude Beatty and Warrender on that bitter December day. There were a number of confused clashes between light forces on both sides and outliers of the High Seas Fleet. Then news reached the British that Hartlepool was under fire. The British heavy ships turned westwards and fanned out so as to be sure of intercepting the returning Germans, with their light cruiser screen scouting ahead. Goodenough in *Southampton*, sighted the returning Germans exactly as planned and began to engage them, but the weather closed in, reducing visibility to not much over one mile. An inexcusable signalling error on the part of Seymore, Beatty's signals officer, caused *Southampton* to disengage and lose touch with Hipper's ships. From that point onward the British blundered about in the mist and rain, searching desperately for the enemy ships, but gained only occasional glimpses of them and never opened fire. The raiding battle cruisers slipped safely home to Germany. From the Royal Navy's point of view this had been a humiliating shambles. The British coast had been cruelly attacked and the enemy escaped unscathed, except for the minelayer, *Kolberg*, which was severely damaged by the heavy seas as it struggled to keep up with the battle cruisers on the return journey. Beatty tried to blame Goodenough. He even wanted to have him dismissed from his command for breaking off his engagement with the enemy, but wiser heads knew that Beatty himself and his signals officer were responsible. In the end, Goodenough was reprieved and the Battle Cruiser Force (as Beatty's command was now called) was moved south from Cromarty to the Firth of Forth so as to be closer to any future potential enemy incursion.

The Germans too were far from satisfied with the outcome of the operation. There was bitter criticism of von Ingenohl for abandoning Hipper in his hour of danger, and Hipper himself knew well that it was only good luck and the thick weather which saved him from an encounter with both Beatty (who he might have been able to handle) and Warrender's battleships (which would have been far too formidable for him). In particular the *Admiralstab* (the German equivalent to the Admiralty) was at a loss to know how the British had known about the coming raid, and were thus able to be prepared to intercept their forces on their way home. The true cause, Room 40's increasing ability to read their signals traffic, seemed too improbable to merit serious consideration. Instead, suspicion fell on neutral trawlers, working on and around the Dogger Bank. Attempts by German light forces to round these up and interrogate their crews in a search for spies had always been frustrated by the presence of British forces patrolling the area. The only viable solution seemed to be a sweep of the Bank in force by battle cruisers, which would cover a large fleet of destroyers and light cruisers, tasked with sweeping up all the fishing boats present and bringing them in for questioning. With luck they might also sweep up some of the British forces in the area at the same time. The High Seas Fleet would not be involved, but would be held ready to come out in the event of serious trouble. The fleet was at the time depleted in any case because the '*Konigs*', the most powerful of the battleships, were away training in the Baltic. The date set for the sortie was 23 January 2015.

The German force consisted of three battle cruisers, *Seydlitz, Moltke, Derfflinger (von der Tann* was in dock) and the heavy cruiser *Blucher. Blucher* had been on the stocks when the Germans first heard about the new breed of ship, the dreadnought battle cruiser, so she was modified to try to bring her as close as possible to battle cruiser standards, but she remained markedly inferior in firepower, in armour and in speed. All the German battle cruisers could exceed twenty-five knots; *Blucher* was hard pressed to make twenty-three. Bringing her on this mission was to prove a costly mistake. Light forces allocated to the sweep consisted of four light cruisers and nineteen destroyers.

The Admiralty, warned of Hipper's forthcoming venture by Room 40, knew exactly what was going on and determined not to fail this time. Beatty's force had been strengthened by the return of *Indomitable* from the South Atlantic, and by the arrival of a new and even more powerful ship – *Tiger*. Unfortunately *Queen Mary*, the one ship with the superior Argo fire control system was absent, undergoing routine maintenance. The British battle cruiser force thus consisted of *Tiger, Lion, Indomitable, New Zealand* and *Princess Royal* – five ships against the German four. Once again British heavy ships were also sent to sea, this time with a screen of obsolete battleships and armoured cruisers standing by to the north of the Dogger Bank in case the Germans attempted to slip away towards the northern tip of Denmark (The Skaw), and even further north Jellicoe with the Grand Fleet was on patrol. To the south the Harwich force of light cruisers and destroyers was also at sea and ready for a fight.

As dawn broke, the Germans began their methodical sweep of the Bank, picking up a handful of suspicious looking fishing vessels, but as the sun came up, the light cruisers flanking both battle cruiser fleets clashed and very soon Hipper was receiving reports of ominous clouds of smoke to the westward. Once again his sortie had been anticipated by the enemy. The weather was clear and bright, so this time there was no chance of slipping away unseen by the superior British forces. Whatever happened he must not let the enemy get between him and his home port. The only course was to turn and run at full speed for home and the protection of the coastal minefields. There then began one of the most thrilling sea chases of recent times. The British *Invincibles*, the oldest of the British battle cruisers, were significantly faster than *Blucher* and the three newest ships could actually achieve almost twenty-nine knots against *Blucher's* twenty-three and were slightly faster than the German battle cruisers. By a supreme effort of their stokers, shovelling good Welsh steam coal into their furnaces in their hellish black stokeholds below the waterline, even *New Zealand* and *Indomitable* were exceeding twenty-five knots, well in excess of their design maximum, throughout the chase. To keep them motivated the 'black gang' were given a commentary on the action and Beatty himself congratulated *Indomitable's* crew on their efforts to keep up. The British ships worked their way slightly downwind of the Germans so as to enable their gunners to take aim with minimum interference from smoke. Inexorably, they drew closer to the fleeing enemy.

The Harwich force had with it seven of the new M Class destroyers, capable of well over thirty knots and these were sent ahead to attempt a torpedo attack from the flank, but they were easily beaten off by *Blucher's* 6-inch secondary armament. By 9 am however, *Lion* and *Tiger* ('The Splendid Cats') were just 20,000 yards astern of *Blucher* and were able to open effective fire, *Lion* leading the column, with Beatty aboard, shifting to *Moltke*, the next ship ahead as *Tiger* caught up. Soon the Germans were replying and both sides were scoring hits. From the pursuer's point of view this sort of stern chase involved the risk of the enemy laying mines in his wake or making a sudden torpedo attack. Ominously Goodenough, observing the enemy from the flank, noticed a flurry of action among the enemy destroyers and informed Beatty, who immediately ordered his escorting destroyers to go ahead and disrupt the enemy manoeuvre. The destroyers were hard pressed to get ahead of the battle cruisers, now making almost twenty-nine knots, but the new M class boats at once showed their mettle. In the event, the enemy threat did not materialize. Probably Hipper's plan was to draw the British on and let loose his destroyers with their torpedoes when dusk fell. The activity observed by Goodenough was only preparatory.

By 9.35 am, all the British ships except *Indomitable*, still a little way behind, were firing on the enemy. A confusing signal from *Lion* (not Seymore's fault this time) caused both *Lion* and *Tiger* to concentrate their fire on the foremost German ship, *Seydlitz*, leaving *Moltke* unmolested and confusing the aim of the two 'Cats' who did not know which splash near *Seydlitz* came from which ship's salvoes. At 9.45 am however, a 13.5-inch shell from *Lion*, fired at a range of 17,000 yards, pierced the armoured deck of *Seydlitz* close to her after turret, setting fire to the charges on their way up to the turret and causing a massive explosion which flashed back into the magazines, putting both aft turrets out of action and killing 165 men. Only amazingly prompt and courageous action by an officer and two petty officers, who flooded the remaining magazines, saved *Seydlitz* from total destruction. As it was, the superbly durable battle cruiser remained in action, her speed unaffected although her firepower was greatly reduced. Hipper however, seeing the battle going against him, sent an urgent signal to von Ingenohl asking for support. The High Seas Fleet had steam up and prepared to put to sea, but was too far away to be of any help.

The British ships were not unscathed. *Lion*, leading the charge, with Beatty aboard, had sustained a hit on 'A' turret, which did substantial damage but did not slow her down or cause a secondary explosion. Then two more hits below the waterline flooded underwater compartments and stopped the port engine, causing her to pull out of line. More hits caused water to deluge into the dynamo room, cutting off all electrical power and making the radio useless. A further hit put 'A' turret out of action altogether. Soon salt water penetrated the boilers and the starboard engine stopped as well. Seeing *Lion* fall out of line, the enemy ships concentrated their fire on *Tiger*. They succeeded in setting the boat deck on fire, causing a spectacular blaze but little serious damage. On the other side poor *Blucher* was now suffering horribly at the hands of *New Zealand* and *Indomitable*. She slowed down, caught fire, and wallowed helpless, far astern of her consorts. Hipper had no option but to leave her to her fate and continue his run for safety. Good luck (or British incompetence) however, was to come to his aid again.

As *Lion* was slowing down and the other ships surged past her, Beatty spotted what he thought was the periscope of a submarine close off his starboard bow. Horrified that he was being led into a trap he signalled a sharp turn to port, swinging his ships away from their pursuit of the enemy. No one else saw this periscope, it was probably imaginary, but Beatty knew well the dangers of an enemy mine or submarine trap and dare not risk his fleet. Even so, the turn to port was a serious mistake. If the object had been a submarine at such close quarters it would have been better to turn towards it and ram than to turn away. Beatty then tried to get his ships to continue the hunt by signalling at the same time 'Course northeast' and 'Attack the rear of the enemy.' These signals were made by flag, no other method being available in the absence of electrical power for the ship's radio. None of the four following, and substantially undamaged, battle cruisers knew what they meant. The enemy rear was the disabled *Blucher* and she was to the northeast, were they meant to attack her again, or continue after the three fleeing battle cruisers? Admiral Moore, Beatty's second in command, simply did not know what to do, but deciding that Beatty must have had some reason for his signals and the sharp turn to port, resolved to concentrate on *Blucher*. Under the guns of four British battle cruisers and the torpedoes of several smaller ships, she caught fire, rolled over and sank, taking over 900 men with her. This diversion and delay left the three remaining German battle cruisers free to escape to the safety of their own minefields and the Jade Estuary. They had a lucky escape. *Seydlitz* and *Derfflinger* were both badly damaged, and the *Moltke* alone could hardly have resisted the four remaining and largely undamaged British ships, all of which had their turrets still serviceable.

the terrible explosion on *Seydlitz* and studied carefully the procedures used in the Battle Cruiser Force to handle ammunition in battle. He found that the men working in the magazines, below sea level, would remove the cordite charges from the containers in which they were stored within the magazine itself, instead of delivering them inside their containers to the handling room. The charges themselves were then stacked up in the handling room and in the aisles within the magazine. Packed in each of the silk bags that held the cordite was the sixteen-ounce pouch of gunpowder which acted as a detonator. This charge was protected by a thick paper barrier, which was supposed to be removed in the gun breech immediately before the breech was closed for firing. Instead of this, the crews in the handling rooms were in the habit of removing the protective paper before placing the cordite charge in the hoist up to the gun turret, leaving a deadly trail of gunpowder on the floors and on down into the handling room. Bags of cordite in this condition also were accumulated within the turret itself, waiting to be loaded into the breeches. These extremely dangerous practices were adopted to try to achieve a higher rate of fire, but in practice they did not improve fire rate at all. Grant managed to get the correct procedures introduced on *Lion*, probably saving her from destruction when she was hit on one of her turrets at Jutland. *Lion* was able to prove that using them she could achieve as good a rate of fire as any other ship, whilst remaining much safer. Tragically, Beatty seems to have taken very little interest in details of procedure like this and made no move to introduce the '*Lion* procedure' onto other ships under his command. Many brave men were to pay dearly for such carelessness.

Although side armour of the British battle cruisers was reinforced after the Dogger Bank battle, deck armour was not, nor were turret disciplines changed. Many of the officers involved in the battle sent detailed reports and recommendations regarding tactics and procedures in to the Admiralty, but these were ignored. Worst of all very little was done to improve the shooting of the Battle Cruiser Fleet. Target practises were still carried out using slow moving targets and exercising very strict economy in the use of ammunition. Continued nagging on this issue by Jellicoe did not produce any results until 1916, when it was planned that individual squadrons would move to Scapa for practise with the main battle fleet.

Both sides were astonished by the ammunition consumption in this short running battle, and the ammunition complement of all ships was increased by both the British and the Germans.

The Dogger Bank affair also seems to have been an example of shoddy planning on the part of the Germans. Surely there were better ways of questioning suspicious fishing boats than by cruising about the Bank in battle cruisers? Why was the High Seas Fleet not ready to back up the battle cruisers? And why were the *Konigs* allowed to disappear on a training exercise when a major action was in the offing?

Tactical blunders were far from being the monopoly of the Germans. Beatty had had as fine an opportunity as he could have wished for to damage the enemy battle cruiser fleet and he had comprehensively muffed it. The Dogger Bank battle shows how completely inappropriate British naval training and practice was for twentieth century warfare. In a fast moving, long- range battle there should have been no room for muddlers like Seymore or admirals like Moore, who had no concept of seizing the moment, as Nelson would have done in the circumstances, and overhauling the fleeing enemy. Added to this, it was obvious that the standard of gunnery in the Battle Cruiser Force was deplorable. How could *Tiger* possibly have misjudged the range by 3,000 yards? Beatty defended himself by pointing out that there was no firing range suitable for his heavy guns on the Forth where he was based and eventually it was agreed that ships of the BCF should go by turns to Scapa and undertake live firing practise. All this took a long time to organize and did not start until spring 1916, but eventually, as events at Jutland were to prove, it was very effective. Had Beatty been more of a team player and less jealous of losing control, even for a short time, of some of his ships, a better standard of shooting might have prevailed throughout his fleet.

There could not have been a better illustration of how inappropriate the Royal Navy's disciplines and practices were for twentieth century warfare than the Dogger Bank action. Significantly it was the first time in history that the great 'Castles of Steel', the dreadnought warships, exchanged fire, and in the battle the fate of *Blucher* gave a terrible illustration of the horrors of twentieth century warfare and the pitiful fate awaiting ships not fit for their purpose. There were lessons to be learnt on both sides and the

Germans were more ready to learn them than their opponents. One vital piece of intelligence did entirely elude the Germans however. Hipper was at a loss to understand how the enemy could have guessed his intentions and been waiting for him at the Dogger Bank. An intensive search was made for spies and traitors, but it never occurred to anyone that the signal codes were now totally cracked.

These three actions in the North Sea, the Yarmouth Raid, the Scarborough Raid and the Dogger Bank were forerunners of Jutland. The first two illustrate clearly the strategic situation faced by both antagonists. The Germans were trying to draw out a small portion of the British fleet so that they could bring it under the guns of the High Seas Fleet and so maul it that the naval strength of both powers would become more equal. This achieved, they would be able to risk a major fleet encounter, in which they believed that their superior gunnery and more durable ships would give them the advantage. It was actually a sound strategy, but it failed to achieve the desired result because the Kaiser was so unwilling to risk his battleships and because von Ingenohl's nerve seems to have failed him at the critical moments. The Kaiser's caution was caused partly because he hated the thought of his expensive navy being lost and partly because he hoped to use his fleet as a negotiating counter in any forthcoming peace negotiations. His caution was misplaced. The loss of some, or indeed most, of the High Seas Fleet would have certainly been a blow to German morale, but it would have had minimal effect on the course of the war. The ships of the High Seas Fleet were playing no role in the execution of Germany's war plans and the potential war winning naval weapon which the Germans did possess, the U-boats, would have operated just as effectively if no High Seas Fleet existed. For the British, the exact opposite was the case. The Grand Fleet was the ultimate weapon, which gave the nation the ability to protect her own vital maritime commerce, to deploy reinforcements from her overseas Empire and Commonwealth and to import war materials and food from America. Without it, enemy commerce raiders would be free to roam the oceans and starve Britain out of the war. At the same time Britain's distant blockade of Germany would be broken so that German forces and citizens would not have to suffer first, 'turnip winters', then actual starvation and a critical shortage of raw materials. Jellicoe understood all this clearly, hence his caution in the deployment of his force and refusal to be drawn into some of the foolish schemes proposed frequently by Churchill and even occasionally by Fisher. There was another flaw in the Kaiser's strategy. By keeping his fleet inactive he allowed the British to increase their numerical superiority. With much greater shipbuilding capacity than Germany and better access to raw materials, Britain was continually adding new and better ships to her fleet, so that while her advantage in dreadnoughts was marginal in August 1914, by the end of May 1916, Britain had brought into service thirteen new battleships and battle cruisers, while Germany had managed only five. Ship's names as follows:

- British: *Benbow, Emperor of India, Tiger, Barham, Queen Elizabeth, Valiant, Warspite, Malaya, Revenge, Royal Oak, Royal Sovereign, Canada, Erin.*
- German: *Markgraf, Kronprinz, Derfflinger, Lutzow, Bayern.*

From the German point of view the best chance to win at sea had come and gone by January 1915.

One class of vessel was significantly absent from all three actions; the submarine. Both sides had expected submarines to play an important part in defensive naval operations and be a potent factor in fleet actions. British subs had failed to defend their east coast bases effectively during the German raids on British shores and German ones had turned out to be no use whatever in the battle cruiser sorties. They were too slow and vulnerable on the surface and too blind and restricted under water, and their communications were too uncertain for them to be able to participate in a fast moving fleet action. It was however, to submarines that the Germans turned after the Dogger Bank debacle.

Deprived by the Kaiser of the option of deploying the High Seas Fleet, the *Admiralstab* looked about for another way of making a contribution to the war effort. The obvious answer was to match Britain's distant blockade of Germany with a blockade of their own, enforced by mines and torpedoes deployed by submarines. Little thought had been given to this strategy before the war, but experience gained in the first six months showed that it could be extremely effective. On 18 February 1915, Germany declared the waters around Britain a war zone in which merchant shipping might be sunk without warning. This was the first phase of unrestricted submarine warfare. The move was a matter of hot dispute within the German administration. Military leaders, convinced that the policy would bring Britain to its knees in six months, supported the policy strongly, whereas the Prime Minister, Bethmann-Hollweg and the Foreign Minister, Jagow, warned that the campaign would bring the United States into the war with fatal consequences for Germany. The doubters were proved correct. The sinking of *Lusitania* and *Arabic*, two large undefended passenger liners with a total of 131 American lives lost, struck horror into the hearts of the American public, and allowed Britain to condemn the perpetrators as shameless pirates. The Kaiser lost his nerve and by August 30, after some 900,000 tons of British shipping had been sunk, he called a halt to unrestricted submarine warfare, to the fury of his generals and admirals. From then on, submarines would have to restrict themselves to sinking only British and French merchant ships, avoiding passenger liners altogether. The U-boat campaign staggered on under these restrictions until the French passenger ship *Sussex* was torpedoed by *UB.29*, resulting in more American deaths. Strong protests from the highest levels of the US government forced the *Admiralstab* to restrict further its submarine operations and revert to internationally agreed norms of conduct. Under these, a submarine was forced to surface beside a merchant vessel, establish its nationality, cargo and destination and then give the passengers and crew time to evacuate before sinking it. Under these restrictions a submarine blockade was totally impractical. Reinhardt Scheer, who took command of the High Seas Fleet in January 1916, ordered all submarines to cease their campaign against merchant shipping.

Far away from the North Sea, in the approaches to the Dardanelles, events were taking place which more than justified Jellicoe's determination to avoid losing a significant proportion of the Grand Fleet as a result of headlong pursuit of an enemy. On 18 March 1915, a combined force of French and British pre-dreadnought warships was ordered to approach close to the Turkish forts near Kephez Point on the Asiatic shore of the Dardanelles Straight. As they closed their objectives, the Allied ships were overtaken by a series of tragic disasters. First the French battleship *Gaulois* was hit by the shore batteries and badly damaged; she was beached to avoid sinking and re-floated later to be towed home for repairs. Built in 1895 she was no great loss to the fleet, which steamed on undeterred towards the forts. They were in fact steaming directly into exactly the sort of trap that Jellicoe so rightly feared. A small Turkish steamer, under command of Lieutenant Colonel Geehl, had sown a field of twenty moored mines in the very area from which the combined fleet was intending to launch its attack. First the French battleship *Bouvet,* then the British pre-dreadnought *Irresistible* succumbed to mines, then another British battleship *Ocean* was disabled by gunfire and a mine strike and had to be abandoned. Worst of all, the dreadnought battle cruiser *Inflexible,* one of the most modern and powerful ships in the Royal Navy, was disabled and had to retire to Malta for extensive repairs. The attack on the forts had to be abandoned and the fleet retired disconsolately to Murdros Island, out of harm's way. Nor was this the end of the British humiliation by the supposedly insignificant Turkish Navy. On 12 May, the German built Turkish destroyer *Muavenet* stole out of the Dardanelles during the night and torpedoed and sank the battleship *Goliath.* She had only been a hundred yards offshore when the three torpedoes struck home and she sank quickly. Tragically, all but 180 of her 750-man crew were carried away by a strong current and drowned. On 17 May 1915, *U21,* a German submarine fighting with the Turks, torpedoed and sank the battleship *Triumph* as she stood off Anzac Beach providing fire support to the troops on land, and the very next day another battleship, *Majestic* suffered the same fate. Fortunately, most of the crews of these last two ships were rescued. Altogether five British and two French battleships and a British battle cruiser had been lost of put out of action in a few months, almost entirely by underwater weapons.

After these tragedies there was no option but to withdraw the whole fleet to a safe anchorage, leaving the armies ashore deprived of heavy gun support. The soldiers complained that the Royal Navy had run away, and so it had. *Queen Elizabeth,* the most powerful battleship then afloat, was immediately recalled all the way to home waters. The place of the capital ships was eventually taken by monitors, too shallow draft and too well protected under water to be easy victims for torpedoes, and by old cruisers hastily fitted with underwater anti-torpedo bulges. The monitors particularly were able to provide the army with much of the firepower it needed. However, the lesson of the Dardanelles was clear. Capital ships simply could not be risked close to enemy coasts or within reach of stealthy mine layers. A small, insignificant naval force could now defeat a powerful, well-armed opponent. *Audacious*, a new dreadnought, had been sunk by a mine in 1914 off the coast of Ireland, proving that even the most modern British ships were vulnerable to underwater weapons. Losses in the North Sea on anything like the scale of those in the Aegean would have deprived Britain of maritime superiority and the war would have been lost. Caution must be the watchword. Fortunately, the lesson was not lost on the commander of the Grand Fleet. Jellicoe had no intention of losing the war in an afternoon.

Chapter Four

The Build Up

S cheer had been a surprising choice for command of the High Seas Fleet. His abilities were widely recognized, he was popular among his naval colleagues, but he had been considered too bold and headstrong to hold a high command. He had differed strongly with the Kaiser and with von Pohl and von Ingenohl on many occasions, always advocating a more active, aggressive role for the fleet. On taking command he had obtained the Kaiser's permission to resume the tactics used in 1914, making hit and run attacks on the English coast so as to force the British to divide their forces to such an extent that the strength of the Grand Fleet could be nibbled away.

Very soon the British presented him with a superb chance to nibble. On 25 March 1916, the seaplane carrier *Vindix* was at sea, aiming to make an attempt to raid the German Zeppelin hangers at Hoyer on the Schleswig coast. Beatty, with the Battle Cruiser Fleet, was at sea to the north of *Vindix* to guard against an attack by enemy battle cruisers, and the Harwich force provided close protection. The raid itself was a failure as the position of the Zeppelin sheds given to the aircrews was incorrect. In the end, only one of the five seaplanes involved found the sheds, but failed to bomb them because the bomb release mechanism jammed. The weather was turning rough with snow squalls, and through these the Germans launched a counter-attack with destroyers and their own seaplanes, hoping to knock out *Vindix* or some of her escorts. The counter-attack was also a failure; it was virtually impossible for aircraft to hit a ship at sea with bombs using the equipment available at the time. In their efforts to avoid bombs however, two British destroyers collided leaving one, *Medusa*, so badly damaged that she had to be towed home. Another attempted enemy destroyer attack resulted in the ramming of the German destroyer *G194* by the cruiser *Cleopatra*. *G194* sank, but *Cleopatra* was herself hit by another British light cruiser, *Undaunted*, whose bows were stove in, reducing her speed to six knots. In this shambolic situation Scheer saw a golden opportunity. The radio intercept station at Neumunster had intercepted signals which told him that the British Battle Cruiser Fleet was at sea. If they could get to the scene quickly, Hipper's battle cruisers could make light work of the British light cruisers and Beatty with *his* battle cruisers would join the foray to find himself face to face with the whole High Seas Fleet, which was preparing to sally out from the Jade. It was not to be. Hipper, emerging from the swept channel into the teeth of the gale that was now blowing, reported that conditions were impossible. The fleet turned round and went home, leaving *Vindix* and the somewhat battered British light forces free to limp back across the tempestuous North Sea.

The next venture of the German fleet closely followed the pattern that had been set in 1914. The battle cruisers, commanded this time by *Konteradmiral* Boedicker (Hipper was away sick) would raid Lowestoft and Yarmouth, while Scheer with the High Seas Fleet, would lie in wait near the Terschelling light, about seventy miles off the English coast, ready to pounce on any British force attempting to chase the attackers home. The German strength was now five battle cruisers, *von der Tann, Moltke, Derfflinger, Seydlitz* and the new and powerful ship *Lutzow*. The chosen date, 24 April, was supposed to coincide with the Irish Easter Rising, which was intended to receive substantial support from Germany (in fact it never arrived). As usual Room 40 knew about this plan in advance and made arrangements to handle it.

The voyage started badly for Boedicker. In the early afternoon *Seydlitz*, his flagship, ran onto a mine which had been put down during the previous November by the British. British mines at that time were notoriously unreliable, but this one seems to have worked well, exploding thirteen feet below the waterline, killing eleven men and tearing a fifty-foot hole in the hull so that 1,400 tons of water flooded into the ship. Her speed was reduced to fifteen knots, and she turned round and limped back home escorted by destroyers. Boedicker shifted his flag to *Lutzow* and initially turned his force round so as to keep clear of further mines and a suspected submarine trap. At about 4 pm he sighted his own battle fleet and turned round again onto a westerly course towards Lowestoft. At dawn the next day, there was a brush between light forces on both sides, Tyrwhitt's Harwich force retreating when they saw the four great battle cruisers ranged against them. Soon Lowestoft was in Boedicker's sights and a brief bombardment ensued, during which three civilians were killed. The raiders then moved north to Yarmouth; they started their bombardment in poor visibility, doing no damage. Boedicker was then distracted by a message telling him that his cruiser screen to the south was under fire from British light forces. He turned and engaged Tyrwhitt's cruisers, one 12-inch shell causing serious damage to the flagship, *Conquest*. This was an excellent opportunity to press home his advantage and mop up most of Tyrwhitt's force, just as Beatty had done during the Battle of the Helgoland Bight. Boedicker however, was no Beatty and he had orders to avoid losses at all costs. He turned round and headed back towards Scheer and the High Seas Fleet. As soon as the battle cruisers were in sight, Scheer, warned by Neumunster that the Grand Fleet was at sea (in fact it was 300 miles away battling through a rough head sea), turned for home.

The results of this enterprise were unsatisfactory to the Germans. *Seydlitz* would require at least a month in dock, two supporting submarines had been lost, and negligible damage had been done to the enemy (Apart from *Conquest's* damage, one British submarine had been destroyed, nothing of military importance on land had been damaged). Most important of all, the British had refused to fall into the trap of dividing the Grand Fleet so as to protect the East Coast. To satisfy public opinion, seven old pre-dreadnought battleships and *Dreadnought* herself were sent to Sheerness; and at Beatty's urging 5BS, Evan-Thomas's 15-inch, fast battleships, were moved from Scapa to the Forth to join the battle cruisers, thus allowing units of the Battle Cruiser Force itself to be sent north for much needed gunnery practice.

Scheer did not give up after the disappointing assault on Yarmouth and Lowestoft. His next plan was indeed far more ambitious. He would use his battle cruisers to attack Sunderland, an important industrial town and shipyard, and once again try to lure the British Battle Cruiser Fleet onto his battleships waiting just over the horizon, before the Grand Fleet could intervene. Sunderland had the advantage of being quite close to the Forth, only 100 miles, so Beatty would be sure to launch himself into Scheer's trap. This time however, the Germans would bring two new weapons into play. The first was the Zeppelin force. The Zepps would patrol the east coast of Scotland on the lookout for any movement south by the Grand Fleet and also keep an eye on the battle cruisers in the Firth of Forth. If Scheer knew exactly what the enemy was doing he would at least not make Von Ingenohl's mistake of running home before it was necessary. The long daylight hours in late May would help to make such reconnaissance effective. The other new factor was his submarine force. Released from their assault on British commerce, the U-boats could lie in wait off the English coast, ready to report movements of British warships and to torpedo them if possible. Some boats would make their way right into the estuaries where the British fleets were based. At the same time, mine laying U-boats would be ready to lay minefields in the path of warships putting to sea. It was a bold and ingenious plan, but no sooner was it hatched than things began to go awry. Firstly the repairs to *Seydlitz* took longer than expected, delaying the start of the operation from 17 to 23 May. *Kapitan zur See* Bauer, in command of U-boat forces, suggested that his boats should sail immediately, regardless of the delays in bringing *Seydlitz* into service, so as to reconnoitre the proposed operational areas and harry any British warships at sea. This was agreed. Ten boats put to sea with orders to patrol the northeast coast of England, then on the 23rd to take up station exactly on the route usually taken by the battle fleets moving south. One further boat, the minelayer *UB.27*, was to pick its way right into the Firth of Forth, where Beatty was now based. Three more large mine laying U-boats set off to lay their eggs off the Forth, the Moray Firth and the Orkneys. Two more boats sailed from Bruges to cover the mouth of the Humber, where the Germans wrongly suspected that some heavy ships were moored and a further three patrolled off Harwich to impede the progress of the Harwich light forces moving north. All these boats were ordered to keep hidden until they received a radio message warning them that the High Seas Fleet was putting to sea, unless there was a good opportunity for a torpedo attack on a large enemy warship.

Soon after the first of the U-boats sailed, another problem arose for the High Seas Fleet. *Seydlitz's* repairs were completed on schedule, but as soon as she was tested they were found not to be watertight. She had to return to dry dock. This caused a further postponement of the operation, leaving many of the patrolling U-boats getting close to their limits of endurance. At last on 30 May all was ready and Hipper's battle cruisers, followed by the High Seas Fleet, got ready for sea.

All was not well however. The U-boats had suffered a number of breakdowns and operational problems, and thick weather had made it impossible for them to carry out a successful reconnaissance. No enemy ships had been successfully attacked. One of the minelayers had been sunk by armed trawlers, and another, *U.75* had laid her mines in completely the wrong place (The mistake was fortuitous however. It was one of these mines, west of the Orkneys, which was to sink the cruiser *Hampshire* carrying General Kitchener to Russia). Later *UC.3*, a large minelayer, disappeared altogether; probably she struck a British mine. *U.27*, the boat charged with entering the Firth of Forth, got tangled in a fishing net, damaged a propeller and had to limp home. The submarine operation was rapidly falling apart. Worse news still came from the Zeppelins. Strong northeast winds made flying extremely difficult and there was no chance of a reconnaissance of the Scottish coast. This was the final nail in the coffin of the Sunderland plan. It would have been foolhardy to close the English coast without some observation screen on the northern flank, especially in view of the experience the German fleet had of the British always being ready (or almost ready) for them. Scheer however, was not a man to give up the chance of a battle easily. He had another plan up his sleeve. Instead of attacking Sunderland, Hipper would cruise ostentatiously up the west coast of Denmark and into the Skagerrak (the stretch of sea separating northern Denmark from Norway). Here he was pretty certain to encounter British cruisers enforcing the distant blockade. These could be dealt with, causing Beatty to sortie from the Forth seeking a fight with Hipper, but instead of Hipper he would find himself facing the full might of the High Seas Fleet, which would be cruising fifty miles behind the battle cruisers, keeping well out of sight of prying eyes on land. Jellicoe's battleships would be too far from Beatty to intervene. The great advantage of this plan was that the starboard (eastern) flank of the German fleets would be close to Denmark, therefore unthreatened by the enemy. The western flank could be guarded by a screen of light cruisers and destroyers, so Zeppelin observation was unnecessary. At 3.30 am at first light on 31 May, the German fleets, 100 ships in all, finally weighed and steamed majestically out of the Jade. (See Appendix V for full order of battle for both sides). One German destroyer broke down and pulled out of line as she was leaving harbour.

Scheer's command consisted of sixteen German dreadnought battleships (one, *Konig Albert* was in dock) plus the 2nd Battle Squadron consisting of six pre-dreadnoughts, Admiral Mauve's obsolete Deutschland class battleships, supported by six light cruisers and thirty-one destroyers. Subordinate to Scheer, but operating independently was Hipper with his five battle cruisers, five light cruisers and thirty-one destroyers. Scheer has rightly been criticised for bringing Mauve's pre-dreadnoughts with him. Their fighting value was far inferior to that of the dreadnoughts and they were slow, only capable of eighteen knots, slowing the whole fleet down by two knots. They were also vulnerable. Scheer had taken them with him in a rare fit of sentiment. He had commanded them himself early in the war, and had given way Mauve's pleading not to be left behind.

One crucial ship missing from Scheer's order of battle was the newly commissioned *Bayern*. She had been completed in March and was still working up in the Baltic. It was lucky for the British that she was not available for battle as she was a fine ship with 15-inch guns. (She was in many respects the prototype for the two World War II battleships *Bismarck* and *Tirpitz*). The Germans were meticulous about the process of working their ships up and training crews before they were committed to battle, taking much longer about the process than the British. It was decreed that a ship not fully worked up could only be made operational if the Fatherland itself was in mortal danger.

In Britain, as usual Room 40 had been aware that something was afoot for several days. They had noted the submarine activity and the busy radio traffic in the Jade, and learnt that the High Seas Fleet and the battle cruisers were ready for sea. Early in the morning of 30 May they picked up a message to the ships of the High Seas Fleet ordering them to assemble in the Jade, and a little later an instruction to open 'most secret order 31 GG 2490.' No one knew what this meant, but it was obviously an operational order of some kind. Soon afterwards another intercepted signal ordered ships to pass the Jade lightship at 3.30 am. No one knew where they were going to head for, but intensive minesweeping activity off the Schleswig coast suggested that they might head north for the Skagerrak. Jellicoe was ordered to sea at 10.30 pm on the 30th, about five hours before the Germans were to leave the Jade. He had actually been planning a sortie into the Skagerrak himself to try to lure the German fleet to sea and had his plans ready. Appendix V shows the full order of battle of the Grand Fleet and the High Seas Fleet and highlights the vast superiority of the British to the enemy in both numbers and gun power. Especially important is the total weight of firepower that it could deploy – over twice as much as the High Seas Fleet. Jellicoe's plan was quite simple (See Chart 1). The battleships of the Grand Fleet would assemble in the Long Forties, an area of sea 100 miles east of the Scottish coast, and Beatty would push further ahead to a position about 100 miles south west of The Scaw. If he encountered the enemy fleet he would try to draw them towards the Grand Fleet and total destruction. If there was no sign of them he was to return northwards to join Jellicoe and the whole fleet would move into a position off the Horn's Reef where they would be between the High Seas Fleet (if indeed it had put to sea) and its base. The Grand Fleet comprised twenty-eight battleships, nine battle cruisers, eight armoured cruisers and twenty-six light cruisers, seventy-eight destroyers, a minelayer and a seaplane carrier.

There were a few shortcomings in the British fleet. The armoured cruisers were of little potential use; they were too slow to perform effective scouting duties, their firepower was of little value and their protective armour inadequate. They were nothing but a liability. Only one of them, *Minotaur*, seems to have had a useful role to play. She acted as a communications ship for the flagship, *Iron Duke*, Jellicoe's flagship, sending, receiving and relaying radio traffic. Another deficiency was the absence of one of the two aircraft carriers allotted to the Grand Fleet, *Campania*, which should have sailed with Jellicoe. *Campania* was a modified ocean liner, adapted to handle seaplanes and also fitted with a primitive flight deck so as to be able to handle conventional wheeled aircraft. Somehow, she missed the signal to sail and failed to notice that the ships around her were getting under way on the night of the 30th. When, in the morning, she found what had happened she was too late to catch up with the fleet. Possibly her aeroplanes might have been useful to Jellicoe had they been available. The ship had recently been modified and given an extended flight deck so as to enable larger machines to take off and land on her, although she had no such aircraft embarked at the time.

With such comprehensive knowledge of the enemy's movements and overwhelming superiority of force (151 ships against 100) however, what could possibly go wrong for the Grand Fleet? Even the weather was favourable, with a slight sea running, moderate visibility and too much cloud cover for Zeppelins to operate effectively. Jellicoe steamed eastward from Scapa, meeting up with Admiral Jerram's battleships, which had been stationed at Cromaty, while Beatty's fast battleships and battle cruisers sped towards the Scaw. Scheer's carefully laid submarine trap and minefields proved totally ineffective. *U.32* did get a sight of one of Beatty's light cruisers, *Galatea*, and fired two torpedoes that missed. None of the mines was detonated. Several of the U-boats saw British warships at sea and reported this to Scheer, but the U-boat commanders could see so little from their small, low, boats that their reports did not lead the admiral to believe that any major British operation was afoot. Unknown to either side, the British and German fleets were on a collision course. Had Scheer known this, his only option would have been to turn and run for home. Jellicoe on the other hand would have seized the opportunity, increased speed, recalled Beatty to join up with the main body of the Grand Fleet, and tried to get between the High Seas Fleet and its base and catch it before it reached safety.

In fact Jellicoe would have had a good idea of where the enemy was if it had not been for an absurd misunderstanding in the Admiralty. On the morning of 31 May, Jellicoe, who had been at sea for twelve hours, signalled the Admiralty and asked for any news of the High Seas Fleet. This signal was received as normal, not by Room 40, but by the Operations Division, which came under control of Admiral Henry Oliver. Oliver's director of operations, Captain Thomas Jackson, went to Room 40 and asked what proved to be a disastrously wrong question, 'Where is the call sign DK coming from?' DK was the call sign of Scheer's flagship. He was answered 'Wilhelmshaven', at which he turned round and left the room. Now the Room 40 staff all knew quite well that the call sign DK was always transferred from the flagship to the duty guard ship in the Jade as soon as the High Seas Fleet put to sea. A new call sign, RA, was given to the flagship when she was at sea. Jackson however, did not know this and did not ask. He sent a signal to Jellicoe telling him that the High Seas Fleet was still in the Jade at 11 am, possibly delayed because they had been unable to make an effective aerial reconnaissance. In fact, of course it was almost 150 miles to the north, having put to sea in the small hours of the morning. Jellicoe was astonished and disappointed.

Was he engaged in yet another fruitless sweep of the North Sea? Would the enemy ever come out and offer battle? He reduced the speed of the fleet to fifteen knots to preserve the destroyer's fuel. If the information from the Admiralty was correct, Scheer could not possibly be anywhere near the Grand Fleet or its battle cruisers until nightfall at the earliest. The Grand Fleet dawdled towards its rendezvous with the Battle Cruiser Force.

As we have seen, Jackson's information was wrong, or at least misleading, by about nine hours. He has been strongly criticised and accused of arrogance, stupidity and carelessness. These accusations do not fit well with what we know of the man. He had been an observer at Tsushima where he impressed the Japanese with his coolness under fire, and he was quite a popular and trusted officer. His failure on this occasion must be attributed to poor organization in the Admiralty and insufficient co-ordination between intelligence and operations staff. In the new era of radio communication, interception and intelligence close co-operation between signals, intelligence and operational staff was vital, but the Admiralty's organizational structure did not allow for this.

Jackson's message had said nothing about Hipper's battle cruisers, so it still seemed quite possible that Beatty might encounter them before his planned reversal of course to join up with Jellicoe. This was not a source of anxiety. Jellicoe knew that the Germans had five, or just possibly six ships (The Admiralty believed, wrongly, that *Hindenburg* was now in commission, in fact she was not operational until 1917), but Beatty's six battle cruisers and the 5th Battle Squadron, consisting of four formidable fast battleships with their 15-inch guns, should be more than a match for Hipper, with or without *Hindenburg*. Jellicoe however, had not taken into account Beatty's shortcomings as a leader. Astonishingly this admiral, the hero and darling of the Press and of the British public, had totally ignored Rear Admiral Hugh Evan-Thomas, the commander of 5BS, when he had arrived with his ships in the Firth of Forth. The two admirals had not discussed tactics, procedures or how best to employ the various ships in the command. This omission was to cost Beatty and his subordinates dear.

Chapter Five

The Run to the South

To understand the battle which was to rage during the following hours, it is important to remember the weather conditions prevailing and difficulties of navigating a ship and grasping the tactical situation in the days before radar and GPS. During the afternoon of 31 May the sea was calm, but banks of haze came and went so that visibility could vary quickly between one mile and over ten miles. Through the haze the flashes of gunfire were sometimes possible to see but the outline of ships was often hidden, making identification difficult. Very seldom was it possible for any ship to see any but the two or three ships, enemy or friendly, nearest to it. The sun, slowly sinking into the western horizon, would at one moment illuminate one column of warships, making them relatively easy targets, and then a few minutes later that column would be hidden and their opponents would stand out clearly. As soon as any action started, the visibility would be further obscured by gun smoke billowing out downwind from the ship in action, and by funnel smoke from the great coal burning furnaces which drove the ships forward. All of this made it extremely difficult for an admiral to make a clear appreciation of what was going on. To make matters worse for the commanders on both sides, navigational plots were seldom completely accurate, depending as they did, on dead reckoning based on a fix obtained many hours ago when a seamark or sight of land may have given an accurate position. Celestial navigational plots were almost impossible to make in the prevailing conditions. Enemy action could make things even more difficult. A navigating officer on *Lion* (W.S. Chalmers) described graphically how a shell strike beneath the bridge, occurring while he was working on the chart, buckled the structure slightly and caused all the portholes to fall in, exposing the chart to the full force of the wind. It tore in half and in spite of his efforts to catch it, disappeared into the great ship's slipstream. He reported to the ship's navigator (Arthur Strutt) who was busy on the bridge, and had with him his notebook in which he had jotted down all changes of course and speed since leaving Rosyth. Handing it to Chalmers he told him to get out a spare chart, and re-plot the whole voyage. Under such conditions it is easy to understand how navigational errors crept in. Radio navigation was available to British ships at that time, thanks to the direction finding radios installed on the east coast of England which could get an accurate bearing on a ship's radio transmissions. Unfortunately this technology was in its infancy and navigating officers seem to have mistrusted it. In any case, radio bearings at that time were prone to error, and the transmissions were liable to give away one's position to the enemy.

At 2 pm, Beatty's force, having seen nothing, was preparing to make its planned turn to the north to join Jellicoe. It had been zigzagging at about nineteen knots on a mean course of a little south of east, with destroyers on each flank and a light cruiser screen ahead, covering a front of about thirty-five miles. 5BS was about five miles astern of the battle cruisers. Beatty now thought he was close to the turning point, although he was in fact some fifteen miles short of it, and ordered the turn towards Jellicoe. This was the first of the navigational errors which were to plague both British and German fleets throughout the action. At this point the two opposing battle cruiser fleets were about fifty miles apart and converging rapidly, the Germans on a course of north north-east. Hipper might have crossed ahead of Beatty without seeing him (See Chart 2) had not a small Danish steamer *N J Fjord* appeared about halfway between the cruiser screens of the two fleets. She was sighted first by the German light cruiser *Elbing*, which ordered two destroyers to investigate. They went alongside the Dane, which stopped, blowing off steam as she did so. Her plume of steam was immediately sighted by the British light cruiser *Galatea* which, with her sister ship *Phaeton*, set off to investigate. As soon as she saw the enemy destroyers, at about 2.15 pm, she opened fire, at the same time signalling 'Enemy in Sight' to Beatty. Four light cruisers from the German screen came to the aid of the destroyers and a running battle developed between the light cruisers on both sides. *Galatea* was hit once by a shell which failed to explode. Beatty had made his turn to the north to meet Jellicoe at 2.15 pm, but on receipt of *Galatea's* signal he turned his ships around from their northerly course, which was taking them towards the planned rendezvous, and steered south south-east to try to get between the German ships and their base. At this point a crucial signalling error was made. As he turned the battle cruisers onto their new course, he signalled Evan-Thomas's battleships, also now on a northerly course towards the Grand Fleet, to follow him. The signal was made by flags and the procedure was that the flag signal should be hoisted, acknowledged, then acted upon only when the original signal flags were lowered. Seymore, or one of his team, true to form, forgot to lower the flags. As a result, while Beatty steamed south eastwards toward the action, the battleships of 5BS were drawing away from the battle cruisers, the gap between the two increasing at almost a mile a minute. After some six minutes Evan-Thomas realized that something was wrong and turned round to follow Beatty, but the damage had been done. The battleships were over ten miles behind, and even at their best speed, it was going to be a struggle to catch up with the impending encounter between the two battle cruiser fleets.

Neither Beatty nor Hipper knew anything at this point about the strength of the enemy force they had encountered. Beatty decided to launch one of *Engadine's* seaplanes to have a look. *Engadine* had been, in civilian life, a Channel ferry. She had been pressed into war service as a seaplane carrier attached to the Battle Cruiser Force. Unlike *Campania* she had no facility to handle wheeled aircraft.

The Short seaplane (No. 10) got airborne at 3.10 pm. The pilot was Flight Lieutenant Rutland ('Rutland of Jutland' he was called ever afterwards) and his observer was Assistant Paymaster Terwin, selected because of his exceptional eyesight. Besides observing, Terwin had the unenviable task of signalling in code from the draughty, uncomfortable cockpit using an unreliable radio. As soon as they saw the frail aircraft, the enemy put up a vigorous but ineffective barrage, causing a good deal of turbulence and forcing Rutland to take evasive action. Visibility from the air was only about four miles, but that was enough for Terwin to see and report the enemy's course and speed and to determine that a number of big ships were involved. His signal got through to *Engadine*, but she seems to have failed to pass it on successfully to Beatty on *Lion* either by radio or later by signal lamp, so in effect the flight was rendered useless. On his way back to his ship Rutland lost engine power and had to land on the sea. Clambering out onto a float he found a broken fuel pipe, possibly caused by the buffeting the machine had suffered from enemy gunfire. Luckily, he had with him a length of rubber pipe with which he was able to repair the Sunbeam engine, re-start it and taxi back to his ship. He wanted to take off again and continue his observation, but he was ordered to come alongside and be hoisted in. So ended the first aviation involvement in a fleet action.

While this was going on the two fleets were still unaware that they were encountering anything more than a light cruiser force of the enemy. Commodore Alexander-Sinclair in *Galatea* attempted to lead the enemy light cruisers onto Beatty's battle cruisers, but they returned to their battle stations, flanking the capital ships. Gradually, smoke from larger ships appeared on the horizon and it became clear to the Commodore that a more significant enemy force was at large. Both battle cruiser fleets were now converging: Hipper on a north-easterly course and Beatty now steering due east, probing for a position between the enemy and his base. As soon as Hipper sighted Beatty's big ships he realized that he was in danger of being cut off, and turned south, towards the approaching battleships of the High Seas Fleet which were still some fifty miles away. His intention was to lead the British battle cruisers towards Scheer and certain destruction. As he had expected, Beatty turned south too so as to steer on a course roughly parallel to Sheer, with the Germans slightly ahead and on his port side (See Chart 3). Gradually, the two lines of battle cruisers converged. Ahead of the British ships, on their starboard bow, Goodenough with his 2nd Light Cruiser Squadron was scouting. The British battle cruisers, to the west of their opponents, were silhouetted against the hazy, sunlit, sky whereas the Germans were quite difficult to see clearly. At about 20,000 yards both sides had a reasonably clear view of each other, although British sighting was interrupted for a time by smoke from a destroyer flotilla. The battleships of 5BS had by now turned round and had managed to close the gap between themselves and Beatty to about six miles by steering a steady course while Beatty was weaving from side to side as he tried to get a clear sight of the enemy. Beatty was also hoping to take advantage of the longer range of his 13.5-inch guns, by opening fire from a position just out of range of the enemy, as Sturdee had been able to do during the Falklands battle. In fact, the extreme range of the British guns was about 23,000 yards and the Germans mostly 18,500, but poor visibility in the North Sea was to render this advantage useless. British ships, painted black, were in the prevailing conditions, easier to see than the Germans, which were grey. (After the battle the Royal Navy also adopted 'battleship grey' paint). By about 3.40 pm, both battle cruiser forces were in line of battle formation, ready to open fire. Beatty at this stage could hardly believe his luck. Here was another chance, as favourable as he had had at the Dogger Bank, to chase the enemy home, destroying some of their number on the way; even better, this time he had the fast battleships behind him to make doubly sure of the job. Neither he nor anyone else on the British side had any suspicion that the battleships of the High Seas Fleet were just fifty miles away, steaming towards him at seventeen knots. After all, Jackson's signal, which Beatty had read, had made it clear that they were still in the Jade at 11 am, so they could not possibly be less than 150 miles away at 3.50 pm. More probably, he thought, they had not put to sea at all.

Jellicoe himself was certainly not expecting to meet any significant German force in the next twenty-four hours. The Grand Fleet steamed slowly towards the meeting point, speed reduced to fifteen knots. This was necessary to conserve the fuel supply of the destroyers, which he expected might have to last them for a further two days at least. He also diverted light forces several times to examine passing merchant ships, thus further delaying progress. As soon as he knew that Beatty was in contact with enemy heavy ships and was trying to cut off the German retreat, he determined to make sure that the enemy force which the Battle Cruiser Fleet had encountered, whatever it was, did not slip away to the north, round the Scaw, so he sent Admiral Horace Hood, with his three Invincible class battle cruisers, fresh from their gunnery training at Scapa, and attached to the main body of the Grand Fleet in place of 5BS, on a course to block that route. He himself with the Grand Fleet continued to steam steadily, in cruising formation, towards the rendezvous point. A few minutes later, when the content of the signals made by Beatty's light cruisers reached him, he ordered an increase in speed to eighteen knots.

In the two battle cruiser fleets excitement was mounting. On the British ships most officers and men had been expecting the operation to turn out to be 'just another boring sweep' and even the sight of a few enemy light cruisers scampering about did not convince them that they were going to meet the enemy in force, but smudges of smoke on the horizon told a different story. This was the day that they had been waiting for, 'Der Tag' they called it, on which they were at last going to meet this upstart enemy and give him the drubbing he deserved. Defeat, or another German escape, was unthinkable. The German sailors felt differently. They knew their whole fleet was at sea and this was as good a chance as they were going to get to reduce the Royal Navy's superiority. They had an enormous respect for British naval traditions, but nevertheless they were confident in their own ships and in their professionalism. When the alarms for action stations sounded, many British officers still assumed that this was just another drill until they looked out through rangefinders, periscopes and binoculars to the eastwards and actually saw the menacing grey shapes and funnel smoke of the heavy enemy ships. They steeled themselves for a ferocious battle.

The German line consisted of *Lutzow, Derfflinger, Seydlitz, Moltke* with *Von der Tann*, the oldest ship, bringing up the rear. Hipper was flying his flag in the leading ship, *Lutzow*. The British were also led by their Admiral in *Lion*, followed by *Princess Royal, Queen Mary, Tiger, New Zealand* and *Indefatigable*. (It is interesting to note that on both sides the senior officer was in the leading ship, on an exposed bridge, facing the greatest personal danger. In this respect naval practice differed from that of land forces in which the custom was to keep generals well behind the front. Scheer and Jellicoe, in command of the main battle fleets, both sailed in ships near the centre of their respective fleets so as to get the best possible view of what was going on and to enable their signals to be most easily read. Both however found themselves in the thick of the fighting). A light west wind caused drifting funnel smoke to obscure the vision of the British ships from time to time. *Lutzow* opened fire at 3.48 pm, the British replying a few seconds later. Range was about 16,000 yards, although the British rangefinders had indicated 18,000. At this range, guns were elevated to give a very high trajectory, so that shells were plunging quite steeply onto their targets, providing a severe test for lightly armoured decks. Officers on the British light ships screening the battle cruisers were unpleasantly surprised by the rapidity with which the enemy seemed to find the range and the steadiness of their ripple salvoes. The first British salvoes were well over their targets, so much so that the enemy light cruisers, sheltering two miles on the disengaged side of the Germans, thought they must have been aimed at them. It took the British nine salvoes to correct the range and the Germans only five. Once again, as in the Dogger Bank encounter, there was confusion among Beatty's ships concerning who should engage each ship in the enemy line. With six British ships against five German, the Admiral had intended that the first two of his line, *Lion* and *Princess Royal* should engage the leading German, *Lutzow*, while the following British ships each engaged the next ship in the line; thus *Queen Mary*, the third British ship should have engaged *Derfflinger*, the second German. Somehow, *Queen Mary* misunderstood her instructions and engaged the third German ship, *Seydlitz*, leaving *Derfflinger* unmolested. The next British ship astern, *Tiger*, made the same mistake, firing on *Moltke*, which was also being targeted by *New Zealand* which had correctly understood the procedure. This dangerous situation continued for at least ten minutes, during which the fortunate *Derfflinger's* fire was extremely effective. It is astonishing that Beatty's captains, all experienced and supposed to be a closely knit team, made such elementary errors both at the Dogger Bank and now again at Jutland. It is difficult not to come to the conclusion that training and teamwork within the Battle Cruiser Force was inordinately slack. The Germans made no such mistakes.

The first hit was on *Princess Royal*, probably by *Derfflinger*. This shook the ship, but did no serious damage. Immediately after it a far more damaging blow was struck on *Lion* herself when a plunging shell from *Lutzow* struck the top corner of her Q turret and ignited the explosives inside. With a terrific roar, flames and smoke shot upwards and almost everyone in the turret was killed instantly. One of the survivors, Major Harvey of the Royal Marines, gave the order to flood the magazine, probably saving the ship from destruction. Harvey had lost both his legs in the explosion and died soon afterwards. He was awarded a posthumous VC. *Lion's* machinery was undamaged and she continued to engage the enemy with her remaining 13.5-inch guns. An officer on the bridge described events graphically:

'At about this time a bloodstained sergeant of Marines appeared on the admiral's bridge. He was hatless, his clothes were burnt and he seemed somewhat dazed: on seeing me he approached and asked if I were the captain ... I asked him what was the matter, in a tired voice he replied "Q turret is gone Sir. All the crews are killed and we have flooded the magazines."

I looked over the bridge. No further confirmation was necessary: the armoured roof of Q turret had been folded back like an open sardine tin, and thick yellow smoke was rolling up in clouds from the gaping hole and the guns were cocked up in the air awkwardly ...

By a bit of bad luck the shell had happened to strike the turret at the joint between the front armour plate and the roof plate. If it had struck either of these plates a direct blow the thickness of the armour would have prevented any serious damage being done ... The shell detonated inside the turret, killed the entire gun's crew and caused a fire in the gun house ... By the time the flash reached the handling room the crew of the magazines had just closed the doors, some were found dead afterwards with their hands on the door clips ...'

Things would probably have gone a lot worse for *Lion* if Warrant Officer Grant, her chief gunner, had not made his careful study of gun loading procedures and observed how proper ammunition handling practices were being ignored in the Battle Cruiser Fleet. He had, as we have seen, forced *Lion's* turret crews to revert to standard ammunition handling discipline under which only one set of propellant charges for each gun would be in the working chamber, and the covers over the igniter charges were not removed until the charge was actually in the gun house. Magazine doors were kept shut except when ammunition was actually passing through them. It is a sad commentary on management practices in the Battle Cruiser Fleet that Grant's disciplines were not instituted on all other ships. The consequences of not doing so were cruelly demonstrated only a few minutes after the hit on *Lion*.

Von der Tann with her 11-inch guns had to elevate the barrels to near their maximum of twenty degrees (this had been increased slightly after the Dogger Bank battle) to achieve the range needed for the opening stages of the action. Last in the line, she engaged *Indefatigable*. At about 4.03 pm, a plunging salvo of three of her shells crashed through the lightly armoured deck of her opponent penetrating deep into the ship and exploding in X magazine. *Indefatigable* reeled out of line, sinking by the stern; the next salvo struck the helpless ship near A turret. There was a tremendous explosion and the 17,000-ton warship lurched over and sank, taking all but two of her 1,019-man complement with her. Now it was five ships against five. It was at about this time that Hipper's ships attempted to use their submerged torpedo tubes; at least four torpedoes were fired, one passing clean under *Princess Royal* amidships. *Princess Royal's* crew saw the torpedo tracks in the water, but for some reason thought they had come from the starboard (disengaged) side and could only have been fired by a submarine. There was a general outbreak of 'U-boat-itis' several imaginary boats being spotted from many of the capital ships on both sides throughout the rest of the day. In fact none were anywhere near the action.

Beatty realized that he was getting too close to the enemy line and turned one point to starboard, hoping once again to take advantage of the greater range of his larger calibre guns. He had also noticed that the German ships were starting to make use of their 6-inch secondary armament, which unlike the British, they kept manned throughout the battle. This would give them a firepower advantage at closer ranges, making it important for the British to keep well away from the enemy.

Elated by his success against *Indefatigable,* Hipper kept his ships firing steadily, each one engaging its opposite number in the British line. *Seydlitz* had had one turret put out of action by *Queen Mary*, but otherwise everything was going well when at 4.05 pm, a nasty surprise presented itself in the form of enormous splashes from shells coming from the north. Though still 19,000 yards astern of the rearmost German ship, Evan-Thomas's mighty 15-inch battleships were opening up a deadly barrage. Until that moment Hipper had had no idea that British battleships were at sea; his scouting forces, all being ahead or to the east of him, had seen nothing of the approaching menace in the north west. Evan-Thomas was an exemplary commander and he had made sure that his gun crews were thoroughly trained and well drilled. Now it was time for the Germans to admire the superb shooting of 5BS as the great ships opened fire on the rear of their line. The flagship, *Barham* straddled *Von der Tann* at 19,000 yards, then shifted her fire onto *Moltke*, hitting her immediately and knocking out one of her turrets, while *Warspite* and *Malaya* were left to deal with *Von der Tann*. She also lost a turret and was damaged below the waterline, taking on 600 tons of seawater. *Seydlitz* was the next to feel the punch of the 15-inch guns, suffering severe damage. Had it not been for the poor performance of the British shells, wrote Commander von Hase, gunnery officer on board *Derfflinger*, Hipper's ships would have been facing disaster.

While the battleships charged towards the melee, at the head of the battle cruiser columns the fight between the rival battle cruisers remained savage. The British had by now found the range and began to inflict some serious damage on their opponents. It was notable that *Queen Mary* and *Princess Royal*, both fitted with the Argo fire control system, were shooting much more accurately than the rest of the Battle Cruiser Fleet. *Queen Mary* had scored at least four damaging hits on *Seydlitz* when disaster struck her. With *Lion* temporarily out of action dealing with her turret fire and *Indefatigable* gone, both *Derfflinger* and *Seydlitz* turned their fire on her and at 4.26 pm, a 12-inch salvo from *Derfflinger* struck her amidships. There was a burst of flame and many of her guns were dismounted by the blast, the ship stopped and heeled over so that men escaping from the turrets and from below decks could not stand on deck but fell headlong into the sea. Then another massive explosion broke the ship in half and the two halves plunged to the bottom. The two following ships, *Tiger* and *New Zealand*, only just managed to avoid colliding with the wreck. Only 19 men out of 1,275 survived. A new and efficient ship, she was a much more serious loss than *Indefatigable*. It was as she went down that Beatty is supposed to have made his oft quoted remark '*There seems to be something wrong with our bloody ships today, Chatfield.*' One of *Queen Mary's* survivors, a petty officer in charge of a turret described his experience:

'*The Gun's crew were absolutely perfect, inclined to be a little swift in loading, but I gave them a yell and pointed out to them that I wanted a steady stride, and after that everything went like clockwork, until suddenly both rammers gave out, my gun going first. This was caused by No 3 opening the breech before the gun had run out after firing; the carrier arm part of the breech must have hit the rammer head and slightly metal-bound it. I dropped the elevating wheel, got hold of a steel pinch bar, forced the end behind the rammer head, at the same time putting the rammer to "Run out." Out went the rammer, and I rushed it back again, and then out again, and all went gay once more. My No. 3 said to me "Petty Officer Francis, can you see what we are up against?" Well I had been anxious to have a look, but could not spare the time, but as soon as my gun had fired and while loading was being completed I had a quick look out through the periscope. It seemed to me that there were hundreds of masts and funnels. The transmitting station reported that the third ship of the (enemy) line was dropping out. First blood to Queen Mary. The shout they gave was good to hear … Then came the big explosion, which shook us a bit, and on looking at the pressure gauge I saw that the pressure had failed.* (He was referring to the hydraulic pressure that powered the turret).

Immediately after that came what I term the big smash, and I was dangling on a bowline, which saved me from being thrown on the floor of the turret: these bowlines were an idea I had brought into the turret and each man in the gun house was supplied with one.

Everything in the ship went quiet as a church. The floor of the turret was bulged up and the guns were absolutely useless. I mention here that there was not a sign of excitement. One man turned to me and said, "What do you think has happened?" I said "Steady I will speak to Mr Ewart." I went back to the cabinet and said, "What do you think has happened Sir?" He said, "God only knows." "Well Sir" I said, "It's no use keeping them all down here, why not send them up round the 4-inch guns and give them a chance to fight it out. As soon as the Germans find we are out of action they will concentrate on us, and we will all be going sky high." He said, "Yes good idea, just see whether the 4-inch guns aft are still standing." The after 4-inch turret was smashed out of all recognition. I told Lieut. Ewart the state of affairs. He said, "Francis, we can do no more than give them a chance; clear the turret." "Clear the turret" I called out and out they all went.

P.O. Stores was the last I saw coming up from the working chamber, and I asked whether he had passed the order to the magazine and shell room, and he told me it was no use, as the water was right up to the trunk leading from the shell room, so the bottom of the ship must have been out of her. Then I said, "Why didn't you come up?" He simply said, "There was no order to leave the turret."

P.O. Francis managed to get off the sloping deck and was eventually picked up by the destroyer *Petard*. His eyes were damaged and his nerves temporarily shaken, but he was soon back on active service. He was convinced (and he was almost certainly correct) that the cause of the explosion was a hit on

B turret, setting off the ammunition stored in the working chamber and flashing down into the forward magazine.

Just before *Queen Mary* went down, Beatty had given an order that opened up a new dimension in the battle. His escorting destroyers were instructed to pull out ahead of the battle cruisers and launch a torpedo attack. Immediately the order was given, the little ships built up to thirty-five knots and cut across the bows of the flagship in line astern, bow waves creaming and sterns buried deep in the water, each ship with her 25,000 HP turbines driving her through the small waves, furnaces roaring, flags snapping fiercely on their halyards. Officers on the battle cruisers remarked on what a fine sight they made. The destroyers were determined to show what they could do in action. They were soon between the two fleets of battle cruisers, manoeuvring to get close enough to the Germans to deliver an effective torpedo attack. The ideal position would be just ahead of the enemy on his starboard bow.

Hipper however, saw what was happening and countered by sending fifteen of his own destroyers, led by the light cruiser *Regensburg*, to intercept the attackers. The German force consisted of a mix of classes, mostly much smaller ships than the British, but including a number of the formidable new S53-66 Class. There were thus some thirty small ships charging towards each other at a closing speed of some seventy knots, while the heavy shells of the great battle cruisers whizzed overhead and splashes of their secondary armament erupted all round the destroyers. A fierce firefight soon broke out between the rival destroyer forces, blazing away at each other at point blank range. The German *V29* was hit by a torpedo, probably from *Petard* (Lieutenant Commander Evelyn Thompson) and *V27* by gunfire, but the guns of *Regensburg* proved devastatingly effective, disabling the British *Nomad*. Six of the Germans got close enough to the British battle cruisers to launch ten torpedoes, but all missed and the first German attack petered out. About fifteen minutes later, another group of German destroyers got a better opportunity as the British battle cruisers passed the four fast battleships of 5BS. These large ships passing each other presented a very good target. Seven more torpedoes were fired which all missed.

On the British side, *Nestor* and *Nicator* got within 6,000 yards of the German battle line, and fired torpedoes that failed to hit their target. They then turned away, regrouped, and fired again from a closer range at *Lutzow* and *Defflinger,* again without success. The little ships then blazed away with their 4-inch guns at their adversaries, scoring several hits but doing little damage. *Nestor* suffered a hit from *Regensburg's* guns and was brought to a stop.

Nestor's captain (Commander Edward Bingham) described his experiences as follows.

'At 4.50 pm the enemy's destroyers turned tail and fled ... Thus I found myself with the solitary Nicator *hot on the track of the fleeing destroyers, and now rapidly approaching the head of the German battle cruiser line, who were not slow in giving us an extremely warm welcome from their secondary armament. At a distance of 3,000 or 4,000 yards* Nestor *fired her third torpedo, and immediately afterwards at 4.58 turned away eight points to starboard in order to get clear of the danger zone and to regain the line of the British battle cruisers.*

Suddenly from behind the head of the enemy's line there came a German light cruiser who opened hot fire and straddled us. It was just about 5 o'clock when two boilers were put out of action by direct hits. From the bridge I saw that something of the kind had happened ... Nothing daunted, the engine-room staff applied themselves with all the means in their power to the work of setting the engines in motion. But it was without avail ... Seeing our plight Petard *(Lieutenant Commander E.C.O. Thompson), now retreating from the chase of the major portion of the German flotilla, gallantly offered a tow; but I had no hesitation in refusing an offer which would have meant the exposure of two ships to the danger that properly belonged to me ... But crippled though we were, we had guns which were still intact, and a hostile destroyer, swooping down on what she thought was an easy prey, was greeted with volleys of salvoes from our invaluable semi automatic guns. After such a warm reception, the German destroyer sheered off post haste ... Whilst lying helpless and broken down we saw the opposing forces of battle cruisers retracing their tracks to the north-west and we were left with the ocean to ourselves. But it was not for long. Fifteen minutes later my yeoman of signals reported: "German battleships on the horizon shaping course in our direction." Very soon we were enveloped in a deluge of shell*

*fire … Bethel (the First Lieutenant) was standing next to me, I turned
to him with the question, "Now where shall we go?" His answer was only
characteristic of that gallant spirit, "To heaven I trust Sir." We gave our
gallant but cruelly short lived ship three rousing cheers.'"*

By this time, Beatty had ordered the destroyers to break off their action, but
like excited terriers they were deaf to his orders, and *Petard* and *Turbulent*
made two further torpedo attacks, the second one on *Seydlitz*. This time
one of the torpedoes, probably fired by *Petard,* whose torpedo team seem
to have been crack shots, struck home, doing extensive damage. Although
Seydlitz was able to resume her place in the line after a few minutes, the
damage was considerable; one 5.9-inch gun was dismounted, the outer hull
was ruptured and severe leaks were started which eventually put much of
the electrical gear on the ship out of service, disabling her turrets.

While this action was in progress, Goodenough in *Southampton*,
accompanied by *Birmingham*, was performing exactly the function for which
light cruisers were intended, scouting well ahead of the battle fleet. A little
after 4.30 pm, from the frail bridge of his lightly armoured ship, he made
out dense clouds of funnel smoke to the south. He held on his course to see
a sight never seen by a British ship before that day, a column of German
battleships steaming at full speed (actually just less than eighteen knots,
hampered as they were by the pre-dreadnoughts), into action. Undeterred,
he held his course so as to get a better look and report accurately on the
enemy's strength, course and speed. At 4.38 pm, he sent his signal to Beatty
which was also picked up by Jellicoe; 'Have sighted enemy battle fleet
bearing SE course N.' This was the point at which it became clear that a
major fleet action was imminent, and that Beatty's force would very soon be
under the guns of twenty-one battleships. Goodenough was now only about
12,000 yards from the leading enemy battleships. Heading directly towards
them, the silhouette of his ships had not been visible to the Germans who
mistook them for their own light cruisers, but as soon as *Southampton*
and *Birmingham* turned side on to the enemy, revealing their telltale four
funnels, all hell broke loose. One hit from a heavy shell would have disabled
a light cruiser, so the two British ships had to dodge and weave violently,
their engines at emergency full speed, to avoid destruction. Everyone on the

bridges was soon soaked from nearby shell splashes, and splinters whizzed around their ears and clanged on the ship's hull. Miraculously there was no major damage. Goodenough steamed out of range but continued to shadow the enemy battle fleet. One of his junior officers wrote later:

> 'I attribute our escape, as far as we were able to contribute towards it, to the very clever manner in which our navigator zigzagged the ship according to where he estimated the next salvo would fall. It was possible to forecast this to some extent as it was obvious that the Huns were working what is technically known as a "ladder." That is to say the guns are fired with an increase of range to each salvo until the target is crossed, and then the range is decreased for each salvo until the splashes are short of the target once again … The best way to avoid it is to sheer towards the enemy when the groups of tall splashes are coming towards the ship, and as soon as they have crossed over and begin once more to come towards the ship, then reverse the helm and sheer away from the enemy. The fascination of watching these deadly and graceful splashes rising mysteriously from the smooth sea was enormous.'

We should now return to the destroyer action. Returning to station, *Petard* as we have seen, offered to tow the disabled *Nestor*, but the offer was refused, and just at that moment the terrifying sight of funnel smoke from the German battle fleet appeared over the horizon. After her highly successful venture, Petard returned to station, to starboard of the battle cruisers. One destroyer, *Moorsom*, had decided not to use her torpedoes against Hipper's ships but to concentrate on a shooting match with his destroyers. After a spirited action she was about to retire when the High Seas Fleet hove into view to the southward. On his own initiative the captain, Commander John Hodgson, swung his little ship towards the enemy and made two torpedo attacks at extreme range (8,500 yards), on the advancing line of battleships. The torpedoes missed and *Moorsom* had a hot time of it as both the main and secondary armament of the battleships were turned on her. She was hit once 'A gentlemanly knock' as one of her officers described it, which brought down her mast and made holes in her superstructure slightly hurting one seaman. She then came across the damaged *Nomad*, but could do nothing for her. *Moorsom* was able to regain her place in the line without further damage.

Chapter Six

The Run to the North

When Beatty received Goodenough's signal telling him that the High Seas Fleet was at sea and would shortly be upon him, he could scarcely believe it. Misled by Jackson's signal, he had been led by Hipper directly into the jaws of a deadly trap and in the process had lost two of his ships. Already the guns of the High Seas Fleet's battleships were probing towards *Lion* and *Princess Royal* at the head of the British battle cruiser line. There was only one possible action. He must order a turn in succession through 180 degrees and steam at full speed towards Jellicoe (See Chart 4). By doing this, he himself might be able to lead the whole High Seas Fleet to their doom. In turning north with his battle cruisers, Beatty met 5BS steaming south, heavily engaged both with the enemy battle cruisers and now with the leading elements of the High Seas Fleet coming towards them. He ordered them to turn in succession and take station astern of him so as to take the pressure off his battle cruisers. Turning in succession meant that each ship turned through 180 degrees on the same spot when it reached it. Evan-Thomas asked him which side of the battle cruisers he should pass and Beatty replied, 'Pass me to port.' Passing portside to portside is the normal and seamanlike thing to do, but in this case it was a serious mistake as it placed the damaged battle cruisers between 5BS and the enemy, forcing the battleships to stop firing and exposing the battle cruisers to further punishment.

Beatty's turn to the north marked the end of the first phase of the Battle of Jutland. So far there could be no doubt that the victor had been Hipper. Besides the two battle cruisers sunk, both *Lion* and *Tiger* had been damaged (*Lion* suffered another damaging hit just after she had reversed course). Probably, the Germans had scored forty-four hits on the British battle cruisers, against eleven by the British, plus a further six by 5BS during their so far brief involvement in the action. All of Hipper's ships had been hit, but were still able to steam and fight, and he had successfully led Beatty's force towards the High Seas Fleet, exactly fulfilling his mission. What he did not know was the presence of another, even more powerful force approaching at speed from the north. He turned his ships round, and steamed north leading the High Seas Fleet in pursuit of Beatty's battered command, and into the jaws of the trap which had been prepared for him. The navigating officer of *New Zealand* wrote of this moment.

'About 15 minutes after the loss of the Queen Mary we saw on our port bow the German battle fleet coming to the rescue of the battle cruisers and an imposing sight they looked, ship after ship in single line melting away into the haze and all showing up white, lit by the sun. Their arrival put a different complexion on the fight and at the decided moment the Lion led us round on the opposite course and we proceeded to the north keeping at long range from the German battle fleet but still continuing our fight with the German battle cruisers which also turned to the north. Soon afterwards, at about 4.55, the Fifth Battle Squadron, consisting of four Queen Elizabeth class battleships, under Rear Admiral Evan-Thomas came up and passed us, still steering to the south towards the enemy. They turned up and formed astern of us and engaged the van of the High Seas Fleet, drawing most of the fire off us onto themselves.

They looked a fine sight as they came down past us, steaming at high speed, their turrets all trained towards the enemy and their guns cocked up high, firing strongly. Apparently our squadron also looked pretty fit still, for one of the navigating officers of the Fifth Battle Squadron said to me after the action "The battle cruisers were a splendid sight as we passed them, firing fast and furiously, in perfect station, with the blank spaces of the Queen Mary and Indefatigable filled up, and seemed to be as full of fight as ever."'

5BS had not escaped the attentions of the enemy gunners, but was so far substantially undamaged. As they turned in succession they found that the enemy was firing at the turning point uncomfortably accurately, and that by the time they reached it, it was within range of the battleships of the High Seas Fleet as well as the battle cruisers and a salvo was crashing into the water every ten seconds. *Barham* was hit hard as she turned and there were near misses on *Warspite* and *Valliant*. The last ship of the line, *Malaya*, wisely decided to ignore normal fleet practice and turned a little early, thus escaping what might have been a severe and concentrated barrage. Now began what is known as the 'Run to the North' with 5BS hotly engaged with the enemy battle cruisers and battleships on the starboard quarter. The British battle cruisers, leading the column, were further away from the action and often out of visual contact, so that they were only firing occasionally. Beatty was doing his best to lead the High Seas Fleet onto the Grand fleet, just as they had led him onto their own battleships. He opened fire again on the enemy battle cruisers as the visibility briefly improved at about 5 pm, but *Lion* and *Tiger* were both hit before Beatty's superior speed enabled him to open the range, causing Hipper and the foremost of Scheer's battleships to concentrate their fire on 5BS. Evan-Thomas's leading two ships, *Barham* and *Valiant*, engaged Hipper, while *Warspite* and *Malaya* fired at long range on the powerful *Konigs*, in the van of the main enemy fleet. *Lutzow*, *Derfflinger* and *Seydlitz* were all hit severely and among the battleships *Konig*, *Grosser Kurfurst* and *Markgraf* also felt the impact of the 1,920lb, 15-inch shells. Once again the excellent training of Evan-Thomas's gun crews was evident. Several of the German ships pulled out of line for a time to repair damage and Hipper gradually slowed down so as not to get too far away from the protection afforded by Scheer's battleships. Beatty then skilfully altered course a little to the eastwards to make sure that his ships obscured the oncoming Grand Fleet, still about twenty-five miles to the north, from Hipper so that he could not warn Scheer of their approach.

As he pulled ahead of the Germans, Evan-Thomas began to move out of range of Scheer's ships and switched all his fire again onto the enemy battle cruisers, scoring more hits on *Lutzow*, *Derfflinger* and *Seydlitz*. *Seydlitz* was also hit by an opportunistic salvo from *Princess Royal*. Hipper's ships were now in a sorry state. Only *Moltke* was still able to use most of her main armament, *Von der Tann* had none of her turrets in working order but she kept in line, bravely, to draw the fire from her comrades. The other three all had much reduced firepower, nevertheless these superbly built warships were still able to keep going, their engines and boilers intact, hulls damaged but still serviceable and soon they restored at least some of their fighting

Inflexible. One of the first generation of battle cruisers, which astonished the world by her speed, gun power and ability to steam fast for days on end. She was damaged in the Dardanelles but survived Jutland unscathed. The quick firing guns shown here on top of her turrets were later removed. Note the director position at the top of the foremast.

Queen Mary. Probably the most efficient of the British battle cruisers, she was fitted with the Argo director system which was much more efficient than the standard Admiralty controller. She made excellent shooting during the run to the South until a shell from Derfflinger struck her on B turret, penetrated into the turret and set off a magazine explosion, wrecking the ship completely.

Warspite became the most famous British warship of the 20th Century. Oil powered and extremely fast for her time, she was fitted with 15-inch guns and proved able to take terrible punishment as she held off the leading battleships of the High Seas Fleet during the run to the north. Damage to her steering engine forced her to retire from the battle. Fourteen of her crew were killed and thirty-two wounded, a relatively light casualty list considering that she suffered fifteen heavy shell hits. She herself fired 259 15-inch shells during the battle and her shooting, like that of the other ships in 5 BS was good.

Nassau was the first German dreadnought; she was launched in 1907. Although piston engined, more lightly armed and slower than British dreadnoughts, she was a formidable ship and extremely well protected both above and under water. She played little part in the daytime encounters at Jutland but was prominent in the night action, making use of her main and secondary armament. She rammed the destroyer *Spitfire*, disabling her and suffering minor damage herself. Note the cloud of black smoke from her coal burning furnaces.

Moltke and *Von der Tann* suffered less than the other German battle cruisers at Jutland, receiving five and four heavy hits respectively, whereas their fellow battle cruisers were each hit over twenty times. *Moltke*, shown here, hit *Tiger*, her opponent, thirteen times in the space of 30 minutes during the first phase of the battle. Note the large cranes amidships which should have made German ships relatively easy to identify.

In 1914 the German Navy became concerned that their "Torpedo boats" were much smaller and had less gun armament than their British counterparts. They were also unable to operate in heavy weather. Fortunately two German yards, Blohm & Voss and Vulcan, had recently built large destroyers for the Russian navy so that designs and some components were already to hand. *V100* was one of the eight ships built for this programme. Six of them formed part of II Torpedo Boat Flotilla which could have presented a severe danger to the Grand Fleet during its voyage home after the battle, had the flotilla not decided to make its own way home via the Scaw prematurely.

Abdiel was a destroyer leader converted for mine laying. Too fast to be intercepted by the enemy, she was one of the most successful small ships in the Royal Navy. She entered the German Bight on sixty-eight occasions laying thousands of mines and making any sortie by the High Seas Fleet extremely hazardous. The only German dreadnought battleship seriously disabled at Jutland, *Ostfriesland*, was a victim of one of her mines.

The light cruiser *Southampton* performed excellent service throughout the battle. She was heavily damaged during the night action but sunk *Frauenlob* with a torpedo. Light cruisers were fast and agile; they played a major part in the battle acting in a scouting role and as guards against enemy destroyers and submarines.

Petard leads a column of M class destroyers. The most successful British destroyer at Jutland, she was built by Denny and launched in 1916. She may have sunk an enemy destroyer and probably was responsible for the torpedo which severely damaged *Seydlitz*. She picked up a handful of survivors from *Queen Mary*. Her torpedoes exhausted, she continued with the Grand Fleet and took part in the night action. Able to make 34 knots and well armed with 4-inch guns and 21-inch torpedoes, M Class destroyers were a key part of the light component of the Grand Fleet.

potential. Beatty's ships, though reduced in numbers, were now in much better shape than their opponents. A vivid description of this phase of the battle was written by a turret officer in *Malaya*. At the rear of the British column, she was nearest to the German battleships and therefore in the thickest of the fighting.

'*5.20 pm I saw a large column of water rise up between my guns and felt the turret shake heavily. We had been hit abreast the turret below the waterline and so heavy was the shock that I feared that our loading gear must be damaged and so our fighting efficiency greatly impaired, although the shell had not pierced into any part of the turret. I went down into the gun house to enquire whether all was well below and received the report that they had been somewhat shaken but that everything seemed all right. This proved to be over optimistic for when the main cage arrived in the working chamber it was found that the shell could not be withdrawn and that was a proper jam up. I dashed down and we worked like niggers to clear it. After what seemed an age, but could not really have been so very long, we managed by extemporary means to get the cage into working order again.*

During this time the secondary or hand method of loading was in use for the right gun and although five rounds had had to be loaded in this manner, the turret never missed a chance to fire which was very pleasing as the secondary method is generally considered such a slow one. The men had to work at tremendous pressure to keep the guns going, everybody available in the turret assisting at loading the right hand gun, including the midshipman, armourer, torpedo man etc. I thought their success a great credit to them.

On going back into the turret I found everyone very cheery and full of go. They had no thought that we should come off worse than the enemy but only wanted to know how many German ships were left afloat and requiring to be finished off. They were full of confidence that every shell was doing its bit and many and varied were the benedictions they sent with each round fired. When things were at their hottest I heard one man in the gun house call out to the others "Don't get rattled you're putting your bleeding feet all over the blooming paintwork."

Those in the shell room had had a fairly good shock when the salvo pitched abreast of them, several being actually knocked over. However they all treated it as a joke and their one idea was to send up as many shells as possible. I think the lot of those in the magazine was the hardest for it is no easy job to handle cordite for a 15-inch gun and the atmosphere down below becomes after a time extremely oppressive.

Until about 5.40 pm the enemy firing continued to be very brisk and to fall all round us, the visibility for us had been getting steadily worse, in fact ever since 5.15 we had rarely been able to see anything but the flashes of the German guns. We were several times hit, to what extent I could not tell, but I saw that the ship had dropped astern of station, and that we had a considerable list to starboard. Reports were continually coming into the Commander so we were not kept so very long into suspense as to the damage done to the ship. I heard reports coming through of a fire and later that it was being satisfactorily dealt with, reports that a certain compartments had been flooded, or water was leaking into others, reports about the casualties dressing stations being full, the clearing of wounded and dead and so on. It all came through in the most matter-of-fact way seeming nothing out of the ordinary as though we made and heard those sort of reports every day of our lives. The Commander had to go and investigate on two or three occasions but the general rule was he was able to control everything from the turret.'

In fact *Malaya* had not been seriously damaged at this stage. Two shells had struck her below the waterline, causing some flooding and contaminating oil tanks with water. The flooding caused a four degree list, but this was corrected by pumping fuel to the port side. The hit which disrupted the management of B turret seems to have been a glancing blow which distorted the armour plating and sent shock waves into the turret but did no very serious damage. The *Queen Elizabeths* were made of strong stuff. *Malaya* actually suffered a total of seven heavy shell hits, all from the 12-inch guns of the High Seas Fleet. The only adverse effect on her performance on that day was to her oil burning apparatus, which had to be shut down. She had sixty-three men killed and sixty-eight wounded during the whole course of the battle. As the rear ship in the British force during the 'Run to the North' she was most exposed to enemy shellfire.

As poor visibility gradually brought the combat between the forces running to the north to an end, another alarming development was taking place to the north east of Hipper's ships. Hood's squadron of three old battle cruisers, *Invincible, Indomitable* and *Inflexible* had been sent to block his escape into the Skagerrak. Finding no sign of him there, they were ordered to return to join Beatty's depleted battle line. Their approach took them straight across the path of the German battle cruisers (see Chart 5). The first contact occurred when Hood's escorting light forces consisting of two light cruisers, *Chester* and *Canterbury* and four destroyers were detected by the light cruisers scouting to the east of Hipper's force. The Germans now knew the British recognition signals, thanks to Neumunster's intelligence gathering, and were able to get very close to the unsuspecting British before opening fire. There was a fierce engagement between *Chester*, from Hood's screen, and four German light cruisers. *Chester* was severely damaged before Hood himself, with his accompanying destroyers, drove the Germans off, disabling *Wiesbaden* and severely damaging *Pillau* and *Frankfurt* in the process. *Chester* was holed and had lost three of her 5.5-inch guns, suffering thirty-five men killed and forty-two wounded. She was ordered home. Among those killed was Boy Seaman Jack Cornwall who received a posthumous VC for continuing to fight his gun even when terribly wounded. The British advance was halted when the enemy mounted a torpedo attack, which forced the battle cruisers to comb the torpedo tracks, while the surviving German light cruisers fled for the safety of their own line. Boedicker, in command of the light cruiser force, signalled to Hipper that he had encountered 'battleships' causing Hipper to turn his force south again so as to be close to the protection of the High Seas Fleet. This turned out to be a move of great significance, as it prevented Hipper from seeing the Grand Fleet in the murk ahead of him, and so he was unable to give Scheer warning of the terrible danger ahead. Boedicker ordered a further torpedo attack on Hood's squadron, supported by the light cruiser *Regensburg*. This led to the destruction of the British destroyer *Shark*, which by a fearless assault on the enemy, successfully frustrated the torpedo attack. Commander Loftus Jones of the *Shark* had put up a most gallant fight in this action, refusing to be taken off his sinking destroyer while a single gun was still working. All this high speed activity in a confined area set up a severe swell in the area later to be known as 'Windy Corner.' Another of Hood's destroyers that came to grief at this time was *Acasta*, which had accompanied *Shark* in her assault on the German light forces. She got away a torpedo, but was hit heavily in the engine room and was unable either to steer or to control her speed. She very nearly collided with *Lion* then managed to stop her engines and lay motionless in the path of the Grand Fleet battleships. She found herself directly ahead of *Marlborough* just as the battleship was torpedoed and her officers swore that the *Marlborough* would have run them down if the torpedo strike had not pushed her off course (a description of *Marlborough's* adventures at this time is given below). Aware of the dramatic possibilities of the occasion, *Acasta* got every fit man on deck, lining her rail from stem to stern and they heartily cheered each battleship as it forged past her. Her officers described it as 'Reviewing the Fleet.' After this, they managed to fill some of the holes in the hull, and working now by candlelight as the dynamos had been destroyed, got the ship slowly under way. Eventually *Acasta* encountered the destroyer *Nonsuch*, and was towed home.

Another British destroyer, *Onslow*, commanded by Lieutenant Commander Tovey distinguished herself at about this time. She was steaming northwards in the van of Beatty's force when an opportunity seemed to present itself for a 'freelance' torpedo attack on the German battle cruisers. In company with *Moresby* she set off to attack. The two were driven off by accurate defensive gunfire; *Moresby* fired one torpedo that missed. Re-joining the British battle line, the two were at first mistaken for Germans and subjected to a heavy but inaccurate barrage from *Lion*. Very soon afterwards they got their first glance of the Grand Fleet steaming south to meet them. As the two battle lines veered to the eastwards *Onslow* spotted a seemingly disabled German light cruiser between the rival fleets, unable to steam but in a perfect position to fire torpedoes. This was the unfortunate *Wiesbaden*. *Onslow* attacked with gunfire, further damaging the light cruiser. She then found herself close enough to renew her attack on the enemy battle cruisers. Just as she got away her first fish she was hit amidships by a heavy shell that put her boilers out of action and reduced her speed to ten knots. In this condition she swung round and fired a second torpedo, this time successfully, at the now heavily damaged *Wiesbaden*. Tovey was extremely doubtful if his little ship, now almost immobile in the middle of a clash between the two biggest battle fleets in the world and already severely damaged, was going to survive. He had however, two torpedoes left and he was not the man to waste them. One of his officers wrote later:

'Again we were on the enemy's bow in a good position for a torpedo attack. The Captain explained to me his reasons for going in to attack after being partly crippled, in case I might be a survivor and he himself killed, so that I would be able to justify his decision and answer any charge of foolhardiness. He pointed out that the policy was sound as we were in a position of torpedo advantage and if we cleared out without firing our two last torpedoes they would be wasted, for we were far too damaged to take any part in the action later on. The probability was that the ship would be lost, as our reduced speed made us an easy target, but what was one destroyer more or less compared to a torpedo hit on one of the enemy battle line? So we steered again towards the enemy.'

The torpedoes were aimed at *Derfflinger*; they probably did not hit her. *Onslow* refused the offer of a tow at first, but when her engines failed completely, she fell in with another crippled destroyer and together they staggered to Aberdeen, *Onslow* being towed by means of her anchor chain, the only line that would hold her in the rising gale.

This action had little significance in the battle, but it tells an important story. Tovey, a young man of the 'small ship navy' did not wait for orders or slavishly follow his leader, he took his own decisions and used his ship in a way which he judged would be most productive. He went on to be one of the most successful and admired admirals in the Second World War. His conduct at Jutland serves as a stark contrast to that of many of his seniors.

While *Onslow* was engaging the enemy, Hood's force had fallen in with Beatty, and Hood's three ships took station ahead of *Lion*. This was at about 6.32 pm. They were immediately hotly engaged with Hipper's still formidable battle cruisers (Chart 5). Visibility conditions now favoured the British and the Grand Fleet, and deploying into line of battle just to the north, was able to get its first ranging shots away, the first shots indeed which the Grand Fleet's battleships had fired at an enemy. Fresh from gunnery practise at Scapa and stationed ahead of the Grand Fleet, the *Invincibles* made notably good shooting. Von Hase, aboard *Derfflinger* commented that his ship was heavily hit several times during this encounter and had to pull out of line. Range was down to 9,000 yards and with the advantage of the light silhouetting their target against the evening sky, the British gun crews were perfectly positioned. Hood himself congratulated the gunnery officers on their performance. '*Your firing is very good*' he said, '*Keep it up as fast as you can, every shot is telling.*' These were the very last words of a popular commander sometimes described as 'The beau ideal of a naval officer.' At about 6.34 *Invincible* was struck by a salvo from either *Derfflinger* or *Lutzow* (both were firing at her) that struck and destroyed Q turret, full of ready to use ammunition. Like her two sisters, *Indefatigable* and *Queen Mary*, she blew up, the cordite in her magazines ripping her apart. Her well-aimed shells had shaken and damaged their opponents, but they had kept on fighting. One accurate salvo from the enemy was enough to destroy *Invincible* completely. Just six men out of 1,032 survived, including her gunnery officer Commander Hubert Dannreuther. Interestingly, he was a German and son of a famous musician. Richard Wagner was his godfather. His distinguished career as a loyal officer in the Royal Navy is a testament to the close ties that had existed between Queen Victoria's Britain and Germany, less than twenty years before this bloody conflict. It was reported by an officer of the destroyer *Badger* which picked him up:

'*He was marvellously self-possessed. I can hardly understand how a man, after going through what he had, could come on board from a raft just as cheerily as if he was joining a new ship ... He had merely, as he put it, stepped into the water when the fore-top came down.*'

With their popular leader gone, the remaining two *Invincibles* of 3 BCS (*Indomitable* and *Inflexible*) continued their charge towards the enemy, and Hipper's Scouting Force retired towards the High Seas Fleet, battered, but still full of fight. The rest of the BCF fell into line behind the remaining *Invincibles*.

We must now return to the Grand Fleet and its meeting with the German battle fleet. Jellicoe had taken in Goodenough's signals about the presence of the enemy battle fleet and as early as 4.47 pm had warned his fleet to expect to be in action later that day, but he still had no idea of the outcome of the battle between the rival battle cruiser forces and only the vaguest notion as to where the enemy fleet was. His cruiser screen had been ordered to scout ahead, but now that the Grand Fleet's battleships were making twenty knots, the obsolete armoured cruisers could only draw ahead very gradually. Beatty had successfully led the whole enemy force towards him, but he had been less successful in communicating his own position or that of his opponents. Also, at about 5.00 pm, he had lost sight of the enemy, and did not regain it until about 6.15, when the engagement in which *Invincible* was lost was beginning. Goodenough did manage to keep in sight of Scheer's battleships, but was unclear about his own position. Beatty's signals to the Grand Fleet gave only the most cursory glimpse of the situation, as he himself understood it. For example 'Enemy battle fleet bearing south east' is hardly useful unless accompanied by an accurate estimate of one's own position, enemy course, speed and range. Further confusion was caused by the armoured cruiser *Black Prince* which was on the starboard wing of the cruiser screen ahead of the Grand Fleet. She sighted and reported battle cruisers in the mists ahead without making clear in her signal whether they were British or German. In fact they were British. Yet another confusing factor was that both Beatty and Jellicoe were several miles out in their dead reckoning plot of their own positions. Jellicoe, still with his ships in six columns in cruising formation, was thus left in the unenviable situation of knowing that twenty or more battleships and five battle cruisers were approaching him at a closing speed of over forty knots, through thick weather, without having the information he needed in order to deploy his fleet to meet them. Even when he himself sighted Beatty, now well to the north of Hipper, he had no clear idea of Scheer's whereabouts, but it was imperative that he should deploy into line of battle immediately. He could hear the sound of gunfire in front of him and things were clearly about to start happening very quickly. Fortunately, he kept his head. His overriding objective was to get between the enemy and the route home to the Horn Reefs. With deteriorating visibility and nightfall only a few hours away he wanted to cut off their retreat and finish them off on the morning of the next day. He therefore gave the order for his ships to deploy to port, forming a line of battle astern of *King George V*, which had been leading his port (eastern) column, with the battle cruisers positioned slightly ahead of the main force (Charts 5 and 6). The course would be east or south east. After the battle much was written about this deployment by people like Churchill, who had scant grasp of the basic principles of warfare at sea and by Beatty and his supporters, who thought that they had a case to make at Jellicoe's expense. Why did he not deploy to starboard, as the enemy fleet were approaching from the starboard bow? There were two good reasons. First a deployment to starboard would have brought him within easy torpedo range of the Germans, a situation which was one of his first principles to avoid. Second, his starboard column, which would have been nearest to the enemy, consisted of his weakest ships, and they would have been manoeuvring within just over 10,000 yards of the powerful *Konigs*, at the head of the German fleet. This was just the chance that Scheer was looking for to cut the Grand Fleet down to size. As it was, just as the great ships swung into line, they began to catch glimpses of Scheer's force approaching, and at about 6.30 pm, opened fire. This was the first (and only) time in history in which two great fleets of dreadnoughts clashed in battle. Jellicoe's deployment had placed his ships in an excellent position, crossing the bows of the German fleet, thus putting Scheer's leading ships in a dangerous situation. This time British gunnery was good and a devastating fire rained down on *Konig*, *Grosse Kurfurst*, *Kronprinz* and *Markgraf*, the leading ships of the High Seas Fleet.

For Scheer himself this was a terrible surprise. Up to this point he had been totally unaware that Jellicoe was at sea with the Grand Fleet and had been quite confident that he could go on damaging the relatively small British force which he had so far encountered, fulfilling perfectly his objective of reducing the numerical superiority of the enemy. Indeed reports from his submarines had clearly indicated that only a fragment of the Grand Fleet was actually at sea. Suddenly everything had changed and for Germany's navy it was now a question of survival. To make matters worse for him, smoke and the dying light made it difficult for his ships to make any effective reply to the fire of Jellicoe's battleships. He wrote later:

'*It was quite obvious that we were confronted by a large portion of the English fleet. The entire arc stretching from north to east was a sea of fire. The flash*

*from the muzzles of the guns was distinctly seen through the mist and the
smoke on the horizon, though the ships themselves were not distinguishable.'*

An unprecedented level of excitement reigned throughout British naval
circles. On board *Iron Duke*, Jellicoe's flagship, the captain, Captain Dreyer,
was watching from a position a few feet behind the gunnery officer. '*Beautiful,
beautiful*' he exclaimed as he watched the fall of shot, '*Just like a rose grower
at a show*' as the gunnery officer remarked later. Even ashore on the North
Sea coast there was now a general air of excitement and indeed relief that at
last the enemy fleet had come out of port to face the drubbing it deserved.
Tugs and minesweepers were getting up steam to help damaged ships home,
dockyards were preparing to receive large ships and Commodore Tyrwhitt,
at Harwich, was in a frenzy of excitement, wanting to join the fun and
actually ordered his force to sea, only to have his order countermanded by
the Admiralty.

The only German ships which could see the enemy at all, were those at the
head of the column and their vision was often blinded by smoke and mist.
Ships in the centre and at the rear of the column were anyhow obstructed
by those ahead of them. The *Konigs* did open fire however. Lieutenant von
Schoultz, despite his German name, an observer from the Russian navy,
aboard the battleship *Hercules*, described it thus:

*'Just at this moment we fired our first salvo … The heavy shock lifted me
involuntarily into the air … My attention was distracted by enemy shells
shrieking over the ship. I see a splash very close to our port side which gives
me a thorough shower bath. Other shells are falling to starboard of us. The
German gunnery must be particularly good. Hercules was not hit.'*

Schoultz continued:

*'I decide to go onto the upper bridge again, and there find our bugler, a youth
of fifteen. When I ask him what he is doing there I notice tears in his eyes
and realize that the poor lad, whose duty it is to pass on signals, is terrified
by the gunfire and probably still more by the loneliness, for not a soul is to
be seen on deck.'*

In spite of the bugler's tears, Scheer was in an impossible position. He had to get away from the fearsome line of battleships ahead of him, but how to do so? To turn in succession, as Beatty had done a few hours earlier would have spelt disaster, with the turning point under fire from a whole fleet's broadside. Only one course was open to him, the *Gefechtskehrtwendung* or 'battle turn away'. This was an extremely difficult manoeuvre in which all the ships in a column reversed course. First the rear ship would turn and as soon as it did so, the next ship ahead would follow suit until the whole fleet had turned through 180 degrees. This was a difficult evolution to get right at the best of times with a constant possibility of collisions, accidents and a whole chapter of errors. It must have been doubly difficult when under effective enemy fire and in poor visibility, but the High Seas fleet executed it perfectly, steaming away into the mist on a south-westerly course. Interestingly, several of Scheer's ships, including some of the pre-dreadnoughts at the rear of the line, missed the signal to turn, but nevertheless did so, the captains using their own initiative, a clear indication of the contrast between German and British fleet practices. The High Seas Fleet would never have made the sort of blunder which Beatty and Evan-Thomas made, when 5BS steamed away from the opening rounds of the 'Run to the South.' Now, shielded by the murk, the High Seas Fleet was safe for the time being, but their course was taking them directly away from their route home. A destroyer attack, ordered to cover the *Gefechtskehrtwendung*, was unsuccessful as the British battleships were able to spot incoming torpedoes from their mast tops and turn away or dodge to avoid them. The destroyers were however able to drop smoke floats that helped to cover the retreat and their presence caused disruption in the British line and delayed its progress. At the same time there was a sudden deterioration in the natural visibility, so that all the British guns fell silent. Many of the German ships were now in a bad condition, particularly the battle cruisers which had been in action almost constantly for three hours, much of that time facing 13 and 15-inch gunfire. *Lutzow*, Hipper's flagship, was making water and badly down by the bow. She could hardly manage fifteen knots and even at that speed her bulkheads were in danger of giving way. She fell out of line. *Derfflinger*, the 'Iron Dog' as she was christened, was almost as bad. She too was making water fast through a great gash in her bows, and all her communications gear was destroyed.

Seydlitz was almost a wreck, her guns out of action and her steering gear damaged. Water was penetrating her generators and control gear and she was losing all electrical power. *Von der Tann* and *Moltke* were both working to repair damaged turrets, but were still capable of steaming and fighting. This left Hipper himself in a difficult position. He could no longer command his battle cruisers from *Lutzow* and he ordered a destroyer, *G39*, to go alongside and take him to *Derfflinger*, but finding her in such a poor way he had to search for another ship on which to hoist his flag. Eventually, he settled on *Moltke*, the least damaged of his fleet, but it was to be some time before he could actually get aboard her.

Scheer's leading battleships, the *Konigs*, had been hit hard. *Konig* herself was in a bad way but could still steam, *Markgraf* had lost her port engine and could hardly keep up. *Grosse Kurfust* was badly holed and was shoring up bulkheads. The ships that had been astern of them had mostly been invisible to the British and escaped serious damage. With Mauve's pre-dreadnoughts in the van, after the hasty about turn, the High Seas Fleet drew away south westwards, relieved to be disappearing into the gathering sea mist and smoke.

Chapter Seven

Clash of the Battle Fleets

At about the same time as the Grand Fleet was deploying, several exciting goings on were taking place close to 'Windy Corner'. The first was an extraordinary manoeuvre on the part of Rear Admiral Robert Arbuthnot. Arbuthnot was known as a hard man, something of a bully. He had command of the 1st Cruiser Squadron, consisting of *Defence, Warrior, Duke of Edinburgh* and *Black Prince,* all obsolete armoured cruisers actually incapable of playing any useful part in the battle. This squadron was stationed on the starboard side of the Grand Fleet, the side nearest to the enemy. Just after 6.15 pm, *Defence* caught a glimpse of a German light cruiser which was scouting in front of Hipper's battle cruisers. *Defence* immediately opened fire, whereupon the enemy slipped away into the mist. Arbuthnot gave chase at maximum speed, cutting dangerously across the bows of *Lion* as he did so and making clouds of black smoke, thus obscuring the approaching enemy battle fleet from the Grand Fleet which was just starting to open fire. He was unable to catch up with his quarry, but instead came across the *Wiesbaden*, already badly damaged by Hood's ships and by *Onslow*. Arbuthnot decided to slow down so that both *Defence* and *Warrior* could open fire on the luckless *Wiesbaden*. Suddenly, out of the mist appeared the leading ships of the German battle fleet. Two almost stationary 15,000-ton warships was too good a target to miss and the German battleships poured heavy shells into the elderly cruisers. *Defence* blew up almost at once, taking all of her 903-man crew with her. *Warrior* was terribly damaged, but water flooding into her magazines probably prevented her from exploding, and she lay helpless and immobile in the path of the enemy. At that moment however, the Germans found a bigger fish to fry. Close to *Warrior* they spied *Warspite*, the mighty fast battleship, inexplicably going round and round in small circles.

This extraordinary situation was caused by an unlucky accident aboard the mighty battleship. 5BS, after a spirited fight with the High Seas Fleet and with Hipper's battle cruisers, had been ordered to fall in at the rear end of Jellicoe's battle line. As they were on a northerly course this meant a turn to starboard. At that point *Warspite* had suffered several heavy hits, but was not seriously damaged. In the general commotion around 'Windy Corner' however, *Warspite's* helm was put over too hard, the helmsman being worried that the ship was dangerously close to *Malaya*. This violent application of helm at high speed caused the steam steering engine, which operated the rudder, to fail, leaving the rudder jammed fifteen degrees to starboard. The probable cause of the failure was the distortion of the bulkhead on which the steering engine was mounted, causing a bearing to run hot and seize up when the helm was altered quickly. The captain immediately ordered his engineers to try to restore control of the rudder. Meanwhile, he tried to control the ship's head using the engines. All this time, *Warspite* was right in the path of the High Seas Fleet. Seeing her plight, the leading German ships lost no time in selecting her as a target and subjected her to a terrible barrage of fire, leaving *Warrior* to limp away unmolested. Using her engines to steer, *Warspite* eventually pulled away from the enemy and became obscured by the mist and smoke. A reserve steering engine was available to cope with such an eventuality, but the ship's troubles were not over. The reserve steering had been wrongly connected and she started to circle again, this time to port. Eventually this problem was sorted out and steering fully restored. Damage to the hull and engine rooms however, restricted the ship's speed to sixteen knots, so as she could not keep up with the fleet she limped back to the Forth. The Germans were convinced that *Warspite* had been sunk, but actually the damage was not too severe; only fourteen men being killed and thirty-two wounded. Her antics had had one positive effect; they had saved *Warrior's* crew from certain destruction. She was eventually located by the seaplane carrier, *Engadine,* and towed towards Cromarty, a rising sea eventually made the tow impossible and the crew was taken off. One wounded man fell into the water between the two ships as the evacuation was taking place. Rutland, the pilot of the seaplane, with great bravery plunged into the sea between the two ships and rescued him, receiving a well-earned Albert Medal for his courage.

The battleship *Marlborough* also suffered difficulties at about this time. Leading the right hand column of the Grand Fleet, she deployed into line as ordered, at the head of the rear division. She was able to fire eight salvoes at a *Kaiser* class battleship, scoring as she thought, a number of hits; then she engaged two light cruisers, one of them being the unfortunate *Wiesbaden*. She then seems to have become a magnet for enemy torpedoes. One struck her on the starboard side amidships, causing her to take a list to starboard and knocking out much of her electrical gear. This was soon repaired however, and the ship was able to resume her place in the line, narrowly missing a collision with the damaged destroyer *Acasta* as she did so. She then spent ten minutes dodging at least four more torpedoes, fired by light cruisers and by destroyers. She had a further chance to engage enemy battleships, this time of the *Konig* class, as they swung round to the south-west, and got off a torpedo herself at *Wiesbaden*. A little later, at 7.19 pm, yet another wave of enemy destroyers attacked her. They were driven off by 6-inch gunfire, but not before they had launched another salvo of torpedoes. As *Marlborough* struggled to avoid these, one was seen to break the surface about 500 yards from the ship then make straight for her starboard side amidships. Luckily it passed clean under her, probably suffering from the depth control problems which were plaguing German torpedoes of that time. A junior officer in her foretop described the actions as follows:

'At 6.08 pm we started taking ranges, and at 6.15 we picked up as target an enemy battleship of the Kaiser class and on her we opened fire at 6.17. (Note: These times are probably inaccurate) *She was making a good deal of smoke, but her inclination was quite easy to determine by the trend of smoke from the funnels and by the general look of the ship. After some alterations of range to the guns, at about 6.19 we began to hit … We fired seven salvos at this battleship and the fifth and last were clearly seen to hit, the fifth with a deep red flame and the last with a great cloud of greyish coloured smoke … At 6.54 we were hit by a torpedo. We thought at first it might have been a mine, for we saw no track of a torpedo whatsoever, but we know now for certain that it was a torpedo as bits of one were found later in the ship. It hit on the starboard side, and aloft the top swayed a lot and finally took up a list to starboard, so that I imagined one strut of the tripod mast had been shot away: but looking*

over the side of the top I saw that it was the whole ship that had taken a list to starboard. At about 7.00 pm when we were just getting square again after the torpedo explosion, three tracks of torpedoes were seen approaching on the starboard side, all three apparently going to cross our track. The bridge were informed, and the ship was turned to port so that two passed ahead of us and one astern. Five or ten minutes before this some German destroyers had appeared on our starboard bow, so presumably these torpedoes as well as the one that hit us came from them ... At 7.19 a flotilla of German destroyers were seen on the starboard bow ... Fourteen minutes later (7.33) the tracks of the torpedoes they had fired were seen approaching from the starboard beam. The tracks were quite clear to us from aloft, and could be picked out when nearly a mile away. At once we reported to the bridge, and they altered course to starboard so that No 1 track, the furthest off, passed ahead of us, but No 2 and 3 were nearly on top of us before the ship commenced swinging. No 2 passed so close to the stern that we lost sight of the track from the top and would certainly have been hit if the stern had not been swinging away under the influence of helm. No 3, which I saw break surface, when about 500 yards on our beam, came straight for the ship, and its track came right up against our starboard quarter – it must have been running below its depth and went right under the ship ...'

Marlborough was able to continue operating with the Grand Fleet until 2 am, when water flooding in through the seventy-foot long rent in her side meant that she could no longer keep up and was settling deeper and deeper in the water. She made her way under escort to the Humber for temporary repairs. On her way she met two U-boats, returning from their fruitless patrol off the English coast. One torpedo was fired which *Marlborough* avoided easily.

It was never definitively established which ship fired the one successful torpedo that had hit her, it may possibly have been the last parting shot of *Wiesbaden*. As the narrative quoted above relates, no one had spotted it approaching, and the crew suspected that they had struck an errant mine until bits of German torpedo were found inside the damaged ship on her return.

The older dreadnought, *Neptune*, was luckier. A torpedo fired at her was missed by the lookouts in the foretop but was noticed by a gunnery lieutenant on the bridge, who without standing on protocol, yelled, 'Hard-a-starboard' into the voice pipe. The ship shuddered under the effects of full rudder and emergency full speed, but the turn brought the missile directly astern of her, and it rapidly gained on her as the party on the bridge looked on in horror. It disappeared under *Neptune's* stern and they braced for the shock, but there was no explosion. Either the torpedo was running too deep or it was pushed off course by the propeller wash of the great ship, so she escaped unscathed.

Among the officers in A turret of the battleship *Collingwood*, one of the 12-inch armed older dreadnoughts, stationed just ahead of *Marlborough's* division, was a young officer recovering from a too riotous night out before the fleet had sailed. Just before the clash of the two battle fleets, no one in *Collingwood* realized that the enemy was anywhere near and all expected that they were engaged on yet another fruitless sweep of the North Sea. Uncomfortable in the stuffy heat of the turret on a pleasant afternoon, the officer climbed out onto the turret roof to get some fresh air and sunshine. Just as he settled down, the turret unexpectedly traversed and the ship shuddered as the great guns opened up. The officer, Prince Albert, later to become King George VI of England, fled back to his station, '*like a rabbit scuttling down his hole*' as he described it. Later, he summed up his feelings during the battle. '*All sense of danger and everything else goes, except the one longing of dealing death in every possible way to the enemy.*' It was lucky for him (and as it turned out for Britain) that he was in *Collingwood*, not one of the newer battleships which had B turret 'superfiring' over the top of A. He would have been blown to pieces by the blast from the muzzles above him.

By about 6.40 pm, the opposing battle fleets were out of sight of each other, the Germans away to the south west, taking cover in the rising mist. The sun was sinking in the west and it would soon be dusk. Jellicoe had reason at this stage to be quite pleased with his day's fighting. He was still unaware of the loss of *Queen Mary* and *Indefatigable* and he knew that he had inflicted severe damage on the leading enemy battleships. Considering the likely outcome of a meeting between the two fleets in similar circumstances he had written:

'Nothing but ample time and superior speed can be the answer, and this means that unless the meeting of the fleets takes place fairly early in the day, it is most difficult, if not impossible to fight the action to a finish.'

He also knew that he had got between the German fleet and its shortest route home past the Horn Reefs. At all costs he must avoid the danger of running into a situation in which his superior gun power could not be deployed to full advantage, such as a major night-time encounter or a close range action. Of night action he wrote, 'Nothing would make me fight a night action with heavy ships in these days of torpedo boats and long-range torpedoes. I might well lose the fight. It would be far too risky an affair.' So far however, things seemed to be going well for him. He would now steam on a southerly course and try to remain to the eastward of the enemy during the short summer night, then give battle in the morning. He did need to know which route Scheer would choose for his retreat. This was critically important. On his outward journey Scheer had selected the route to the west of the Amrun Bank and the Horn Reefs. On his return he could take the swept channel east of the Bank and inside the Reefs, passing close to Sylt Island and the Vyl lightship, or again he could stand on further south towards Borkum Island, then turn east, running close to the north German coastline (See Chart 10). Jellicoe had no way of knowing yet which route Scheer would choose. He had no doubt of the outcome of an encounter between the fleets in daylight, but in the darkness things might be different. He knew that the High Seas Fleet had trained intensively in night-time fighting, and feared that they might be much more adept at it than his own command. Also, in darkness, strange things can happen, making it likely that his numerical superiority might be difficult to deploy. He was also acutely conscious of the dangers of pursuing a fleeing enemy fleet. Mines dropped astern of the fleet or a submarine trap could, as he had pointed out himself on many occasions, be disastrous; much better to wait for the enemy fleet to come to him.

That was exactly what Scheer did and sooner than anyone expected.

Goodenough had continued his invaluable role as scout-in–chief for the Grand Fleet and had kept in touch with the High Seas Fleet after its dramatic about turn. This was not a comfortable billet for frail light cruisers, close to enemy battleships, but while he was dodging shellfire, the Commodore had seen that they were steaming on a generally south-westerly course with the pre-dreadnoughts in the van and the *Konigs* in the rear. Hipper's remaining battle cruisers (*Lutzow* had by now fallen out of line) were on their port quarter. Just before 7 pm he saw that the Germans were making another, totally unexpected *Gefechtskehrtwendung* and were heading straight for the Grand Fleet in column, with the *Konigs* and the battle cruisers now in the lead, almost inviting Jellicoe to take a second chance to cross their tee. Goodenough informed Jellicoe immediately. Scheer's reasons for this extraordinary manoeuvre have been a matter for conjecture ever since the battle. He himself justified it by saying that he wanted to have another crack at the British before dark and that he wanted to rescue the smitten *Wiesbaden*. These reasons are both unsustainable. The *Gefechtskehrtwendung* put his battered battle cruisers, which were in no condition to fight, and the *Konigs*, also badly damaged, closest to the British battleships and exposed his fleet to the whole weight of the enemy broadside in the most unfavourable imaginable position. As for *Wiesbaden*, she was a wrecked light cruiser in a sinking condition and no admiral alive would risk a whole battle fleet to save such an inconsiderable prize. It is much more likely that Scheer had misjudged the position of the Grand Fleet and was trying to steal away under its stern for the Horn Reefs. In an unguarded moment after the war, Scheer admitted that if he had carried out such a manoeuvre on a peacetime exercise he would have been sent home in disgrace.

The setting sun now caused the German ships to stand out clearly, making excellent targets for the British gunners. Briefly, the British line was disrupted by a report of enemy submarines in action (there were none in the area), then a withering fire was opened on the leading German ships. *Marlborough, Hercules, Revenge* and *Agincourt*, all ships of Admiral Burney's 1st Battle Squadron making especially good shooting at 8,000 to 9,000 yards, while Gaunt's 5th Division was able to concentrate on the enemy battle cruisers which were too severely disabled to make a serious reply. At least fifteen heavy shells slammed into the leading German ships, the *Konigs*, and the battle cruisers, without any effective response. By about 7.15 pm, almost the whole Grand Fleet was in action against the enemy columns who were unable to reply. Scheer was facing annihilation for the second time that evening, and this time the range was so close that even the defective

British shells had terrific impact and fire was more deadly than ever. He must get away at once. He did the only thing he could do. He ordered a third *Gefechtskehrtwendung*, at the same time commanding the gallant battle cruisers to physically charge at the enemy and thus cover the battleships' about turn. The actual order was '*Ran an den feind*' – 'Charge the enemy.' Command of the battle cruisers was now in the hands of Captain Hartog, the captain of *Derfflinger*, as Hipper was still in his destroyer looking for an undamaged ship to board since *Moltke* was in no condition to accommodate him. Hartog did not flinch from his duty, and the poor, battered ships drove onwards into a veritable firestorm in an action afterwards referred to as 'the death ride of the battle cruisers.' Damaged as they were, their machinery was still in working order and they made as if to try to ram the battleships which were pouring heavy shells into them. *Derfflinger* alone received at least nine heavy hits during her charge, disabling two turrets and smashing her upperworks out of recognition. To make matters even worse, torpedo nets had been blasted loose and were hanging over the ship's side, threatening to foul her propellers. One of her officers wrote:

'The signaller on the bridge read the message – Ram! The ships will fight to the death – Our captain did not bat an eyelid he gave the order "Full speed ahead, course south east"; followed by Seydlitz, Moltke and Von der Tann we headed straight for the enemy's van. Salvo after salvo fell around us, hit after hit struck our ship. A shell pierced Caesar turret and exploded inside. The turret commander, Lieutenant Commander von Boltenstern, had both his legs blown off, and almost the whole gun crew were killed … The burning cartridge cases sent out great sheets of flame which flared up from the turret as high as a house. The great flames killed everyone within their reach. Another shell pierced the roof of Dora turret. The same horrors ensued. From both after turrets great flames were now spurting, mixing with clouds of yellow smoke … I felt a pain in my heart when I thought of what the conditions must be in the interior of the ship … A terrific roar, a tremendous explosion then darkness … The conning tower seemed to be hurled into the air, poisonous greenish yellow gases poured into our control room through the aperture. I shouted "Down gas masks" and at once each man pulled down his gas mask over his face … Whole sections of deck were hurled

through the air, a great concussion threw everything movable overboard ... We could scarcely see the enemy who were disposed in a semi-circle round us. All we could see was great red-gold flames spurting from their guns ... The flashes from the muzzles looked like the opening of two wide blazing eyes and I suddenly remembered where I had seen something of the sort – Sascha Schneider's picture "The Feeling of Dependence" had created the impression of something similar to what I was experiencing. It shows a black monster of shadowy outline, opening and shutting its smouldering eyes and fixing on a chained human form, which is awaiting the final embrace.'

This was the most gallant performance by the Imperial Navy, but it risked the total destruction of the battle cruiser fleet. At the last possible moment, after the ships had sustained further heavy damage, Scheer relented. His battleships, in spite of some confusion and a number of very near collisions, had executed their turn and were steaming away from the enemy, trying to sort themselves into proper order. This in itself had been an astonishingly seamanlike performance, for although Scheer's signals had been confusing, the flag officers commanding the various squadrons used their common sense and there were no casualties. Scheer then called off Hartog's 'death ride' and instead sent the 6th and 9th destroyer flotillas, a total of twenty boats, dashing forward in three distinct waves to cover his headlong retreat. The British saw the attack coming and turned away to 'comb' the torpedo tracks, each ship keeping a careful lookout for approaching missiles. There were several near misses, but no hits on the battleships. Steaming directly away from the source of the threat it was relatively easy to see oncoming torpedoes, as the rate of approach was usually less than twenty knots in the case of torpedoes fired at long range. Probably the battleship's propeller wash was responsible for many of the narrow escapes. Jellicoe counter-attacked using light cruisers and destroyers to drive off this new threat and at least one of the German destroyers, *S35*, was lost and three others severely damaged by a combination of fire from the secondary armament of the battleships and the defending light forces. The 4th Light Cruiser Squadron under Commodore Le Mesurier was especially effective in this engagement.

As they turned back towards the High Seas Fleet, the German destroyers dropped highly effective smoke floats, obscuring themselves and the battleships from the Grand Fleet and the battle gradually fizzled out, the rival fleets separated from each other by smoke and the gathering dusk. This was just as well for Scheer. His fleet was dangerously out of formation and only his older ships, now again at the head of his line, were still largely undamaged and in a condition to continue fighting. These ships moreover, were furthest from the enemy and could do nothing to cover the retreat of the *Konigs*. Of the battle cruisers, only *Moltke* and *Von der Tann* could still fight. *Seydlitz* and *Derfflinger* both had their foredecks awash, their magazines flooded and their turrets largely out of action. It is unlikely that any British battle cruiser would have had the least chance of surviving such a battering as they had endured. Only *Lutzow* was at this point, in sinking condition, limping away from the battlefield with an escort of six destroyers making smoke to protect her (she was finally abandoned and sunk at 2.45 am).

Jellicoe has been criticised for his turn away from the torpedo attack, some critics arguing that he should have turned towards the threat and kept on battering the enemy fleet. Such a move would have been against every principle of his strategy. It would have added almost forty knots to the approach speed of the torpedoes, making them extremely difficult to avoid and it would have risked a spate of mine laying by the retreating destroyers, seriously jeopardizing the safety of the fleet which he had to keep intact at all costs. Torpedoes, it must be remembered, were expected to achieve a thirty per cent hit rate against a column of battleships, so a barrage of thirty of them might have been expected to achieve ten hits, destroying at a stroke, the superiority of the Grand Fleet. Cautious as ever, Jellicoe had thought coolly and quickly and did the right thing.

As the battle faded away, the two battle fleets settled down, with the British on a generally south-westerly course, led by Beatty's battle cruisers, and the Germans steering south, about eighteen miles to the westward, with the remains of Hipper's battle cruisers in the van, on the port bow of the leading battleships (Chart 8). Beatty spotted them briefly and opened fire but achieved no result. He had signalled their bearing to Jellicoe, but unfortunately his reckoning of his own position was badly wrong and contact with the enemy was lost. Beatty then sent a radio message to Jellicoe 'Submit van of battleships follow battle cruisers. We can then cut off whole enemy battle fleet.' Jellicoe consequently ordered the division of battleships closest to Beatty to follow the battle cruisers to the south-west, but in reality Beatty had no more idea of the position or course of the enemy fleet than anyone else, and the battleships he referred to, Admiral Jerram's 2nd Division, never located the Battle Cruiser Force, so could not follow it. Beatty had been hoping to cut across the bows of the High Seas Fleet as it steamed south, but as the light faded, failed to find it again until a squadron of light cruisers (3rd LCS), under Admiral Napier, made contact with its German opposite number (4th Scouting Group). There was an exchange of fire, but fading light soon made accurate shooting impossible. Dashing towards the sound of gunfire, other British light cruisers eventually came into action. These were *Caroline* and *Royalist* of 4 LCS under Captain H.R. Crooke. They got a reasonable sight of the enemy battle cruisers and the pre-dreadnoughts and prepared for a torpedo attack. Jerram countermanded this, fearing that what they had seen were actually Beatty's force. Crooke however, took no notice and the two light cruisers put in a bold torpedo attack at about 8,000 yards. One of *Caroline's* torpedoes was seen to run true, but the enemy turned away and it eventually failed to hit its target. The cruisers escaped through a hail of gunfire. Their attack had come to nothing, but at least they had located the enemy and driven him off to the westward. At roughly the same time, the battle cruisers got a last fleeting glimpse of the main German fleet and were able to report their position accurately (this time!) to Jellicoe. The battle cruisers briefly engaged their old rivals, scoring several damaging hits. Poor light and battle damage prevented any effective reply, but supporting fire from of all things, Mauve's squadron of pre-dreadnoughts, covered a turn away to the westwards and into the darkness and drove off the remaining British light cruisers. The 'five minute ships' had at least done something to justify their inclusion in the German order of battle. They suffered only light damage; *Schleswig-Holstein* and *Pommern* both were hit once and they themselves scored a single hit on *Princess Royal*. As Jerram had been unable to find Beatty, no British battleships were involved in this brief action. If they had been able to locate the battle cruisers earlier, they might have been able to press home an attack. Just as night was falling the enemy battle cruisers were eventually spotted from Jerram's own ship, *King George V*, as they melted away into the dusk. Sub Lieutenant Cunliff aboard the flagship wrote later:

'Saw the silhouettes of three battleships (actually they were probably battle cruisers) about 8,000 yards away on the starboard bow and positively identified them as German by the distinctive cranes between their funnels.'

He reported them to the bridge, but no action was taken and the chance slipped away.

Astern of *King George V* was *Orion*, the flagship of Rear Admiral Leveson. Her lookouts also spotted the Germans through the gathering dusk. Leveson's flag lieutenant, Lieutenant Crooke, turned to him and said, *'Sir, if you leave the line now and turn towards, your name will be as famous as Nelson's.'* Leveson was no Nelson, but an admiral schooled to obey and not to think for himself. *'No.'* he replied, *'We must follow the next ahead.'* This miserable response brought an end to the possibility of a final daylight attack on the crippled German fleet. Had Leveson or Jerram had the spirit that inspired their juniors like Crooke, the outcome of the battle might have turned out much more favourably for the British.

How significant was this episode in the last of the summer daylight? Beatty's instinct that he could get ahead and once again cross the T of the whole German fleet if the battleships joined him was probably sound, but he was taking no account of the inability of British ships to identify each other and distinguish friend from foe in the darkness. A night-time fleet encounter would have been fraught with danger. This does not excuse Jerram and Leveson from not making an opportunistic attack while they could still see, and they would have had a prime chance of sinking at least one of the damaged battle cruisers before darkness fell. It is hard to imagine a commander of the calibre of Hipper or Hartog missing such a chance for aggressive action and the passivity of these British admirals stands in stark contrast to the enterprise and pluck shown by the more junior British officers commanding small ships that evening and earlier in the day.

Scheer now had one objective and one only. He must get away as quickly as possible. Facing a vastly more numerous enemy, it was senseless to continue to try to erode the superiority of the Grand Fleet. The best he could hope for was to get home without further significant damage, but how to do so? He knew that he was separated from two of his routes home by the Grand Fleet, and that he was gradually being edged south-westwards, further and further from his destination, by the sporadic engagements since his third *Gefechtskehrtwendung*. Perhaps however, there might be a chance to turn and slip around the sterns of the Grand Fleet in the darkness. Light forces could spread confusion in the enemy fleet and under cover of night, perhaps get close enough to some of the big ships to do serious damage (Chart 9). The Japanese destroyers had achieved this brilliantly in the night at Tsushima only eleven years ago. Nothing however, must deflect his fleet from its main aim; to get itself safely back to harbour. As night fell he ordered a course of south-east, towards the ten-mile long line of British ships, with the rider '*Durchhalten*' – 'No Stopping'. The new course meant that the two great fleets were converging and would inevitably clash sometime during the night.

Chapter Eight

Night Action

Darkness fell, but it would be light by three in the morning. The British assumed their night cruising formation. The battleships, now in four columns, closed up to each other so as to be easier to protect from torpedo attack and less likely to fire on friendly ships. The battle cruisers formed the vanguard, ahead and slightly to the west of the main body, ready to repel any attempt by the Germans to slip around the head of the Grand Fleet and make off eastwards towards home (Chart 8). Beatty wrote:

'I did not consider it desirable or proper to close the enemy battle fleet during the dark hours. I therefore concluded that I should be carrying out the Commander in Chief's wishes by turning to the course of the fleet (which was southerly) *and reporting to the Commander in Chief that I had done so.'*

Astern of the Grand Fleet the light forces were massed, placed there to try to prevent any attempt by the enemy to cross behind the battle fleet and escape towards the Horn Reefs passage. Jellicoe seems to have thought this an unlikely course of events, but he was aware that his big ships would be too far south to block the enemy's route home in that direction effectively. He had taken the additional precaution of sending three submarines to guard the entrance to the Horn Reefs passage, but these had orders to remain invisible until June 2. This order was issued before Jellicoe knew that the German fleet was at sea and it rendered their voyage useless. As night fell on 31 May, a further obstacle in the form of a new minefield was laid by the fast destroyer *Abdiel*, off the Amrun Bank, in the entrance to the Horn Reefs channel. *Abdiel* had been well prepared for such a mission and had been standing by throughout the action, close to the flagship, waiting for orders.

She was loaded with ninety mines, ten of them of the Leon (free floating) type. Her captain (Commander Berwick Curtis) wrote:

> *'At about 9.30 pm I got orders to proceed to a position south of the Vyl lightship and lay a line of mines. We therefore set off at 32 knots passing on our way several ships in the distance, and also a flotilla of sorts which was making a great deal of smoke, but as we were not making any smoke ourselves, we presumably were not seen. We reached our position at 1 am and laid the mines then returned to Rosyth for another load, passing south of the big North Sea mining area. We had 80 ordinary and 10 Leon mines on board, all primed, so perhaps it is just as well that we weren't hit. The ship did exactly what she was intended to do, justified her existence, that's all there is to it.'*

He was being unduly modest. As we have seen, ships in the North Sea frequently did not know exactly where they were, and navigation on a misty night at high speed is no easy matter, but *Abdiel* found the Vyl lightship, which enabled her to fix her position accurately, and laid a string of eighty conventional mines. Mine laying was a very dangerous business, especially in an area like the Horn Reefs, which was already heavily mined by both sides. A ship that did not know exactly where she was would be in severe danger. Also of course, the enemy might easily set a mine trap himself in an area which his opponent might think suitable for mining. The Commander says nothing about the immense skill required to navigate his ship accurately and safely. *Abdiel* had the great advantage over most of the German destroyers in being an oil burner, hence the relative absence of smoke even at thirty-two knots. She continued to be used to lay mines in enemy waters for the rest of the war, becoming one of the most valuable and deadly small ships in the Royal Navy.

Between his fleet and where he believed the enemy were situated, Jellicoe placed the invaluable Goodenough with his 2nd Light Cruiser Squadron, while the 4th Light Cruiser Squadron scouted ahead.

Scheer laid his plan of escape carefully. He did indeed select the route inside the Horn Reefs and the Amrun Bank, as the entrance to it was nearest to him and it was well protected by his own minefields. At nightfall he was some 100 miles from the entrance to the channel and he planned to reach it by daybreak. He had twice that day been taken by surprise by the Grand Fleet and been at a tactical disadvantage. Another such mistake would be fatal. He had ordered a course of south south-east, which would take him directly to the Horn Reefs. In the van of his fleet were the five light cruisers of the 2nd Scouting Group followed by the eight older dreadnoughts. In the centre of his column were Mauve's six pre-dreadnoughts and in the rear were the seven powerful but wounded *Kaisers* and *Konigs*, followed by the four surviving battle cruisers. It had taken him some time to get his ships into order after the continual turns away from the enemy in the past few hours and this was made more difficult by Hipper who, having at last been able to board *Moltke* and regain command of the battle cruisers, tried to take his accustomed station ahead of the battleships. It was not until after 10.30 pm that things got properly into order. The 4th Scouting Group, consisting of five light cruisers, was to starboard of the column, and would pass closest to the rear of the British Fleet if things went according to Scheer's plan. Still further towards the enemy, destroyers probed the darkness, trying to locate the tail of Jellicoe's columns. Early that night the British had done Scheer a tremendous favour. German ships challenged and recognized each other in the darkness by displaying a sequence of coloured lights when they were challenged. The British challenged and answered challenges by flashing a code using signal lamps. *Lion* had somehow lost her record of the code to be flashed on that fateful night and unbelievably, asked by radio what it was and was answered by another ship. This conversation was overheard by Neumunster radio station, which immediately informed the High Seas Fleet of the British recognition code. Now German ships could pass themselves off as British in the darkness almost whenever they wanted. The Germans had two further great advantages in the quality of their searchlights and in their night fighting procedures. Both sides used electric arc type searchlights; the Germans on their heavy ships had eight 43-inch lights, the British, two 36-inch or 24-inch. Besides this disparity of size and numbers, the German searchlights were fitted with an iris type shutter so that they were lighted before the ships were likely to go into action and could be shone at full power as soon as the iris was opened. The British lights had no iris and would be dim and flickering for a few vital seconds after they were switched on; a grave disadvantage, especially at close quarters. German night action procedure was carefully planned to get the vital first broadside off at the enemy. When an enemy ship was present, the lookout would follow it with his glasses, and the searchlight, with the iris closed, would automatically follow where the glasses were pointing. If the enemy was less than 1,650 yards away the German guns would be loaded and trained to follow the searchlight. A challenge would be made and unless the target instantly gave the correct reply, the searchlight would be switched on and the guns would simultaneously be fired, ensuring a vital advantage in the engagement. These procedures were subject to many, many practise drills and worked very well in combat. The British on the other hand, would make their challenge; then, if it was not correctly answered, turn on their searchlight, which would flicker and splutter, then the operator would have to sweep the sea to find his target before the fire control system could set about aiming and firing the guns. By that time a small ship might have been blown to pieces.

The first night encounter was an abortive skirmish between destroyers during which four German torpedoes were fired ineffectively at close range, then the attackers made off before the British could make any effective reply.

The second night encounter took place at about 11.15 pm when two light cruisers, *Frankfurt* and *Pillau*, came across a flotilla of British destroyers led by *Castor*, a light cruiser, just as the latter was taking station at the tail of the fleet. The Germans launched torpedoes at 1,200 yards range, very close, but fortunately *Castor's* flotilla swung onto their new course immediately after the enemy torpedoes had been fired, so the missiles missed their target. Following behind *Frankfurt* and *Pillau* were *Hamburg* and *Elbing*. Using their knowledge of British recognition signals the Germans closed to about 1,000 yards range then opened a rapid fire on *Castor*. At that range they could hardly miss and *Castor* was badly damaged by at least seven hits. One shell struck her motor boat and set it on fire causing a vivid flame to light up the scene. *Castor* was able to fire back however, damaging *Hamburg* and knocking out one of her guns. She also fired a torpedo which missed. She then turned away to put out her fire and the action fizzled out.

A far more deadly encounter was brewing in the narrowing space between the two battle fleets. Goodenough in *Southampton* with *Dublin*, *Nottingham* and *Birmingham*, had placed himself to the westward of 1st Battle Squadron, which was having trouble keeping up with the fleet due to the torpedo damage suffered earlier by *Marlborough*. (*Marlborough* had to pull out of line and return home later that night). At 11.30, lookouts on *Southampton* sighted five grey shapes close on their starboard beam. At first they could not identify them, then one of the unknown ships hauled up a coloured display of signal lights. This raised the suspicion that they were Germans. Goodenough brought an end to a frenzied argument about their identity on the bridge of *Southampton* by saying '*I can't help it if they are British. Open fire!*' They were in fact the light cruisers *Stettin, Munchen, Frauenlob, Hamburg* and *Stuttgart*. They had been forced to edge well to the east of the main German line to avoid collisions with Hipper's battle cruisers. They immediately switched on powerful searchlights and a venomous fire- fight broke out. *Southampton* and *Dublin* had switched on their searchlights and thus became the focus of the German fire, while the other two British ships remained darkened and were left relatively unscathed as they deluged the enemy with 6-inch shells at point blank range. *Southampton*, as we shall see, was badly mauled and her guns and searchlights put out of action, while on *Dublin* a fierce fire raged below decks. The navigator was killed and his charts destroyed, as was the wireless room. The ship could not communicate or find her way and lost contact with the fleet until mid-morning the next day. The Germans were in an even worse plight. All of their ships had been hit and more or less severely damaged, and one, *Frauenlob*, had been hit by a torpedo fired by a cool headed officer on *Southampton* at the height of the battle. She staggered away, rolled over and sank taking 319 men with her. There were only three survivors.

Southampton's torpedo lieutenant told the story:

'*At about 10.15 there appeared on our starboard beam, scarcely 1,500 yards distant, a line of five ships steering in the same direction as ourselves. We inspected them carefully from the bridge, and officers in the after control position also observed and reported their presence to us. The next few minutes were full of suspense, the newcomers being as unwilling to disclose their identity as were we; meanwhile a cautionary order were passed to the guns and searchlights, and I gave the order to flood the starboard torpedo tube ready for firing. Then the two squadrons almost simultaneously decided that the other was hostile and opened a violent fire.*

Each of the five German ships switched on two groups of lights and opened fire, at least three ships very speedily concentrating on Southampton, which, with her searchlights burning, made an excellent target, the others finding and engaging Dublin, our next astern. Neither Nottingham nor Birmingham showed any lights, with the result that they remained undiscovered and were enabled to pour a heavy fire on the enemy at almost point blank range.

On the bridge the full glare of searchlights of the leading enemy ship was on us, and we could see nothing, but I had already received enough impression of the general direction of advance of the enemy for the purpose of torpedo fire, so I passed down an order to the torpedo flat and waited impatiently for the reply. When it came through – the report "Ready" – I fired at a group of hostile searchlights, which were the only things visible.

The Commodore came over to my side and asked if I had fired. I told him I had, and that the tube's crew were reloading ... I began to look round. It was impossible to distinguish the firing of our own guns from the noise of bursting shells; I remember a continuous screaming noise, apparently caused by "overs", but I could see nothing of the results of our own firing owing to the glare of the searchlights. I received no definite impression that the ship being struck by shell, only a confused uproar. I did not find out the true state of affairs on deck until it was all over. I observed that a fire had started on board somewhere aft, which was hidden by another which shot up just abaft the bridge, nearly to the fore-top. Our firing and the enemy's too now became desultory, and there were brief periods of calm, when there was little else to do but watch the fire, which was within a few feet of the bridge screens, and, having seen three ships blow up earlier in the day, I wondered how long it would be before we made the fourth, and what it would feel like. Just as we had made up our minds that another few minutes would surely see the end of Southampton, the searchlights from the leading enemy ship went out and she sheered off to starboard. She had been torpedoed and was sinking, though we did not know it at the time.'

There were twenty-nine killed and sixty wounded on *Southampton*, and she was badly damaged, her searchlights and all but her forward guns were destroyed and the hull badly holed by three direct hits. The damage was shored up and she could still make twenty knots, so was able to remain with the fleet for the rest of the battle, but fell behind on the voyage home, having to slow down to keep the hull watertight in the heavy weather. She received a hearty and well-deserved cheer when she eventually docked in Rosyth.

While this action drew to an end, the most incredible things were happening a few miles to the south. The German battle cruisers had got split up and were proceeding independently, all roughly following the course set by the admiral. *Moltke*, the least damaged of them, was the first to blunder into the British battle line. At 11.30 pm she found herself steaming almost parallel to four massive battleships. These were Jerram's 2nd Battle Squadron of modern 13.5- inch gun ships and at close range they could have blown even a tough ship like *Moltke* to pieces. Stealthily, *Moltke* drew away, everyone on board praying that they had not been sighted. Actually they had been sighted and identified by the battleship *Thunderer*, but her captain decided not to open fire as he '*considered it inadvisable to show up the battle fleet*'; neither did he make any attempt to report his sighting to Jellicoe. Had he done so it would have become clear that the Germans were steering for the Horn Reefs and at that stage it would have been relatively simple to turn the fleet round and cut them off. Twice more *Moltke* tried the same trick, with the same result. Then she gave up, increased speed and cut round across the bows of the Grand Fleet, making the Reefs in safety. An hour later the heavily damaged *Seydlitz* ran across *Agincourt* and *Marlborough* in the same way, with the same result. Not a shot was fired and no one told Jellicoe. The gunnery officer of *Marlborough* (Ross) had had her clearly in his sights and asked for permission to open fire. '*No.*' said the captain, afraid the ship had been misidentified. '*Of course what I should have done*' wrote Ross afterwards '*was to have opened fire and blown her out of the water, then said sorry.*' Too heavily damaged and thus too slow to follow *Moltke's* example, *Seydlitz* managed to slip through a gap in the British lines and carry on her way unmolested. Scheer, with the main body of the High Seas Fleet, still had no indication of the position of the Grand Fleet and continued his push to the south south-east. At a little after midnight his leading ships were actually crossing the wake of the hindmost British battleships and entering the gap between them and the light forces screening the rear of the Grand Fleet (Chart 9). This was for him an incredible stroke of luck; but as his fleet streamed through the gap, not more than three miles under the sterns of the fast battleships of 5BS, they could not avoid a clash with the destroyers and light cruisers approaching fast on their port quarter.

On *Tipperary*, a powerful destroyer leader at the head of the westernmost column of the destroyer force, all lookouts were concentrating on the western flank, where it was assumed the enemy fleet was lurking. At 00.03 hours, the captain sighted the indistinct forms of a column of large ships on a course converging with his own. He was unable to identify them and unlike Goodenough, unwilling to assume that they belonged to the enemy, although he was in an ideal position to launch torpedoes. After a few minutes he flashed a recognition signal. Seconds later a searchlight came on and a storm of heavy and shells crashed into the destroyer, her bridge was swept away and her oil fuel caught fire. Her opponents, the battleships *Westfalen*, *Nassau* and *Rheinland* and assorted light cruisers, then turned their guns on the next destroyers in line, *Spitfire*, *Sparrowhawk* and *Garland*. These managed to get off two torpedoes, but the battleships turned away westward to avoid them. *Spitfire* had to make a sharp turn to avoid the wreck of *Tipperary*, then swung round to try to pick up survivors, all the time hammering at the great battleships with her 4-inch guns. At close range these were unexpectedly effective, putting two searchlights out of action and causing some forty casualties. Her luck could not last and suddenly she found herself right in the path of *Nassau*, which had resumed her original course after turning away from the torpedoes. There was a terrible crash as the two ships, one of 1,000 tons and the other of 21,000 tons met, *Nassau* lurching over ten degrees and losing twenty feet of her port side armour plating onto *Spitfire's* deck. Her guns, fired at maximum depression, could not hit her victim, but blast from the muzzles swept away Spitfire's masts, bridge and foremost funnel. She limped away to commence a hazardous voyage home. Meanwhile the savage battle in the darkness raged on. The light cruisers *Elbing*, *Stuttgart*, *Hamburg* and *Rostock* were on the port side of the battleships, and found themselves dangerously close to the British destroyers. Turning away to avoid torpedoes brought them close aboard their own battleships and *Elbing* collided with *Posen* and was totally disabled; she may also have been hit by one of the British torpedoes and she eventually sank. At the same time the destroyer *S32* was hit by fire from British destroyers and lost all power.

After the loss of *Tipperary*, the destroyer column re-formed astern of *Broke*, a sister ship. At 00.40 hours, *Broke* sighted a large ship with two funnels and massive cranes amidships. This profile should have given her away as German, but *Broke* flashed a challenge that was answered by a storm of shellfire from the battleships *Westfalen* and *Rheinland* and from the light cruiser *Rostock*. *Broke* was reduced to a wreck, everyone on the bridge was killed and the helm jammed hard to port. *Sparrowhawk*, close astern of her and turning to fire torpedoes found *Broke* out of control and heading for her at full speed. The two destroyers smashed into each other, the shock throwing men from *Sparrowhawk* onto *Broke's* foredeck and the confusion was multiplied as men from the two ships, believing their own vessels doomed, scrambled onto the other, equally damaged, destroyer for safety. To make matters worse, *Contest*, the next boat astern, piled into *Sparrowhawk* jamming her rudder hard over. Eventually the ships were parted and *Broke* and *Contest* managed to limp home. *Sparrowhawk* was abandoned and sank. There were still five undamaged destroyers in the column and these avoided the wrecks and made one further attack on the column of battleships. The battleships turned away from their torpedoes, but the light cruiser *Rostock* was less lucky, she caught a torpedo amidships which put her out of action. Gunfire from the battleship's secondary armament put an end to two of the attackers, *Ardent* and *Fortune*. In these encounters the only German battleship to have suffered any significant damage was *Oldenburg* which was hit on the bridge by 4-inch fire from the destroyers. This killed or wounded most of the bridge party and rendered the ship temporarily out of control. With great courage her captain, Hopfner, though seriously wounded, took over the wheel himself and skilfully avoided a collision.

Steaming eastwards to join the remaining column of destroyers guarding the easterly quarter of the fleet, two of the surviving British destroyers caught a glimpse of what they thought was a German heavy cruiser. In fact it was *Black Prince*, one of Arbuthnot's 1st Cruiser Squadron which had avoided destruction at 'Windy Corner', but had her speed reduced and had been trying to catch up with the Grand Fleet. She found herself close alongside the centre of the High Seas Fleet's battleships and made the mistake of flashing a recognition signal. A terrible storm of fire overwhelmed her, setting ammunition, coal and furnishings alight. Like a ship from hell she careered off into the darkness, her hull glowing red and her upperworks illuminated by a pillar of reeking fire. There were no survivors.

The port (easterly) column of destroyers was led by Commander Goldsmith in *Lydiard*, and had been joined by refugees from the now shattered westerly column. They were steaming about four miles astern of the hindermost British battleships. Goldsmith had noticed a lot of firing to the westward, which he believed was a terrible 'blue on blue' affair between British light forces. He was a little surprised when he saw a column of battleships to starboard, on a parallel course to his own; he assumed they must be the ships of 5BS, which had somehow got astern of station. He led his destroyers round across their bows to take station to starboard of the battleships, but did not realize how long a tail of stragglers had joined him. As a result the last two ships in his line, *Petard* and *Turbulent*, found themselves close under the bows of the battleships and discovered that they were not 5BS at all but the High Seas Fleet led by *Westfalen*. *Turbulent* was rammed and sunk, but *Petard* escaped under a hail of gunfire which swept away much of her upperworks, killing most of the men on deck, but leaving her machinery undamaged. She was unable to attack her tormentor with her own torpedo armament as she had fired the last of them at *Seydlitz* earlier in the battle. Goldsmith has been criticised for not turning the rest of his flotilla round onto a parallel course to the German battleships and attacking with torpedoes. He was in an ideal position to do so. The criticism may be justified, but Goldsmith's failures pale into insignificance compared to the inept performance of some of the senior officers aboard the British battleships.

Losses on both sides during the night so far had been fairly equal. The British had lost four destroyers and an armoured cruiser and two further destroyers had been severely damaged. The Germans had lost two light cruisers and a destroyer with a further light cruiser severely damaged, but the really serious and inexplicable British failure had been one of communication. Jellicoe in *Iron Duke*, near the middle of the British columns, about ten miles to the south of these actions, heard and saw gun flashes behind him but assumed that these were the minor clashes between light forces which he had expected. It was very likely that Scheer would send his destroyers to make an attack on the British columns under cover of darkness and he had disposed his own small ships specifically to fend them off. Incredibly none of the destroyer officers reported to him that they were in contact not with a handful of destroyers, but with the whole enemy battle line, steering south eastwards. On most of the British ships it seems that senior officers just assumed that the admiral knew everything which they themselves knew and would take action at the appropriate time. Jellicoe, stationed near the centre of his battle fleet, of course could not possibly know what was going on behind him in the darkness. Destroyers and light cruisers were supposed to be the eyes and ears of the fleet, yet they said nothing. Even more inexplicable was the negligence of the officers of the rear divisions of the British battleships (5BS and the 6th Division). They actually saw the fighting and could have intervened, using the light of burning ships to guide their fire. Failing that, they could at least have communicated to Jellicoe what they had seen and it would have become clear to him where the Germans were and what their course was. The High Seas Fleet could then have been cut off by the faster British battleships and severely mauled before they reached the Horn Reefs. Instead, 5BS and the 6th Division, both in the rear of the Grand Fleet, sailed sublimely on, following the leader and saying nothing. Jellicoe thus had no cause to revise his original opinion that the main body of the German fleet was somewhere to the west of him and steaming south so as to reach the Helgoland swept channel at daybreak. In at least one case a ship in the rear of 5BS (*Malaya*) did report what was going on to Evan-Thomas aboard *Barham*, ahead of her, by light signal; but Evan-Thomas did not see fit to pass this on to Jellicoe.

Officers afloat were not the only culprits. Room 40 was busy all night intercepting enemy radio traffic. At about 9.00 pm, they picked up a signal from the cruiser *Regensburg* saying that the High Seas Fleet was in square 165y, that is to say 56.33N 5.30E and steaming south. This was duly relayed to Jellicoe. Unfortunately, it was completely misleading and Jellicoe knew it, as he had only recently been in visual contact with the Germans. The reason for the error was that *Regensburg's* navigational plot was wildly inaccurate, so this was hardly Room 40's fault, but this, in combination with the false information which the Admiralty had given Jellicoe about the departure of the

High Seas Fleet from the Jade, had completely undermined his confidence in any information sent to him from the Admiralty. As a result he decided to ignore a further signal sent to him at 10.40 pm which correctly reported the enemy's course and speed, thinking it was probably more 'Admiralty rubbish.' The Admiralty then obtained no less than six new intercepts that correctly indicated German intentions. One ordered an airship to reconnoitre the Horn Reefs, another ordered destroyer flotillas to assemble off the Reefs and four more correctly gave the fleet's course and speed. The Admiralty, once again in the person of the same Captain Jackson who had caused the incorrect information about Scheer's not leaving the Jade to be sent to Jellicoe, did not trouble to pass any of these six to vital messages to the Grand Fleet. Had it done so Jellicoe would surely have realized that this time the information he was getting, far from being 'rubbish', was the key to achieving an historic victory. He bemoaned afterwards *'the Admiralty's withholding from me almost hourly information which would have led me to alter course during the night for the Horn Reefs.'*

The encounter involving *Petard* was not the last of that night. The British 12th Destroyer Flotilla under Captain Stirling in *Faulknor* was the easternmost outpost of the rear of the British Fleet. As the first streaks of dawn appeared in the eastern sky, Stirling saw a line of big ships steering an almost parallel course to his own and recognized them immediately as Germans. Unlike his fellow destroyer commanders he immediately sent an ultra-high priority signal reporting what he had seen and manoeuvred to attack. (Actually his signal was not received on *Iron Duke* due to enemy jamming). At first the Germans were in some doubt as to the identity of the small ships steaming on their flank, then as the truth dawned, they turned away to avoid torpedoes, opening up a heavy fire with every gun which would bear. *Onslaught* was hit and badly damaged, but was able to maintain station as her consorts pressed home their attack. Torpedoes were fired at a range of about 1,000 yards and there were several near misses, one exploding in the wake of *Kronprinz*, only 100 yards astern, probably triggered by her propeller wash. Another ran clean beneath *Markgraf.* German good luck however could not continue and the unfortunate victim was the old pre-dreadnought *Pommern.* Hit by one or possibly two torpedoes, she was not nearly as well protected as more modern ships and the detonation seems to have set off her magazines as there was a series of explosions, tearing the old ship apart and killing every man of her 844 complement. It was never established for certain which destroyer had fired the missile; most probably it was *Obedient*. Apart from this terrible loss of life, the loss one obsolete battleship did not do much to weaken the German fleet. An officer on *Maenad*, one of *Faulknor's* flotilla described the action thus:

'*Maenad was the leading ship of the 2nd Division of the first half of the 12th Flotilla and was stationed on the port quarter of Faulknor the 1st Division being on the starboard quarter of Faulknor ... The short night had been very dark and full of excitement, as splashes, explosions, searchlights and star shells had been constantly visible to the north and west of us, and since all hands had been at action stations since 6 pm on the evening before, nerves were at "concert pitch." The flotilla had been well strafed by some presumed enemy cruisers astern of us at about midnight, but though many shots had fallen before us and alongside, fortunately no one was hit. Course had been altered to the north east and speed increased to 25 knots for some time to draw clear, then the original course and speed reverted to after firing ceased.*

Suddenly at about 2 am some dark objects loomed up on the starboard beam and there was much speculation as to what they were, for it was of course possible that we had unknowingly closed our own battleships. They were exciting moments. Jane's Fighting Ships was on the chart table ready for reference, and the Captain, 1st Lieutenant and Midshipman consulted it eagerly to determine what vessels these might be, but the ships showed themselves to be enemy by giving recognition signals quite different to those used in our service ... The Captain ordered both tubes to be trained on the starboard beam as soon as the first division received orders to attack, and this was done. On we went, the noise of the guns firing, etc. being drowned out by the roar of the engine room fans as steam was raised for full speed. The eagerness of the stokers was so great that soon too much pressure was raised, the safety valves lifted, and all other noises were drowned in the deafening roar of steam at 250lbs. pressure close by the bridge.

We followed Faulknor round, but the turn came unexpectedly and try how they would, the torpedo tube's crews could not train as fast as the ship turned, and only one torpedo was fired. The order was therefore passed to train the tubes to starboard in preparation for another attack, which the Captain said he intended to carry out. While this was being done a big explosion occurred as a result of the flotilla's attacks (since thought to have been Pommern), we then turned a complete circle to starboard, though how we passed through the remainder of our division without a collision we don't know ...

At about 2.25 am the enemy, consisting, as far as we could see, of five Konig or Kaiser class battleships, were sighted again, and course was steered parallel to them when about 2,000 yards off. The enemy were firing hard at us and their shots were falling short and over, and certainly felt as if they were passing close to our heads, but in spite of it all Maenad was not hit anywhere.

We fired two torpedoes in this second attack and then turned away under full helm, and while still turning, right astern, there was a terrific explosion, which at any rate showed that one of our torpedoes had hit the enemy. It was rapidly getting light at this time, and in a few minutes it was broad daylight and we came across Marksman ...'

This second attack was the final encounter and it might well have been significant, as the small group of destroyers, which had fallen in with the destroyer leader *Marksman* had actually blundered into the path of the battle cruisers now bringing up the rear of the German fleet. The encounter was confused and there were many claims as to who had hit what. *Moresby* was certain that she had hit *Von der Tann*, which turned away smoking heavily, but was actually undamaged. The only German casualty was the destroyer *V4*, which blew up and may account for the explosion reported by *Maenad*.

There has been some controversy about the relative performance of British and German destroyer forces at Jutland. The German official history is extremely critical of British destroyer performance, for example Die Krieg der Nordsee states:

'The few successes and exceptionally high losses of British destroyers are, in view of all the facts most surprising. Personal bravery among the senior officers of the flotillas and the captains of various ships was certainly not

lacking, and was indeed acknowledged by the German fleet but..., all the British destroyer attacks showed great lack of training in methods of attacking the enemy and incorrectly understanding the situation as well as the counter measures that the ships attacked might make. All the attacks were delivered separately and while the boats were still closing. The destroyers always approached too close so they were sighted and driven off by gunfire before they could turn and attack on a parallel course ...'

This is pretty ripe coming from the Germans. Their own destroyers, though mostly also handled with great daring during the daytime fighting, did no damage at all to the Grand Fleet during the night when Scheer had confidently predicted that they could inflict serious losses on the enemy. One flotilla (II Flotilla) of twenty powerful destroyers with a full complement of torpedoes actually pulled out soon after midnight and scuttled home via the Skagerrak. Another (VII Flotilla) made an ineffective attack on some British light forces then withdrew. Otherwise the German flotillas seem to have cruised around doing nothing offensive. British destroyers by contrast sank an old battleship *(Pommern)* and two valuable light cruisers, *Elbing* and *Rostock* (*Note: Ebling's* loss may have been caused only by collision), at least one destroyer *(V4)* and disabled another *(S32)* during the night, with the loss of four their own number destroyed and three disabled. In these exchanges the British clearly came off best. In the daylight hours they had also hit *Seydlitz*, *Wiesbaden* and possibly *Lutzow*. It is certainly true however, that the night fighting skills of the High Seas Fleet and the initiative shown by their officers were incomparably better than those of their opponents. Their deployment of searchlights and recognition systems gave them the upper hand in almost every encounter, but there is no evidence whatever of any enemy superiority in handling destroyers. As we have seen, their hit rate with torpedoes throughout the battle was considerably worse than the British. Also German capital ships, with their fearsome complement of 6-inch secondary armament, fully manned, were extremely dangerous to approach too closely. The most serious mistake made by British destroyer officers was their poor ship recognition skills, which were compounded by the German knowledge of British recognition codes.

In fact, the Germans probably misunderstood the role of the British destroyers, which was different to that allotted to their own. Knowing the overwhelming superiority of the British in weight of broadside and numbers of battleships, the High Seas Fleet came to place great reliance (misplaced, as it turned out) on the ability of destroyers to make high speed attacks on the enemy battle line, damaging and slowing down some of the great ships so that they had to pull out of line. For this reason, destroyers were normally massed ahead and astern of the battle line, close together and ready to dash in and make an attack. As we have seen, they did this several times during the battle, but never succeeded in making a hit. (*Marlborough* was probably hit by the stationary light cruiser *Weisbaden*). Conversely, the British saw the main role of destroyers as defensive. They were disposed all round the fleet so as to be well placed to drive off attack from enemy light forces or submarines. Captains were however permitted to take aggressive action if a favourable opportunity arose. They had some success in this mode. Had they had better training in night fighting they might have been extremely effective.

Chapter Nine

Dawn

By the time dawn had finally broken it was obvious that the weather had taken a turn for the worse. A heavy swell from the west indicated the approach of strong winds, and visibility became limited due to mist patches and drizzle. Beatty, who had seen and heard nothing of the night actions, all well to the north of him, thought that the enemy were to the south-west and asked permission to scout in that direction, but Jellicoe was still expecting them to be steaming on a roughly parallel course to his own. He turned the whole fleet onto a northerly course, deploying his ships in column, ready for the action which he still expected. As soon as it was light, Zeppelins appeared intermittently over the fleets, indicating that the Germans now knew the British dispositions. They were greeted with fire from every gun which would bear; but the art of anti-aircraft gunfire was in its infancy and no hits were scored. As the minutes ticked away it became less and less likely that the Grand Fleet would get another chance to engage the enemy; and at 4.10 am Jellicoe received confirmation that his prey had slipped away. This came in the form of a signal from the Admiralty reporting a further intercepted German radio message. The signal read as follows. '*Urgent, at 2.30 am German main fleet in Lat 55.33 N Long 6.50 E course SSE 16 knots.*' That meant that they would by now be past the Horn Reefs, and just entering the passage through the minefields off the Danish coast. In short, they were home and dry. Returning to cruising formation the Grand Fleet could now do nothing but cruise the area of the battle looking for stragglers, then set a course for home, bitterly disappointed. Beatty, when given the news by his chief, showed not only disappointment, but also a rare sign of understanding of the situation. '*There's something wrong with our ships*' he repeated '*And something wrong with our system.*' How right he was on both counts.

There was still, in theory at least, a danger to the returning Grand Fleet from enemy destroyers and submarines. Fortunately for the British the most dangerous of the enemy destroyers, II Flotilla, had departed round the Skaw, and almost all the others had run out of torpedoes and were getting low on fuel. For them a venture into the North Sea to attack British ships on their way home was out of the question. Most of the U-boats deployed before the battle had already returned to base, but there were still some at large and Scheer ordered more to sea to try to pick off some of the returning British ships. Deteriorating weather hampered their progress, but one of the subs already in place made an attack on the damaged *Warspite* as she limped home. Her steering was still damaged and she had to be steered from the engine room. Damage below the water line at first limited her speed to sixteen knots, but the crew managed to shore up bulkheads so that she could increase speed to nineteen knots without risk of flooding and gradually she was able to work up to twenty-two. This was just as well, as she had no escorting destroyers. She was zigzagging at 9.35 am when two torpedoes passed her, one on each side. In the choppy sea then prevailing, the periscope of *U.51* had not been seen, although she had been only 650 yards away when she released her torpedoes. At 11.42 am a periscope was sighted right under *Warspite's* bows. She turned to ram, but the steering, which was still having to be operated from the engine room position, was slow to react and this sub, *U.63*, was missed by a few yards. *Warspite* then opened up with her secondary armament, but the intruder dived and sat safely on the bottom. At the same time as this action was in progress, destroyers from Rosyth arrived and began a depth charge attack, but the *U.63* was able to creep away unharmed. *Warspite* continued her journey, arriving in Rosyth at about 3 pm. Damage was not too serious and she was able to leave the dockyard and re-join the Grand Fleet on 20 July. She had had a shaky start to a career that was to make her the most famous of all British twentieth century warships.

Marlborough, the only other severely damaged British battleship, had remained with the fleet for most of the night, but her steadily reducing speed made her a problem to her own division (5th Division) and to 5BS which was supposed to proceed in concert with it. She was sent home at about 2 am on 1 June. The worst of her damage stemmed from the torpedo, probably fired by *Wiesbaden*. She had a seven degree list to starboard, but it was not considered desirable to counter flood the port wing compartments to correct the list as the extra weight of water would slow her down still more. She had the light cruiser *Fearless* for company on her voyage home. At first she was able to make way at about twelve knots, and headed for Rosyth, but a rising wind and sea was constantly working the shored up bulkheads and she shipped more and more water. At 9.30 am, two conning towers were sighted and she changed course quickly, but in fact these belonged to two British submarines which dived out of the way. Just over an hour later there was a real submarine threat as *U.46* got within extreme range and fired a torpedo at 3,300 yards. This missed by a wide margin and *U.46* did not risk staying on the surface so close to an undamaged light cruiser, so she disappeared and crept away. Just before noon a large submersible pump was lowered into the bilge to clear some of the water and as this started working, speed was increased to thirteen and a half knots, but the extra speed further strained the bulkheads and the pump rapidly became choked with cinders. All this time the sea was rising, putting increasing strain on the damaged hull. Just before midnight the pump shifted, knocking away some of the timber being used to shore up the bulkheads, thus allowing still more sea water to rush into the hull. Floodwater surged around the boilers. Speed was reduced to ten knots, and the ship sought shelter under the lee of Flamborough Head. Some escorting destroyers from Harwich that had now appeared were ordered to come alongside and be prepared to take off the ship's company. *Fearless* stood off to windward to try to flatten the seas that were now coming over the foredeck of the damaged battleship. One of the destroyers laid an oil slick. While this was going on, a diver was getting to work on the shores, reinforcing the bulkheads around the engine rooms and a high-pressure ejector was used to clear the pump. By 4.30 am, the water level had dropped slightly and by 8 am, *Marlborough* staggered into Immingham and safety. Her draft when she arrived was forty feet, eleven feet more than normal. It had been a close run thing.

The rest of the Grand Fleet battleships, with the exception of 5BS, which had born the brunt of the action during the run to the north, had suffered little damage. Apart from *Warspite* and *Marlborough*, all the surviving heavy ships were able to steam at at least twenty knots and were able to retain their correct formation during the long, weary trek back to Scapa, Cromarty and Rosyth, heading into an increasingly angry summer gale in the North Sea

Several of the destroyers were damaged by enemy action or by collision and had hazardous voyages home. The adventures of *Spitfire*, severely damaged in her collision with the battleship *Nassau* and by gunfire, illustrate the problems of bringing these small ships into port. *Spitfire* was a K Class destroyer, built in 1913, rather smaller and less powerful than the M Class ships that made up most of the Grand Fleet destroyers. Her captain (Commander W. Trelawny) had suffered a head wound from a shell that whizzed over the bridge, taking off his hat and causing a shallow flesh wound. He and a lieutenant had been on the bridge at the time of the collision and had been hurled from there onto the upper deck, a distance of over twenty feet; they were shaken but not seriously hurt. All the masts and rigging were gone, the bridge structure wrecked, there were dents all along the hull, and the bows were badly stove in, while on what was left of the fore deck lay a large section of *Nassau's* armour plating. As the two ships had been closing each other at some fifty knots when the collision occurred, it is surprising that the little destroyer still floated at all. While the captain destroyed the ship's confidential papers, the crew rigged a steering position aft with a voice pipe to the engine room and the young surgeon probationer got to work on the wounded. Working in the most terrible conditions he had to amputate a seaman's leg without any anaesthetic. His work and courage were much admired. The ship had been terribly damaged by fires which had broken out below decks, wrecking all the cabins and mess decks. Luckily, the engines and three of the four boilers were intact so there was a possibility of making way and it was decided that, as *Spitfire* was no longer any use as a fighting ship, she would try to make her way home.

As soon as she got under way at six knots there was a fearful scare as a large ship appeared out of the darkness and seemed to make straight for her. As the monster approached, passing a few yards under the stern of *Spitfire*, it became horribly clear that it was a cruiser (actually *Black Prince*) on fire, probably now without a living soul on board. The hull was glowing red hot, and flames poured out of every aperture. A few minutes after the apparition passed, there was a loud explosion and it was seen no more. A horrified watcher on *Spitfire* described the sound of the doomed ship passing as being *'like a motor car in low gear.'*

Spitfire had no means of signalling and only the remains of a patched up chart to steer by, but she struggled slowly westwards into a rising sea. The crew were kept busy stuffing anything movable into the gaping hole in the bow, but it was all soon washed away. Work paused for a short while whilst a most moving funeral service was held for seven men killed in the action. At one point the wounded destroyer came across a Norwegian steamer who offered to take the crew off the ship, but they bravely refused. During the night of 1 – 2 June however, the weather got worse and preparations were made to fire distress rockets. The Captain reckoned they were still about sixty miles off shore, although the navigational plot was extremely uncertain in the absence of proper charts or instruments. However, perhaps there was a chance of being seen by a minesweeper or a patrolling destroyer. Just as the rockets were ready to go, the sky cleared and the wind began to drop, and 4 am found the little ship making ten knots on a course of west south-west. She soon fell in with a drifter, which gave her a course for the Tyne, now only twenty-two miles away. Three hours later, *Spitfire* was safely moored alongside in Jarrow and the exhausted crew were given a good meal and a warm dry bed in the depot ship *Bonaventure*. There was certainly 'something wrong with the system' as Beatty had said, but there was nothing wrong with the spirit and resourcefulness of the destroyer crews.

Scheer had waited at the entrance of the passage home through the minefields, hoping for news of *Lutzow* and of his missing light cruisers. When he heard that the wounded battle cruiser had been finally sunk by one of his own destroyers, he ordered his fleet to proceed towards the Jade. At about 5.22 am there was a violent explosion alongside the battleship *Ostfriesland*. At first this was thought to be a torpedo strike, but then bits of mine were found on deck. She had struck a mine which had been laid by *Abdiel* on a high-speed minelaying mission on 5 May, quite close to the field laid during the night of the 31st. Being a German battleship, *Ostfriesland* had excellent under water protection and was not at first severely damaged. She fell out of line and was escorted by a seaplane and two airships as she made her own way along the channel to the west of the Amrum Bank and Helgoland. She was close to Helgoland when an imaginary submarine was spotted and to avoid the torpedo it was supposed to have fired, she made a sharp turn. As a result of this violent manoeuvre a damaged torpedo bulkhead was ruptured and the ship began to take on water fast. She signalled for help and for the services of a pumping vessel from Wilhelmshaven, but before it could get to her, the leak was partly cured and she managed to limp into the Jade at ten knots under her own power.

Mines and submarines in the Helgoland Bight had been a constant worry for the High Seas Fleet. A flotilla of minesweepers had been at work during the night, but it was impossible for them to locate and sweep every mine laid by fast British minelayers. A floating mine was sighted as the High Seas Fleet entered the swept channel and a mine warning buoy dropped by the leading battleships as they approached the Reefs. As the rest of the fleet turned into the channel this buoy was mistaken by the following ships for a submarine periscope and subjected to heavy fire as the battleships passed. As we have seen, British submarines on station off the Horn Reefs had been instructed to sit on the bottom and they saw nothing of the High Seas Fleet's passing.

Bringing the heavily damaged *Seydlitz* safely home was a triumph for German organization and seamanship. The crew had been constantly at action stations since the first clash of the battle cruisers in the early afternoon of the previous day and must have been utterly exhausted. By early morning of 1 June the ship could barely make seven knots. Most of the fore part of the hull was full of water and as the bows sunk deeper and deeper in the water, more areas gradually became flooded. Steering was difficult, as helm orders had to be passed by word of mouth and voice pipe to the men operating the steering motors in the engine room. The light cruiser *Pillau* was ordered to guide her into harbour, but she was now drawing forty-four feet of water and she grounded gently off Syldt Island just after 9 am. The tide was rising however, and the Captain expected to be able to get afloat again before high water, which was due at about midday. To lift the bows, some after compartments were counter flooded and this, together with the rising tide, was enough to get her off. It seemed however that the channel to the east of the Amrum Bank was going to be too shallow for her to continue by that route, so it was resolved to turn the ship round and make for the passage to the west of the bank, with a division of minesweepers clearing the way. Just as *Seydlitz* was turning round however, a signal was received warning that British warships were to the east of the Horn's reef (5BS was there at about 9 am and had been spotted by a Zeppelin), so the ship had to revert to her original course, with the minesweepers ahead sounding the channel and signalling the depth by means of flags. Several times *Seydlitz* grounded on the soft mud, but pushed herself through the slime by going hard ahead, using maximum engine power. All the time, more water was gushing in and the ship became dangerously unstable, taking a list of eight degrees to port. Attempts were made to tow her by the minesweepers and by *Pillau*, but these were unsuccessful. Scheer ordered that she should be beached so as to be recovered later, but the ever-resourceful *Kapitan zur See* Moritz von Egidy found that by going slow astern and proceeding backwards, the stress on the wounded bows was relieved, somewhat reducing water inflow. No chance remained of entering the Jade on the tide and at 5.30 pm the two pumping ships *Boreas* and *Kraft* came alongside. *Boreas* pumped out some compartments above the armoured deck and in the fore part of the ship, but *Kraft's* pumps failed and she was useless except to nudge the stern from time to time to assist steering.

The extra pumps were just able to hold their own as *Seydlitz* faced another night at sea, but early on 2 June the dirty weather which had plagued Jellicoe's ships reached the Helgoland Bight and the wind reached gale force. Speed was now down to three to five knots (astern), barely enough to stem the tidal stream out of the Jade. *Pillau* however, managed to find a pathway through the off-lying banks and eventually *Seydlitz* was able to anchor off the mouth of the river waiting for the tide. Luckily her anchors, chains and capstans were still working. The wounded were taken off the ship and the powerful tug *Albatross* arrived to help. On the top of the tide, the tug and her charge scraped over the bar, but *Seydlitz* grounded again just inside it, in the grip of a strong tidal stream at about 7.30 pm. As the tide turned, she came off at about 8 pm, but the tug could not hold her against the tidal stream and was itself holed by Seydlitz's starboard outer propeller. The battle cruiser drifted out of control until somehow getting her own engines to run again, she was able to go slow ahead, and at 3.25 am on 3 June, she found a safe place to anchor and divers managed to put some temporary patches on the hull. Weight, including two of her turrets, was removed and *Boreas*, assisted by harbour pumps, cleared out some of the excess water. By 6 June she was fit to be towed by two harbour tugs into the sea locks, proceeding into a floating dock a few days later. By any standards this had been a superb and resolute performance.

All the other German heavy ships (except of course *Lutzow* and *Pommern*) reached harbour safely. *Ostfriesland* and *Von der Tann* were repaired in dry dock at Wilhelmshaven, and were completed by 26 July and 2 August respectively. *Moltke*, the least damaged of the battle cruisers, was dry docked in Wilhelmshaven, then taken to Hamburg for further repairs, which were completed by 30 July. *Markgraf* and *Grosser Kurfust* were also dry docked in Hamburg and were completed on 20 and 16 July. *Konig* was also ready for sea by 21 July. *Derfflinger* was, after *Seydlitz*, the most heavily damaged of the German battle cruisers, having been hit by no less than seventeen heavy shells. One witness wrote:

> *'What had happened to this fine ship? From a distance I could see torn rigging hanging down, but the damage to her hull and inside her was far worse than anything I had seen before. A huge gaping hole was torn through her damaged deck. Two 15-inch shells had penetrated the armour close to each other and one of them had exploded inside. The other lay unexploded in a cabin. The ship had also been struck below the water line by two shells but they had failed to penetrate the rather weak armour at that spot…, but the best example of the force of the shells was to be seen near the bows. One shell had entered the port side and had gone through the forward battery taking a whole armour plate with it. Afterwards it may or may not have exploded outside. The superstructure looked like a madhouse, it had been bent, torn open and broken to bits. All the guns in the casements had been ruined. The barrel of one had been broken off completely so it looked like a howitzer …'*

It was astonishing that the 'Iron Dog' was able to remain at sea with such damage and that she sustained only 157 dead and 26 wounded from her crew of 1,068. Ironically, her turbine machinery that served her so well, was manufactured by Parsons on Tyneside.

The other damaged heavy ships, *Kaiser*, *Oldenburg*, *Helgoland*, *Nassau*, *Reinland* and *Westfalen* were all ready for action on or before 10 July.

On the British side, *Malaya* and *Barham* both had to be dry docked, but were back in service by mid-July. *Lion*, *Princess Royal* and *Tiger* had suffered numerous heavy hits, *Lion* having to have one of her turrets removed for repair. All the battle cruisers were back in service however, by the end of July, so that the Grand Fleet's numerical advantage over the Germans was never compromised by the battle. The fleet reported itself ready for action four hours after its return to Scapa. From that last day of the battle, June 1 1916, for the whole of the rest of the war, the numerical superiority of the Grand Fleet over the High Seas Fleet steadily increased. Scheer's sole object had been to reduce this superiority and he had singly failed.

A summary of the ships on both sides requiring dry docking after the battle is as follows:

British	**German**
Barham	*Derfflinger*
Lion	*Grosser Kurfust*
Malaya	*Helgoland*
Marlborough	*Konig*
Princess Royal	*Markgraf*
Tiger	*Moltke*
Warspite	*Ostfriesland*
	Seydlitz
	Von der Tann

Chapter Ten

Conclusions

The most obvious conclusion from Jutland is that the affair was a terrible waste of lives and materials. Even by the grim standards of the Great War the loss of life, 8,645 killed (6,094 British, 2,551 German), in about twelve hours is horrific and the vast investment in ships and armaments, which had been undertaken by both sides, must have seemed to have yielded a poor return. Initially the German people, especially the Kaiser, were ecstatic about the achievement, as they thought, of their fleet. Hipper and Scheer deservedly became national heroes. An unduly gloomy press release from the Admiralty in London tended to encourage German triumphalism. The British public, expecting another Trafalgar, was surprised and disgusted. There were instances of parties of sailors being booed in the streets and armchair critics of the Royal Navy and its leadership had a field day. A more sober and analytical view of the battle requires a careful examination of the strategy and leadership of the rival fleets, the performance of the people involved in the fighting and the strengths and weaknesses of the ships and armaments that they employed.

German strategy was to isolate and destroy a small part of the Grand Fleet so as to achieve parity of forces in the North Sea and eventually lift the blockade. Conversely, the British wanted to maintain their command of the seas around northern Europe by keeping their fleet vastly superior in numbers and firepower to that of the enemy. Scheer's plan for luring the British Battle Cruiser Force into a situation in which most or all of their ships would be lost was perfectly sound and logical. It had little chance of success however, because unknown to him, the British were reading most of his wireless traffic. Jellicoe's principle of keeping his fleet intact, under his own tight control, was also in the circumstances the correct one although it robbed him of the chance of achieving a devastating victory, especially when the High Seas Fleet steamed straight into his arms at around 7.15 pm.

He was also right to be extremely concerned about the danger of running onto an enemy minefield, which could, at a stroke, destroy his numerical advantage over the High Seas Fleet. The Dardanelles campaign provided a grisly example as to how this might happen.

Scheer's actions after he discovered that the Grand Fleet was at sea were also perfectly logical. He obviously was not going to catch the BCF unsupported that day and he was heavily outnumbered. He had to get home as quickly as possible with minimum losses. He badly misjudged the position of the Grand Fleet when he made his unsuccessful lunge to the south-eastwards at about 7 pm, but otherwise his management of the situation cannot be criticised. Certainly luck was on his side when his ships steamed through the gap between the Grand Fleet battleships and the light forces in the rear; but overall his handling of the night action and the disposition of his ships was masterful. The same can be said of Hipper's execution of his role. His ships fought magnificently against a much more powerful opponent and he made no tactical errors. It is particularly impressive that when he had to disembark from his flagship and was unable to command his ships directly, his second in command, Hartog, took over without any disruption or confusion.

Jellicoe's handling of his command during the battle was equally sound. Faced with incomplete information and poor visibility, he made no major mistakes, although Scheer's good luck during the night-time manoeuvres was the British admiral's misfortune. Beatty's performance during the battle cruiser action was certainly courageous and he did an excellent job of leading the High Seas Fleet onto the British battle line, but there can be little excuse for the fact that ships under his command did not properly understand which enemy ship they were supposed to be firing at, making the same mistake as they had made at the Dogger Bank. It was also not only incompetence on the part of his signals officer, but also poor management on his own part that allowed the battleships of 5BS to stray so far from the battle cruisers when the action was opened. If he had taken the trouble to establish a proper working relationship with Evan-Thomas the problem would never have arisen. It is one of the first principles of warfare that forces should be concentrated, not split up piecemeal; and there can be no doubt that the 'Run to the South' would have turned out very differently if 5BS had been closer to the battle cruisers, so that it could have been involved from the start.

Quite illogically, Beatty became celebrated as a hero; and after the war an unseemly row broke out between his supporters and Jellicoe's. The main casualty of the dispute was any logical, unbiased, understanding of the facts of the battle until many years had passed and the antagonists were both long gone.

To achieve their strategic objectives, both fleets had to establish suitable training regimes and operational procedures. The career of Ned Charlton illustrates the fact that the Royal Navy, though superbly suited to policing duties and fighting colonial wars, had paid scant attention to the serious business of how to fight a formidable enemy in the North Sea. Taking command of the Grand Fleet in 1914, Jellicoe set out to improve standards of gunnery and fleet manoeuvring. Gunnery practise was carried out on a range to the west of the Pentland Firth and also from time to time in Scapa itself. The figures for hits achieved (see the statistics below) indicate that these drills were quite effective, as the shooting of the Grand Fleet was adequate, although that of the BCF was decidedly not up to scratch due to the limited facilities for practise firing on the Firth of Forth. It was much more difficult to arrange realistic rehearsals of fleet manoeuvres than to exercise the guns of the battleships. The Grand Fleet's training mainly involved carrying out the evolutions set out in the Signal Book smartly and correctly under the eye of the admiral. Jellicoe's principle of keeping the fleet together and tightly under his own control could only work in battle if he was kept fully informed of what was going on by his scouting forces, particularly the light cruisers. It seems that the drills and procedures for using these small, fast ships to keep the admiral informed of enemy movements were not properly rehearsed or understood by those involved, with the notable exception of Goodenough, whose 2nd Light Cruiser Squadron was attached to the BCF, not to the main body of the Grand Fleet. For example, light cruisers should have somehow kept in touch with the German fleet during the night and warned Jellicoe of their move to escape to the Horn Reefs; they should have been scouting ahead when the High Seas Fleet approached the Grand Fleet for the first time and Jellicoe was desperately trying to establish the relative positions of the two fleets; incredibly they failed to give the admiral any useful information at all during the night. To be fair, communication by radio, the only system which could be used in the poor visibility prevailing, was cumbersome and slow and also subject to enemy jamming. However, all of these difficulties could have been anticipated and procedures rehearsed, and the light cruiser squadrons given a much clearer picture of their role in a fleet action. This was in fact done in the months after the battle.

Even less excusable was the poor standard of night fighting displayed by the Grand Fleet. It is difficult to understand why Jellicoe, with all his knowledge of the German naval capability, did not place more emphasis on training his ships in night fighting. Granted, he wanted to avoid a night encounter if possible, nevertheless he should have anticipated that a struggle in the darkness might be thrust upon him and it was tragic that the destroyers and cruisers which encountered the enemy ships that night were almost invariably fired on before they felt able to take action themselves. Once again, Goodenough was a notable exception.

The numerous unopposed sweeps of the North Sea carried out by the Grand Fleet during the year before Jutland seem to have taught it nothing at all about night fighting or ship recognition, and the senior officers appear to have learnt one thing only; 'Follow the leader and say nothing.' Obviously Jellicoe could not have his subordinates dashing off and 'doing their own thing' during the night, but on the other hand, simply waiting to be told what to do when an enemy ship was in sight, as happened on numerous occasions, was inexcusable and speaks of poor training.

The High Seas Fleet had an extremely boring regime in wartime, consisting of periods acting as guard ships at the mouth of the Jade, gun drill in the protected waters of the Helgoland Bight, and time alongside in dock during which the crews lived ashore. In spite of this, their fighting spirit seems to have been at least as good as the British. What really distinguished them from their opponents was the aggressive attitude of individual captains and their determination to take matters in hand, seizing the initiative when required. To them the mission was all-important, not conformity to orders and programmes. As Fisher remarked after the Dogger Bank battle '*Any fool can obey orders.*' Being a relatively young navy, they had worked out sensible tactical procedures and systems for working together. Their tactics were based on logical thinking, not on a set of rules evolved many years ago in the age of sail. Their actions, ironically, resembled those of Nelson's 'band of brothers' far more closely than those of their British counterparts. They were not faultless however. Like the British, they failed to use their light forces correctly to scout ahead of the fleet, resulting in nasty surprises when 5BS appeared during the 'Run to the South', and when the Grand Fleet battleships twice emerged out of the mists to cross the German tee.

In addition to the gaps in British training and tactics, important shortcomings in material and technology handicapped the Royal Navy at Jutland. The disparity between the numbers of ships lost on the two sides told a sorry story.

British Ships Lost	German Ships Lost
Battle Cruisers	**Battle Cruisers**
Invincible	*Lutzow*
Indefatigable	**Pre-dreadnought Battleship**
Queen Mary	*Pommern*
Armoured Cruisers	**Light Cruisers**
Warrior	*Wiesbaden*
Defence	*Elbing*
Black Prince	*Rostock*
Destroyers	*Frauenlob*
Tipperary	**Destroyers**
Nestor	*V48*
Nomad	*S35*
Turbulent	*V29*
Ardent	*V27*
Fortune	*V4*
Shark	
Sparrowhawk	

The Germans after the battle, celebrated even more serious British losses, but they were being over optimistic. Neither *Warspite* nor *Marlborough* had been sunk as they confidently claimed. Even worse for them was the situation of the two fleets in the following months. The Grand Fleet still had all but four of its battleships (*Barham, Malaya, Warspite* and *Marlborough*) and four more or less undamaged battle cruisers (*New Zealand, Inflexible, Indomitable,* and *Australia*) ready for sea only hours after its return to Scapa. The Germans had at that point no battle cruisers and only eleven serviceable dreadnought battleships against twenty-four battleships and four battle cruisers with the Grand Fleet. The battle had done nothing to shake Britain's ability to command the North Sea and to continue to enforce the distant blockade. In fact, it had enhanced it by putting the High Seas Fleet out of action for two months, and the much greater pace of British ship construction was to make the German position yet weaker as time went on.

The standard of gunnery on both sides had been a subject for debate, especially since even British officers throughout the action noticed how quickly their opponents found the range and how deadly accurate their salvoes were. The statistics certainly confirm that Hipper's battle cruisers achieved far better results than Beatty's:

	Heavy Shells Fired	*Hits*	*%*
Hipper (1st Scouting Group)	1670	65	3.9
Beatty (1 & 2 BCS)	1469	21	1.4

To be fair to the British Battle Cruiser Force, during the 'Run to the South', where most of the damage was done to its ships, wind direction and light conditions greatly favoured the Germans, however Evan-Thomas's fast battleships, which joined in the closing stages of the 'Run to the South' and all of the 'Run to the North' did far better:

	Heavy Shells Fired	*Hits*	*%*
Evan-Thomas (5BS)	1099	29	2.6

Hood's older battle cruisers, fresh from brushing up their gunnery at Scapa, did even better, again favoured by visibility conditions, and in this instance shorter range:

	Heavy Shells Fired	*Hits*	*%*
Hood (3 BCS)	373	16	4.3

The comparison between the battleships (excluding 5BS) on both sides is also interesting:

	Heavy Shells Fired	Hits	%
German Battleships	1927	57	3
British Battleships (excluding 5BS)	1593	57	3.7

Overall there is hardly a significant difference in gunnery performance between the two fleets. During most of the fighting between battleships, light conditions favoured the British.

	Heavy Shells Fired	Hits	%
All heavy German ships	3597	122	3.4
All heavy British ships	4480	123	2.8

Included in the German hits are thirty-seven hits on the obsolete armoured cruisers *Warrior, Black Prince* and *Defence,* obtained at extremely close range, so the raw figures slightly flatter the German gunnery.

Torpedoes should be considered alongside gunfire. British 21-inch torpedoes had a range of 4,200 yards at forty-four knots or 10,750 yards at twenty-eight knots; the German weapons were similar, mostly achieving 5,450 yards at thirty-five knots and 10,950 at twenty-nine knots, although some of their ships were equipped with an older model. Their torpedoes were mostly 19-inch, but some of the capital ships used 23.6-inch models.

British torpedoes seriously damaged *Seydlitz,* and sunk *Pommern, Rostock, Frauenlob, V29,* probably *Weisbaden* and possibly *V4.* Ninety-four torpedoes were fired, giving a probable hit rate of 6.3%. German ships probably fired 112 torpedoes, damaging *Marlborough* and sinking *Shark* and possibly *Turbulent,* so that their hit percentage was either 2.6 or 1.8%. The German performance was hindered by the faulty depth control mechanism fitted to many of their torpedoes. Torpedoes fired from heavy ships on both sides are included in these figures. None of these scored a hit.

The only conclusion that can be safely drawn from figures of hits by all weapons is that there was no great difference between the marksmanship of the two sides.

As it is clear that the two sides were roughly, equally successful in hitting their opponents with gunfire or torpedoes, it is appropriate to consider why the German fleet was able to do so much more damage to the British and cause so many more casualties than they suffered themselves. Obviously the sinking of the three battle cruisers and two armoured cruisers was the main cause of British losses:

	Killed
Queen Mary	1266
Indefatigable	1017
Invincible	1026
Defence	903
Black Prince	857
Total killed on these ships	5069

A further 603 were killed in small ships sunk and in *Warrior*, which foundered on the way home, making total losses in ships that sank, 5672, that is 93% of all British fatalities. By contrast the Germans lost only two large ships sunk.

	Killed
Pommern	822
Lutzow	115
Total	937

1116 were killed in smaller ships sunk, making a total of 2053 killed in ships that sank, 80% of total fatalities.

Fatal casualties in ships not sunk for both sides were similar:

	Total	Ships with most casualties
Losses in surviving German ships	436	(*Derfflinger* 157, *Seydlitz* 98)
Losses in surviving British ships	422	(*Lion* 99 *Malaya* 63)

It is clear from these figures that the cause of the disproportionate number of fatalities on the British side was the propensity of British ships to sink when hit. The reasons are not far to seek. *Defence, Warrior* and *Black Prince* should never have been involved in the battle and they were handled with the most astonishing recklessness. They were sitting ducks for the High Seas Fleet, and their armour protection was useless against heavy shells. The losses of the battle cruisers were, as we have seen, for two main reasons; they were not designed or built to withstand heavy plunging shells, and their ammunition handling practices were criminally dangerous.

Immediately after Jutland, even Beatty had realized this. He wrote to Jellicoe:

'*Urgent.*

Experience on Lion indicates that open magazine doors in turrets are very dangerous. Present safety arrangements of flash doors are ineffective when turret armour is penetrated. Flash from shell may reach cordite in main cages and thence to handling rooms. This occurred on Lion when turret roof was penetrated, but magazine doors being at once closed saved the magazine from catching fire. Almost certain that magazines of three lost battle cruisers exploded from such cause. Consider it matter of urgent necessity to alter existing communication between magazine and handling rooms by reverting to original system of handling room supply scuttles, which should be fitted immediately. Meanwhile imperative to maintain small stock cordite in handling room for magazine, doors being kept closed with one clip on and opened only for replacement of handling room. Proposed handling room scuttles should be capable of being made watertight at will. Commander Dannreuther of Invincible will report personally on this matter at Admiralty tomorrow Sunday.'

This rather poorly worded telegram makes it clear that Beatty had at least partly grasped the issue which had already been addressed by *Lion's* own gunnery officer, W.O. Grant. The telegram did not address the issue of cordite handling discipline, perhaps because the dangerous practices unearthed by Grant only existed in the Battle Cruiser Force and Beatty wanted to keep it under his hat. An enquiry conducted by Rear Admiral Tudor, the Third Sea Lord, who questioned the survivors of the hapless battle cruisers, made it quite clear that ammunition handling was the root of the problem, but his findings were not published at the time, probably in order to save embarrassment on the part of Beatty and the BCF. As a result, the Grand Fleet remained blind to the fact that ammunition held in the turrets had been responsible for the loss of the three great ships and concluded that inadequate armour protection was at least in part to blame. Nevertheless, the practice of stacking ready to use cordite bags in the turrets and handling rooms was eventually changed in the BCF, and scuttles were fitted as Beatty recommended. If the Admiral had listened to the lowly Warrant Officer after the Dogger Bank encounter, many lives would have been saved. Further consideration of the relative significance of handling practices and inadequate protective armour, the two factors which rendered the British battle cruisers such death traps, makes it clear that by far the most important was the ammunition handling. Actually *Lion* suffered thirteen heavy shell hits during the battle, *Princess Royal* nine and *Tiger* fifteen, all three ships survived and were able to continue fighting. It was simply good luck that no shells penetrated the turrets of *Princess Royal* and *Tiger* and of course *Lion* had adopted different handling procedures so that the hit on Q turret was not fatal to the ship. While many critics of British ship design have pointed to the difference in armour between Beatty's ships and Hipper's, these figures strongly suggest that at least the later British battle cruisers could stand heavy punishment, provided there was no flash back into the magazines. How they would have fared if the enemy had had 15-inch main armament is an open question.

There was a huge disparity in gun power in favour of the British (See Appendix V) and as we have seen, the British fired more heavy shells than their opponents and scored a similar number of hits. The greater calibre of British guns was offset however, by the poor quality of British armour piercing shells, which were too brittle and tended to break up on impact, thus exploding before they had penetrated the hull of the enemy ship. An excellent example of the effect of this was a 12-inch strike on *Derfflinger* by *Bellerophon*. The missile hit the armoured conning tower, causing it to vibrate violently sending clouds of gas and smoke into the ship but doing no serious damage. Similarly, a 12-inch shell from *Agincourt* struck *Markgraf* and broke up on impact on her armour plate, bending it inward and damaging some items on deck, but causing no serious problems. Two hits by the same ship on *Kaiser* made a hole in the casement armour around the secondary armament, but the charge did not explode and burnt out harmlessly. Even the 15-inch shells sometimes caused little damage. A strike by either *Barham* or *Valiant* on *Grosser Kurfust* made a hole in her armour, but seems to have exploded outside the hull, doing little damage and causing no casualties. Three more huge shells from the same source on the same victim did some hull damage and damaged two of the casement guns, but the ship was not seriously wounded. She certainly would have been if the shells had penetrated and burst correctly. The British problem was not that their shells did not hit the enemy, but that when they did hit their target, even the most formidable of them did not penetrate the armour before exploding, negating the value of the much heavier British armament. No doubt the lighter protective armour of the British ships was also a contributory factor in the disastrous vulnerability of British battle cruisers, but it was not the critical one. The problem is very evident when we look at the statistics related to all the battle cruisers on both sides:

	Ammunition Used	*Hits on Ship*	*Casualties*
British			
Lion	326	13	150
Tiger	303	15	70
Queen Mary	150 est	7	1274
Princess Royal	230	9	103
*New Zealand***	420	1	–
Invincible	110 est	5	1027
Indefatigable	40 est	5	1019
Indomitable	175	–	–
Inflexible	88	–	–
German			
Lutzow	380 est	24	165
Seydlitz	376	22	153
Derfflinger	385	17	183
Moltke	359	5	40
Von der Tann	170	4	46

* The Captain of *New Zealand* (Captain John Green) had been presented with a talisman by a Maori chief. He was assured that if he hung it round his neck in battle, the ship and her crew would be quite safe. Although *New Zealand* was in the thick of the fighting the charm seems to have been extremely effective. Unkind observers suggested that it was too strong and worked to protect the enemy too, New Zealand's gunnery being notoriously shaky.

Note: Casualties noted in this table include those killed, wounded and taken prisoner.

Among battle cruisers which did not blow up, casualties on both sides appear to have been similar in the case of ships hit roughly the same number of times, suggesting that the better German protective armour and the inadequacies of British shells were offset by the effect of the heavier calibre of the British guns. There is no evidence here that the British suffered more casualties due to their lighter armour.

The relative vulnerability of British dreadnought ships seems to have been confined to the battle cruisers. In the case of the rival battleships, the most striking fact is that none of the dreadnought battleships involved at Jutland was lost on either side. Three, *Warspite, Marlborough* and *Ostfriesland*, retired with serious damage, but eventually all three of them got home safely. Two of these ships were most severely damaged not by gunfire, but by underwater weapons. It seems that the heavy defensive armour of German battleships was adequate for resisting the British 15-inch shells, and even the more lightly protected British battleships were able to stand up to multiple German 11 or 12-inch strikes without suffering fatal damage. Considering dreadnought battleships on both sides, protection seems to have been more than adequate to stand up to hits from the guns of the time. The situation might of course have been different if British shells had worked properly.

The fast battleships of 5BS and the German *Konigs* bore the brunt of enemy fire and were in the forefront of the fighting, receiving the most severe punishment:

	Ammunition Used	Hits on Ship	Casualties
British			
Warspite	259	15	46
Malaya	215	7	131
Valiant	288	–	1
Barham	337	6	72
German			
Konig	167	10	72
Grosse Kurfust	135	8	25
Markgraf	254	5	24
Kronprinz	144	–	–

Note: Casualties include those killed and wounded and taken prisoner.

By the gruesome standards of the First World War, the casualty figures for battleships on both sides are quite modest. Of these ships only *Warspite* had to pull out of the battle due to her steering problems, but she remained a formidable fighting ship and was never in any danger of sinking.

In summary, it is impossible to avoid the conclusion that there is one clear reason for the heavy British losses at Jutland – the ammunition handling in the battle cruisers. The inadequate protection afforded by their lighter armour was certainly a handicap, but the relatively modest casualty figures in the ships that survived and in the battleships suggest that this was not a critical weakness.

It is always interesting for historians (and perhaps also for their readers), to speculate on what might have happened if some crucial events had turned out differently. Jellicoe had hoped to catch up with the High Seas Fleet on the morning of 1 June somewhere in the Helgoland Bight and inflict a crushing defeat on it, using his commanding superiority in battleships to do so. In the light of the figures for casualties and the quite limited extent of damage done to battleships on both sides by gunfire, it seems a little unlikely that such an outcome could have occurred. Battleships on both sides seem to have had a rather small chance of doing each other fatal damage. Quite possibly the two most severely disabled German battle cruisers, *Seydlitz* and

Derfflinger, would have succumbed to any further heavy shell hits, but indeed so might any of the British battle cruisers in which dangerous cordite was still being held in the turrets. The British battleships would have been able to take advantage of their superior speed (Scheer still being hampered by the pre-dreadnoughts) and firepower to pound the enemy, but the excellent protective armour of their opponents and their proximity to their base might well have saved them from the most serious losses. Possibly Scheer himself might have escaped with his dreadnought battleships, sacrificing the pre-dreadnoughts and his battered battle cruisers in a rear guard action. Jellicoe would have had to take great care to avoid straying into minefields that abounded in the Bight. Any damaged British ships would have had to contend with a rising North Sea gale on their way home. Overall, the possibility of a dawn encounter resulting in a crushing victory for the British does not seem at all certain.

If Jellicoe can be criticised for his handling of the battle, it is in his failure to put more substantial obstacles in the way of the High Seas Fleet's escape to the Horn Reefs. Although he did not expect the High Seas Fleet to take this route home, it was obviously a strong possibility that Scheer might select it. By the evening of 31 May, it was too late to communicate with the submarines waiting under water at the entrance to the passage, but *Abdiel's* exploit showed that aggressive mine laying could be carried out effectively. Mines could be laid in 1916 by surface ships or by submarines and had Jellicoe (or the Admiralty) had the foresight to provide the Grand Fleet with more mine laying capacity, a more extensive mine trap near the Reefs could have done more damage and at much less risk than a surface action. In particular, Britain had five large mine laying submarines in commission (*E41, E34, E45, E46,* and *E51*). Each of these had a capacity for twenty mines as well as their torpedo armament. If some of them had been deployed at the same time as the Grand Fleet put to sea and operated in conjunction with it, they might have been extremely effective. One of the outstanding lessons of naval warfare in the First World War was that mines destroyed far more warships on both sides (150 German and 46 British), than gunfire and torpedoes combined.

In addition to its abysmal failure to communicate accurate information to Jellicoe, the Admiralty has been criticised for holding back the Harwich force of destroyers and light cruisers and using them only to help escort some of the damaged ships home. Tyrwhitt's force were certainly some of the most experienced and capable small ships in the Royal Navy, and had they materialized to the west of the High Seas Fleet on the evening of 31 May they might have done a lot of damage. This possibility however, must be considered in the context of the poor night fighting capability of the Grand Fleet and the difficulty its ships had in distinguishing friend from foe. The appearance of a new British force from an unexpected quarter would have posed some obvious risks, and probably the Admiralty was right to withhold the Harwich ships.

From a strategic point of view, how much did the Royal Navy's failure to overwhelm the High Seas Fleet really matter? Of course a crushing victory would have made wonderful headlines and would have been a tonic for the nation's morale, but it would have made minimal difference to the work of the blockade enforcing small ships which ultimately held the key to Germany's defeat, nor would it have had much effect on the German submarine campaign which was renewed with a vengeance a few months after Jutland. What mattered was that the Grand Fleet survived as by far the most powerful naval force in the North Sea, and the attempt by Germany to challenge it had failed. As one reporter succinctly put it 'The German Fleet has assaulted the jailor but is still in jail.' Not one bag of extra fertiliser, not one pound more food and not a single extra item of machinery reached Germany as a result of the Imperial Navy's efforts at Jutland.

The leading naval strategist of the period, Sir Julian Corbett, put it perfectly with a lawyers precision and economy of words, '*The object of naval warfare must always be, directly or indirectly, either to secure command of the sea, or to prevent the enemy from securing it.*' Britain had command of the sea from August 1914 until the end of the war and the German fleet never came close to wresting it from her. Jutland was a failed attempt to challenge this situation and the failure rendered any further such attempt impractical.

Chapter Eleven

After Jutland

During the remainder of 1916 the German High Command mounted a vigorous and ultimately successful campaign to force the Kaiser to defy his Chancellor, Bethmann-Hollweg, and release the U-boats to conduct unrestricted submarine warfare against Britain, its allies and the neutral ships which supplied war materials and food to them. Until this was achieved however, Scheer determined to continue his policy of attempting to isolate and destroy a section of the Grand Fleet. By August his strength had been supplemented by the addition of two more battleships, *Konig Albert* and the mighty *Bayern* with her 15-inch guns. As he now had only two serviceable battle cruisers (*Moltke* and *Von der Tann*), *Bayen*, *Grosser Kurfust* and *Markgraf* were transferred to Hipper's scouting group on a temporary basis. On 18 August, this force set out on an attempt to carry out the exercise which had originally been planned to take place in May. The scouting group would bombard Sunderland so as to lure Beatty from his anchorage at Rosyth and then lead him onto the guns of the High Seas Fleet's battleships waiting over the horizon. Two lines of U-boats would also be lying off the north-east coast waiting to trap warships coming south. Scheer did not want to run the risk again of encountering the whole Grand Fleet as he had at Jutland, so he insisted on very extensive airship reconnaissance. This meant that clear weather, without too much cloud cover or strong winds, was essential. The plan might have worked if Room 40 had not got wind of what was happening long before the High Seas Fleet sailed. Both Beatty and Jellicoe were well prepared with six battle cruisers and twenty-five battleships at sea even before Hipper was out of the Jade. This time Tyrwhitt was also ordered to move north towards the scene of the action. Submarines were also deployed in the path of the High Seas Fleet.

At 5 am, the British submarine *E-23* hit the battleship *Westfalen* with a torpedo and she had to return to base. An hour later, the light cruiser *Nottingham*, one of Goodenough's flotilla scouting for Beatty, was hit by three torpedoes from *U.52* and sank. Goodenough signalled the news of this to Jellicoe, stating that he did not know if the damage had been caused by mines or torpedoes. Jellicoe, afraid of being led over a mine trap, immediately reversed course and steamed north until Goodenough was able to confirm that torpedoes had certainly been to blame. This suggested that it was safe for the Grand Fleet to forge southwards again towards the enemy, which it immediately did. These manoeuvres seem to have confused the watching Zeppelins, and confusion was increased when another Zeppelin, *L13*, happened to see the Harwich force steaming north. Tyrwhitt's light cruisers were misidentified as battleships by *L13*, which reported them to Scheer. Assuming that this was Beatty's Battle Cruiser Force, Scheer turned south to the attack, but shortly afterwards received an alarming signal from one of his U-boats telling him that the whole Grand Fleet was only three hour's steaming to the north. Now convinced that he was running into a trap, Scheer turned round and returned home, ordering Hipper to follow him. One final disappointment was in store for Jellicoe, who had hoped that this time he might be poised for the decisive victory that had eluded him at Jutland. The light cruiser *Falmouth* was torpedoed and sunk on the way home.

In October, Scheer had one last try, but once again the British were forewarned and this time submarines were deployed into the Bight before the Germans put to sea. The light cruiser *Munchen* was torpedoed by *E-38* shortly after leaving the Jade, and Scheer, believing himself to be trapped in his home port, abandoned the venture.

Apart from some expeditions against the Russians in the Baltic and a few unsuccessful sorties by battle cruisers and light forces, several of which resulted in heavy German ships being torpedoed by the increasingly formidable British submarine force, the High Seas Fleet was confined to port for the rest of the war. Boredom, poor food and inconsiderate treatment by their officers began to take a deadly grip on the seamen. Many of the best officers and men volunteered for the U-boat service. By mid-1918, proud ships like *Von der Tann* and *Derfflinger* had become hotbeds of revolt and when the fleet was ordered to make its final 'Death Ride', charging into the southern North Sea and bombarding the Belgian coast and shipping in the Thames Estuary, the crews simply refused to sail.

While the High Seas Fleet was rusting in port however, the Imperial Navy had developed a new strategy that could, if it had been adopted earlier and pursued relentlessly, have won the war for Germany. Admiral Henning von Holtzendorff, a friend and former commanding officer of Scheer, was the leader of a group of senior officers of both the army and the navy trying to force the Kaiser to lift the restrictions on submarine warfare. Holtzendorff produced a detailed paper proving that if the U-boats could sink 600,000 tons of shipping a month for five months, Britain would be forced to sue for peace. The paper was closely argued and laden with statistics. Furthermore, it asserted that even if (as was likely) unrestricted submarine warfare drove the Americans into the war on the Allied side, they would not have time to mobilize before Britain had capitulated, and in any case it would be impossible for them to ship troops or supplies across the Atlantic due to the danger from U-boats. In January 1917 the Kaiser finally assented, overriding the objections of Bethmann-Hollweg.

From February 1917 onwards, the ferocious war with the U-boats was waged and at first it seemed clear that Holtzendorff had been correct. The U-boats were actually exceeding their target of 600,000 tons a month and the Admiralty was at a loss to know what to do. British food stocks were reduced to a few weeks supply.

At the end of April, after much prevarication and debate, the Prime Minister, Lloyd George, forced the admirals to release destroyers from the Grand Fleet and use them to convoy merchant ships, thus dramatically reducing the chances of a successful submarine attack. At the same time, the Allies undertook the prodigious task of building mine and net barriers across the English Channel, and from the Orkneys to the Norwegian coast. American destroyers joined the convoying forces and American ships and mines and minelayers began to appear in significant numbers. An American squadron joined the battleships at Scapa. Gradually, merchant shipping losses declined and U-boat losses increased. By April 1918, merchant ship new builds were exceeding losses to submarines, thus finally turning the tide of the struggle. Significantly, not a single troopship coming from America was lost in the course of the war. The U-boat offensive was just too little and just too late.

The Admiralty had by 1916, abandoned its opposition to strategic mining, sowing the Bight, and indeed much of the North Sea, with minefields that made any enemy naval operation extremely dangerous. Almost 200,000 British and American mines were eventually laid by the end of the war, more than half of them in the waters adjacent to the German coasts.

The ultimate failure of the U-boat offensive serves to underline the folly of the Kaiser and of Tirpitz in building the High Seas Fleet at all. Building those splendid warships consumed Germany's limited resources of men, raw material and industrial capacity, inhibiting, at least until 1917, her capacity to maximize the strength of her submarine fleet. One single battleship consumed about the same level of resources as twenty submarines and an extra twenty boats in the Western Approaches might well have been enough to turn the course of the war. The Kaiser's court seems to have been incapable of clear strategic thinking in naval affairs and thus squandered the superb skills of German naval engineering and the courage, expertise and devotion of the officers and men of the Imperial Navy. The correct strategy for Germany would have been to build a powerful U-boat force for offensive operations against Allied mercantile and naval shipping and develop a strong coastal defence force of land based artillery, submarines, destroyers, light cruisers and shallow draft gunboats, supported by a massive defensive and offensive mine laying operation using small, fast, expendable ships. As the great Bismarck had stated before he was dismissed, the only effects of Germany's building a battle fleet would be to make an enemy of the British and to divert resources from the army. Events were to prove him exactly correct.

Inconclusive and unsatisfactory as it was, Jutland was a clear statement of British naval supremacy and a vindication of the cautious tactics which Jellicoe had stated so clearly in his communications with his superiors. Even after such a disappointing performance, the Royal Navy still commanded the North Sea and the Western Approaches. The tactical failures and the poor performance of many of the British subordinate commanders in comparison to their German opposite numbers reflected their upbringing in the constricted environment of the Royal Navy in the Victorian and the Edwardian eras, which had proved impossible to correct. For generations British naval forces had been so obviously superior to those of other nations that procedures, attitudes and disciplines had become ossified and unable to arise to the challenge of twentieth century warfare. Even these weaknesses however, did not prevent the Grand Fleet from remaining in control of the North Sea or loosen its stranglehold on German maritime commerce. This was the key to ultimate victory.

Chronology of the Battle

30 May

22.30	Grand Fleet puts to sea

31 May

01.00	Hipper's battle cruisers put to sea
02.00	High Seas Fleet puts to sea
12.00	2nd Battle Squadron from Cromarty meets Jellicoe's fleet as ordered
12.48	Admiralty informs Jellicoe that High Seas Fleet is in Jade
12.00	High Seas Fleet passes Horn Reefs.
14.00	N.J Fjord spotted by German and British light forces
14.15	Battle Cruiser Force turns north to join Jellicoe
14.28	British light cruisers fire on German destroyers
14.32	British battle cruisers turn south
14.38	5BS turns south to follow battle cruisers.
14.51	Rival battle cruisers sight each other
15.10	*Engadine* launches her aircraft
15.40	Hipper turns south to lead Beatty onto High Seas Fleet
15.47	*Engadine* recovers aircraft
15.48	*Lutzow* opens fire on *Lion*
16.03	*Indefatigable* blows up
16.11	5BS opens fire
16.20	Destroyers of both sides launch attack on rival battle cruisers
16.26	*Queen Mary* blows up
16.46	High Seas Fleet sighted, battle cruisers turn north
16.57	5BS turns north
17.40	*Wiesbaden* damaged, Hood's 3rd Battle Cruiser Squadron in action.

17.56	BCF in sight of Grand Fleet
18.15	Battle Cruiser Force junction with Grand Fleet. Destroyers in action.
18.25	*Defence* sunk. *Warspite's* steering problems. *Onslow* attacks. Grand Fleet deploys.
18.33	*Invincible* blows up.
18.35	High Seas Fleet turns south-west.
18.55	Attack by German destroyers.
18.56	Grand Fleet turns south-west to get between High Seas Fleet and its base.
19.10	High Seas Fleet turns eastwards towards Grand Fleet.
19.18	Death ride of German battle cruisers. German destroyers attack.
19.20	High Seas Fleet turns away. German destroyers fire torpedoes. British turn to avoid them.
19.32	German destroyers drop smoke floats.
20.30–21.00	Final actions between light cruisers, battle cruisers and German pre-dreadnoughts.
21.15	Grand Fleet in night cruising formation.
22.45	*Frauenlob* sunk.
23.20 approx.	*Tipperary* sunk, *Elbing* sunk, *Spitfire* damaged by collision with *Nassau*. *Ardent* and *Fortune* sunk.
23. 40 approx.	High Seas Fleet passing between British battleships and light forces. *Rostock* torpedoed.

1 June

00.10	*Black Prince* explodes.
01.45	*Lutzow* scuttled.
02.10	*Pommern* torpedoed.
02.40	*V4* torpedoed.
03.00	High Seas Fleet at Horn Reefs Light Vessel.
05.20	*Ostfriesland* mined.

Appendix II

British and German Dreadnought Battleships

The first generation of British dreadnought battleships, the *Bellerophons*, were virtual repeats of *Dreadnought* herself. Ten guns were mounted in five turrets, three on the centreline and two wing turrets, only one of which could be used at any one time. The secondary armament was rather weak, consisting of sixteen 4-inch guns, eight of which were placed on top of the main turrets, meaning that they could not fire independently of the main armament. These ships saw very little action during the war, except that *Dreadnought* herself rammed and sank a U-boat. *Bellerophon*, *Superb* and *Temeraire* were at Jutland, but not in the thick of the fighting. Between them they fired 188 12-inch shells. *Dreadnought* herself had been detached from the Grand Fleet to support the Dover Patrol and the defences of the English Channel. (Plan 1).

The *Neptune* and *St Vincent* classes were quite similar to the *Bellerophons*, but had an improved layout of the main armament with one after turret superfiring over the top of the other. However, this arrangement could only be used when the guns were firing a broadside. If they were trained fore and aft, men in the lower turret would be concussed when the upper one was fired. All ten guns could fire a broadside together, although this imposed a serious strain on the hull. All six *Neptunes* were at Jutland and fired between them over 500 rounds, suffering no substantial damage. The three later ships in the class, *Neptune*, *Collossus* and *Hercules* had slightly enhanced armour protection, a single mast and slightly more power. (Plan 2).

The four ships of the *Orion* class were a substantial improvement on those that had gone before. Fitted with ten 13.5-inch guns in five turrets, all mounted on the centreline and which were designed to withstand the shock of superfiring, they could in practice, bring far more weight of fire down on an enemy ship. They also had better protection than the *Neptunes*. All four fought at Jutland, suffering little damage and getting off almost 200 rounds. They were followed by the four ships of the *King George V* class that were almost identical, except that they mounted an improved version of the 13.5-inch gun, giving a slightly higher velocity. One of them, *Audacious*, was mined and lost as a result of an inexcusable failure to close watertight doors in 1914. The other three fought at Jutland. They were the last battleships completed before the outbreak of war. (Plan 3).

The *Iron Duke* class closely followed the *King George V's* and had a very similar layout, but incorporated better secondary armament of twelve 6-inch guns and three anti-aircraft guns. Three of the four ships were at Jutland, *Marlborough* being the only one to suffer serious damage. They fired almost 300 13.5-inch rounds between them.

The five fast battleships of the *Queen Elizabeth* class were a leap forward in warship design. Much faster and more powerful than their predecessors, they also mounted eight 15-inch guns, the most formidable weapons at sea at that time. They were oil burners, thus saving much weight and space and giving scope to add extra protection. They were intended to act as a powerful forward element of the battle fleet, carrying out a scouting as well as a fighting role. (Plan 4). They were followed by five similarly armed ships of the *Royal Sovereign* class, which were slower and less powerful, being intended to form a part of the main battle fleet formation. The *Queen Elizabeths* played a pivotal role in the Jutland battle, showing their formidable firepower and also demonstrating their ability to absorb terrible punishment whilst sustaining relatively few casualties. At least twenty-four hits were scored by them during the 'Run to the South' and the 'Run to the North' phases of the battle. *Royal Oak* and *Revenge*, of the Royal Sovereign class, fought at Jutland, firing 38 and 102 15-inch rounds respectively. They probably scored fourteen hits between about 6.15 pm and nightfall, although some of these 15-inch hits may be attributable to the *Queen Elizabeths*. (Plan 5).

The Germans were horrified when they heard of *Dreadnought* as it rendered their whole, recently built battle fleet, obsolete. They eventually resolved to convert ships already on the drawing boards to dreadnought standards, the first of these, *Nassau* being completed in 1909, three years after *Dreadnought*. The *Nassaus* were specifically designed to fight in the North Sea and it was decided that as visibility there was seldom more than ten miles, guns did not require very long-range capability. They therefore settled on twelve 11-inch main armament. The turrets were so positioned however, that only a maximum of eight guns could be used at a time. To deal with any attacking destroyers they had twelve 5.9-inch and sixteen 3.4-inch secondary armament. The 5.9's were extremely effective weapons with a range of over 14,000 yards (later increased to over 16,000) they could and did, play a part in the actions between capital ships, as well as driving off intruding destroyers. The *Nassau's* reciprocating engines limited their speed to below twenty knots. Initially they burnt coal only, oil injection was added later in an attempt to increase maximum speed. Their great strengths were their formidable defensive armour and their excellent underwater protection. Making use of their eighty-nine foot beam, their hulls were divided into many watertight compartments, and longitudinal torpedo bulkheads ensured that damage from mine or torpedo strikes would be minimized. The four *Nassaus* all fought at Jutland, getting off between them 245 rounds and sustaining no very serious damage. (Plan 6).

The next generation of battleships, the *Helgolands*, were virtually a scaled up version of the same design. (Plan 7). They mounted twelve 12-inch guns as their main armament and were both longer and broader in the beam, giving space for more powerful engines and making them about half a knot faster. Once again the layout of the main battery meant that only eight guns could bear at a time. The *Helgolands* played an important part in the Jutland battle, *Helgoland* suffering a 15-inch hit from 5BS, but sustaining little damage. *Ostfriesland* was seriously damaged by a mine.

In 1910, a major step forward was made in battleship design with the *Kaiser* class. These were turbine powered and consequently faster than their predecessors, achieving up to twenty-three knots, far in excess of their design specification. They had an improved main battery layout with one of the aft turrets superfiring over the other, and two wing turrets. This allowed the main armament to be reduced from twelve guns in previous classes to ten without reducing the weight of broadside. In theory all ten guns could bear on a target on the beam, although in practice this was seldom achieved as it involved one wing turret firing across the deck of the ship. (Plan 8). They fired between them over 620 rounds at Jutland and absorbed numerous hits themselves without suffering severe damage.

The *Konigs* represented another major step forward. Once again there were only ten guns in the main battery, but these were all mounted on the centreline, allowing a genuine ten-gun broadside. (Plan 9). Even better protected than their predecessors, they were to bear the brunt of the fighting between the main battle fleets as they were invariably stationed in the van of the fleet. They sustained numerous heavy hits from 12, 13 and 15-inch British guns and *Konig, Grosser Kurfust* and *Markgraf* were all seriously damaged, but remained able to steam and to fight.

Bayern and *Baden* were extremely formidable ships with good protection and 15-inch main armament. They were not ready for Jutland and never became involved in a fleet action.

	Hp	Engine	Speed	Main Armament	Turret Armour	Deck Armour	Wt Of Armour	War Displacement	Armour % Displacement	Fuel
British Dreadnought Battleships										
Dreadnought	23,000	Turbine	21Kt	10 X 12 Inch	11-4 Inch	4 Inch	5000	21845	22.9	Oil/Coal
Bellerophon	23,000	Turbine	20.75Kt	10 X 12 Inch	11-9 Inch	4 Inch	5430	22102	24.6	Oil/Coal
Superb	23,000	Turbine	20.75Kt	10 X 12 Inch	11-9 Inch	4 Inch	5430	22102	24.6	Oil/Coal
Temeraire	23,000	Turbine	20.75Kt	10 X 12 Inch	11-9 Inch	4 Inch	5430	22102	24.6	Oil/Coal
Collingwood	24,500	Turbine	21Kt	10 X 12 Inch	11-Inch	3 Inch	5590	23030	24.3	Oil/Coal
St Vincent	24,500	Turbine	21Kt	10 X 12 Inch	11-Inch	3 Inch	5590	23030	24.3	Oil/Coal
Vanguard	24,500	Turbine	21Kt	10 X 12 Inch	11-Inch	3 Inch	5590	23030	24.3	Oil/Coal
Neptune	25,000	Turbine	21Kt	10 X 12 Inch	11 Inch	3-4 Inch	5562	22720	24.5	Oil/Coal
Colossus	25,000	Turbine	21Kt	10 X 12 Inch	11 Inch	3-4 Inch	5562	23050	24.1	Oil/Coal
Hercules	25,000	Turbine	21Kt	10 X 12 Inch	11 Inch	3-4 Inch	5562	23050	24.1	Oil/Coal
Conqueror	27,000	Turbine	21Kt	10 X 13.5	11 Inch	2.5 Inch	6560	25870	25.4	Oil/Coal
Orion	27,000	Turbine	21Kt	10 X 13.5	11 Inch	2.5 Inch	6560	25870	25.4	Oil/Coal
Monarch	27,000	Turbine	21Kt	10 X 13.5	11 Inch	2.5 Inch	6560	25870	25.4	Oil/Coal
Thunderer	27,000	Turbine	21Kt	10 X 13.5	11 Inch	2.5 Inch	6560	25870	25.4	Oil/Coal
Ajax	31,000	Turbine	21Kt	10 X 13.5	11 Inch	4 Inch	7080	25700	27.5	Oil/Coal
Audacious	31,000	Turbine	21Kt	10 X 13.5	11 Inch	4 Inch	7080	25700	27.5	Oil/Coal
Centurion	31,000	Turbine	21Kt	10 X 13.5	11 Inch	4 Inch	7080	25700	27.5	Oil/Coal
King George V	31,000	Turbine	21Kt	10 X 13.5	11 Inch	4 Inch	7080	25700	27.5	Oil/Coal

Name										
Benbow	29,000	Turbine	21.25Kt	10 X 13.5	11 Inch	2.5 Inch	7925	30380	26.1	Oil/Coal
Iron Duke	29,000	Turbine	21.25Kt	10 X 13.5	11 Inch	2.5 Inch	7925	30380	26.1	Oil/Coal
Emperor Of India	29,000	Turbine	21.25Kt	10 X 13.5	11 Inch	2.5 Inch	7925	30380	26.1	Oil/Coal
Marlborough	29,000	Turbine	21.25Kt	10 X 13.5	11 Inch	2.5 Inch	7925	30380	26.1	Oil/Coal
Barham	76,575	Turbine	24Kt	8 X 15	13 Inch	3 Inch	8900	33000	27.0	Oil
Malaya	76,575	Turbine	24Kt	8 X 15	13 Inch	3 Inch	8900	33000	27.0	Oil
Queen Elizabeth	76,575	Turbine	24Kt	8 X 15	13 Inch	3 Inch	8900	33000	27.0	Oil
Warspite	76,575	Turbine	24Kt	8 X 15	13 Inch	3 Inch	8900	33000	27.0	Oil
Valiant	76,575	Turbine	24Kt	8 X 15	13 Inch	3 Inch	8900	33000	27.0	Oil
Ramilles	40,000	Turbine	22Kt	8 X 15	13 Inch	4 Inch	8380	31200	26.9	Oil
Resolution	40,000	Turbine	23Kt	8 X 15	13 Inch	4 Inch	8380	31200	26.9	Oil
Revenge	40,000	Turbine	23Kt	8 X 15	13 Inch	4 Inch	8380	31200	26.9	Oil
Royal Oak	40,000	Turbine	23Kt	8 X 15	13 Inch	4 Inch	8380	31200	26.9	Oil
Royal Sovereign	40,000	Turbine	23Kt	8 X 15	13 Inch	4 Inch	8380	31200	26.9	Oil
Agincourt	40,279	Turbine	22.4Kt	14 X 12	9 Inch	2.5 Inch	N/A	30,350		Oil/Coal
Canada	37,000	Turbine	22.42Kt	10 X 14	10 Inch	4 Inch	7000	32120	21.8	Oil/Coal
Erin	26500	Turbine	22Kt	10 X 13.5	11 Inch	3 Inch	4,207	25250	16.7	Oil/Coal

German Dreadnought Battleships

	Hp	Engine	Speed	Main Armament	Turret Armour	Deck Armour	Wt Of Armour	War Displacement	Armour % Displacement	Fuel
Nassau	22000	Piston	19.5Kt	12 X 11	11 Inch	3.15 Inch	6537	21210	30.8	Coal
Posen	22000	Piston	19.5Kt	12 X 11	11 Inch	3.15 Inch	6537	21210	30.8	Coal
Rheinland	22000	Piston	19.5Kt	12 X 11	11 Inch	3.15 Inch	6537	21210	30.8	Coal
Westfalen	22000	Piston	19.5Kt	12 X 11	11 Inch	3.15 Inch	6537	21210	30.8	Coal
Helgoland	28000	Piston	21Kt	12 X 12	10.6 Inch	3.15 Inch	8212	24312	33.8	Coal
Ostfriesland	28000	Piston	21Kt	12 X 12	10.6 Inch	3.15 Inch	8212	24312	33.8	Coal
Thuringen	28000	Piston	21Kt	12 X 12	10.6 Inch	3.15 Inch	8212	24312	33.8	Coal
Oldenburg	28000	Piston	21Kt	12 X 12	10.6 Inch	3.15 Inch	8212	24312	33.8	Coal
Kaiser	31000	Turbine	21Kt	10 X 12	11.81 Inch	4.72 Inch	10100	27400	36.9	Coal
Friedrich Der Gross	31000	Turbine	21Kt	10 X 12	11.81 Inch	4.72 Inch	10100	27400	36.9	Coal
Kaiserin	31000	Turbine	21Kt	10 X 12	11.81 Inch	4.72 Inch	10100	27400	36.9	Coal
Konig Albert	31000	Turbine	21Kt	10 X 12	11.81 Inch	4.72 Inch	10100	27400	36.9	Coal
Prinzregent Luitpold	26000	Turbine	20Kt	10 X 12	11.81 Inch	4.72 Inch	10100	27400	36.9	Coal
Konig	31000	Turbine	21Kt	10 X 12	11.81 Inch	3.94 Inch	10440	28148	37.1	Oil/Coal
Grosse Kurfurst	31000	Turbine	21Kt	10 X 12	11.81 Inch	3.94 Inch	10440	28148	37.1	Oil/Coal
Markgraf	31000	Turbine	21Kt	10 X 12	11.81 Inch	3.94 Inch	10440	28148	37.1	Oil/Coal
Kronprinz	31000	Turbine	21Kt	10 X 12	11.81 Inch	3.94 Inch	10440	28148	37.1	Oil/Coal
Bayern	48,000	Turbine	22Kt	8 X 15	13.78 Inch	4 Inch	12000	31691	37.9	Oil/Coal
Baden	48000	Turbine	22Kt	8 X 15	13.78 Inch	4 Inch	12000	31691	37.9	Oil/Coal

Appendix III

British and German Battle Cruisers

The three *Invincibles* were the first battle cruisers. (Plan 10). They were also the first warships able to maintain a speed for twenty-five knots for sustained periods in almost any weather conditions, thanks to their turbine engines, thus they were the perfect ships for operations like the Falklands battle. They were more than a match for any heavy cruiser, and offered the possibility of sustained command of the world's oceans. Longer and more powerful than contemporary battleships, they were extremely impressive, but their relatively light armour and poor underwater protection made them vulnerable in action against any ship with comparable armament. *Invincible* was lost at Jutland due to poor protection and dangerous ammunition handling practices. *Inflexible* was severely damaged by a mine in the Dardanelles. At Jutland, they were sharply engaged with the leading ships of the High Seas Fleet and with the enemy battle cruisers, firing at least 370 rounds. Their shooting seems to have been extremely good; they achieved sixteen hits, a better performance than any other squadron, British or German. *Inflexible* and *Indomitable* were not seriously damaged in the battle.

The *Indefatigables* were essentially slightly scaled up *Invincibles*. They made use of the extra twenty-five feet of length to give more space and a better arc of fire to the two wing turrets. They suffered the same deficiency in protective armour as their predecessors, *Indefatigable* herself blowing up at Jutland. *Australia* missed Jutland, being under repair after a collision with *New Zealand*. *New Zealand* survived the battle virtually unscathed having expended 420 rounds, more than any other British ship. (Plan 11).

The *Lion* class (Plan 12) were much bigger, faster and more heavily armed than previous battle cruisers, in fact they were bigger than the *Orion* class battleships. They were better protected than the *Invincibles*, but protection was still much inferior to that of the German battle cruisers. Their eight

13.5-inch guns were all mounted on the centreline, *Lion* and *Princess Royal* both had one turret mounted between their funnels, *Tiger* and *Queen Mary* had both fore and aft turrets superfiring and used a later mark of gun firing a slightly heavier shell. (Plan 13). All these ships were in the thick of the fighting at Jutland, *Queen Mary* being destroyed by a magazine explosion. *Lion* was the most severely damaged of the survivors, having been hit on a turret by a 13.5-inch shell from *Lutzow*, but she avoided disaster thanks to her better ammunition handling discipline and the prompt flooding of the magazine. Nevertheless, the single hit on her turret killed eighty crewmen.

German battle cruisers were designed from the first to be able to form part of a major battle fleet, acting as a fast scouting squadron and taking their place in the battle line. They were intended to fight primarily in the North Sea, not, like their British counterparts, to range the world's oceans. News of the British *Invincibles* convinced the *Admiralstab* that their own battle cruisers should be armed with eight 11-inch guns and be able to achieve a speed of at least twenty-four knots. This high-speed requirement dictated that they should be the first German turbine powered large warships. In practice their turbines were able to drive them at well over their designed speed.

The first of this new breed of ship was *Von der Tann*, (Plan 14) which came into service in 1911. Her fore and aft turrets were on the centreline and she had two wing turrets, able to train on either side so as to provide a full eight-gun broadside. The principle difference between *Von der Tann* and her British rivals was her far greater weight of armour both underwater and on her deck, turrets and sides. After the Dogger Bank action had shown that naval battles might be fought at ranges of more than 20,000 yards, her turrets were altered to enable the guns to be elevated to more than twenty degrees so as to increase effective range from 20,700 yards to 22,900 yards. She proved to be an excellent ship, tough, durable and fast, and her plunging shells, fired at high elevation, were extremely effective against weak British deck armour. At Jutland she was responsible for destroying *Indefatigable*, but was severely damaged by hits from *Barham*, *Tiger* and *Revenge*. All her turrets were put out of action for a time and her speed reduced, but she remained in the battle line.

Moltke and *Goeben* (Plan 15) were similar to *Von der Tann*, but increased in size and even more heavily armoured. They had ten 11-inch guns with one rear turret superfiring over the other, and two wing turrets. *Goeben* was transferred to Turkey in 1914, but *Moltke* played a major part in the Jutland battle and although hit at least five times by British shells, four of these being 15-inch rounds fired by 5BS, she was the least severely damaged of Hipper's force and became his flagship during the latter part of the battle.

Seydlitz was larger than *Moltke* but had similar armament, the extra weight being devoted to yet more protective armour and more powerful engines. Hit by one torpedo and over twenty heavy shells at Jutland, she was jointly responsible for the sinking of *Queen Mary* and possibly of *Invincible*. The amazing story of her return to harbour is narrated in the text.

Derfflinger, *Lutzow* and *Hindenburg* (Plan 16) were probably the best battle cruisers built by any combatant during the war. Originally, they were to be fitted with diesel engines for cruising, but this project was abandoned in favour of pure turbine power with furnaces burning both oil and coal. Turbines at the time had the disadvantage of rather high fuel consumption at cruising speeds, largely because the propellers were directly driven by the turbine shafts without a reduction gear. This meant that the propellers had to be very small and rotate extremely fast. Their armour was similar to that of *Seydlitz*, but their heavy guns were increased to eight 12-inch so as to give the possibility of successfully engaging British battleships. For the first time, all the turrets were mounted on the centreline. In service they were able to achieve twenty-eight knots, a full two knots more than their design speed. *Hindenburg* was not ready in time for Jutland, but *Derfflinger* and *Lutzow* were heavily engaged. *Derfflinger*, together with *Seydlitz*, was firing on *Queen Mary* when she blew up and was probably responsible for destroying *Invincible*. She herself was hit twenty-one times by heavy shells including nine devastating strikes during the 'death ride' at about 8.15 pm, after which she was virtually incapable of firing her main armament. She lost 157 dead and 26 wounded. Her condition after the battle is described in the text. *Lutzow* was the only German dreadnought lost at Jutland. She was initially Hipper's flagship, but when her wireless room was destroyed he had to leave her and search for a less damaged ship. In the first phase of the battle she hit *Lion* and *Barham*, and probably destroyed the hapless *Defence*. Together with *Derfflinger* she hit and destroyed *Invincible*. She herself was severely damaged by Hood's 3rd Battle Cruiser Squadron then mauled again during the 'death ride'. Altogether she suffered twenty-four heavy hits and became virtually helpless, taking on 2,300 tons of water. As most of the flooding was in the forward compartments she was severely down by the bows and any attempt to go ahead caused further damage and flooding. She attempted to make way astern, but soon the rudders and propellers lifted out of the water and her situation became hopeless. She was sunk by torpedoes from the destroyer *G38*. She suffered 128 casualties.

	Power	Engine	Speed	Main Armament	Wt Of Armour	War Displacement	Armour % Displacement	Fuel
British Battle Cruisers								
Indomitable	41,000	Turbine	25Kt	8 X 12	3460	20125	17.2	Oil/Coal
Inflexible	41,000	Turbine	25Kt	8 X 12	3460	20125	17.2	Oil/Coal
Invincible	41,000	Turbine	25Kt	8 X 12	3460	20125	17.2	Oil/Coal
Indefatigable	44,000	Turbine	25Kt	8 X 12	4000 Est	22080	18.1	Oil/Coal
Australia	44,000	Turbine	25Kt	8 X 12	4000 Est	22080	18.1	Oil/Coal
New Zealand	44,000	Turbine	25Kt	8 X 12	4000 Est	22080	18.1	Oil/Coal
Lion	76,000	Turbine	27Kt	8 X 13.5	6000 Est	35160	17.1	Oil/Coal
Princess Royal	76,000	Turbine	27Kt	8 X 13.5	6000 Est	35160	17.1	Oil/Coal
Queen Mary	83,000	Turbine	27Kt	8 X 13.5	5140	32160	16.0	Oil/Coal
Tiger	108,000	Turbine	29Kt	8 X 13.5	6000 Est	35160	17.1	Oil/Coal
German Battle Cruisers								
Von Der Tann	42,000	Turbine	27.75Kt	8 X 11 Inch	6201	21700	28.6	Coal
Moltke	52,000	Turbine	28Kt	10 X 11 Inch	7000 Est	25300	27.7	Coal
Gorben	52,000	Turbine	28Kt	10 X 11 Inch	7000 Est	25300	27.7	Coal
Seydlitz	63,000	Turbine	28Kt	10 X 11 Inch	7500 Est	28500	26.3	Coal
Derfflinger	63,000	Turbine	26.5Kt	8 X 12 Inch	7500 Est	31200	24.0	Oil/Coal
Lutzow	63,000	Turbine	26.5Kt	8 X 12 Inch	7500 Est	31200	24.0	Oil/Coal
Hindenburg	72,000	Turbine	27Kt	8 X 12 Inch	7500 Est	31500	23.8	Oil/Coal

Note: Speeds Given Indicate Design Maximum. In Service Some Of These Ships Were Able To Exceed These Speeds By At Least 2 Knots. Turbine Engines Often Delivered Well In Excess Of Their Rated Power.

Light Cruisers and Destroyers

Light Cruisers

Light cruisers on both sides played an important part in the battle in spite of their failure to scout as effectively as had been hoped. Many different designs were current, British ships being generally bigger and more heavily armed than the earlier German light cruisers, but quite similar to the more recent designs. Some examples of light cruisers at Jutland are as follows:

	Built	*Armament*	*Tons*	*Engine HP*	*Speed kt.*
Southampton	1912	8 x 6-inch	5,400	25,000	26.5
Birmingham	1913	9 x 6-inch	5,440	25,000	25.5
Chester	1915	10 x 5.5-inch	5,185	31,000	26.5
Elbing	1913	8 x 5.9-inch	5,252	30,000	27.5
Wiesbaden	1913	8 x 5.9-inch	6,601	31,000	27.5
Frauenlob	1901	10 x 4-inch	3,158	8,000	24.7

Light cruisers had poor armour protection, typically 3-inch belt armour and 1-inch deck. Gun crews were not in armoured turrets, but stood behind gun shields with their legs exposed to terrible damage by splinters. *Chester* for example, survived seventeen hits from 5.9-inch shells, suffering twenty-nine men killed and forty-nine wounded, the wounded mostly losing legs. All ships carried torpedo armament as well as guns.

Light cruisers were generally reasonable sea boats, but were not able to keep up with battle cruisers in rough weather.

The Germans lost four light cruisers at Jutland; *Wiesbaden, Elbing, Rostock* and *Frauenlob*. There were no British losses, although *Chester* and *Southampton* were badly damaged.

Destroyers

Most of the British destroyers at Jutland were of the 'K', 'L' or 'M' class. The main armament for all destroyers was their complement of torpedoes, but British destroyers also carried formidable gun armament that was occasionally effective against much larger ships. The Germans still referred to destroyers as 'Torpedo boats', emphasizing the importance they placed on underwater armament. In the early part of the war, German destroyers were much smaller than their British rivals, but by 1916 some much larger and formidable ships such as the S 31-36 class were joining the fleet.

There was no German equivalent to the British destroyer leaders which were all ships ordered by foreign navies before the war and completed to British requirements. The light cruisers used by the Germans to perform this role proved very effective in battle as was shown by *Regensburg's* exploits during the 'Run to the South'.

	Armament	*Tons*	*Knots*	*Torpedo Tubes*
K Class	3 x 4 inch	950	31	2 x 21-inch
L Class	3 x 4 inch	1,000	29	4 x 21-inch
M Class	3 x 4 inch	1,000	34	4 x 21-inch
Marksman class	4 x 4 inch	1,600	32	4 x 21-inch
G37–42	3 x 3.5 inch	8–950	33	6 x 19.7-inch
S31–36	3 x 3.5 inch	810	36	6 x 19.7-inch
V2–V6	2 x 3.5 inch	569	30	4 x 19.7-inch

In both navies, individual destroyers of a particular class might vary considerably. The figures given are typical of the class. Destroyers would become severely hampered in bad weather and often sustained damage; in heavy gales they had to adopt survival tactics.

The nomenclature of the German ships is a little confusing. The initial letter indicates the builder, the number the serial number of the order. B = Blohm & Voss, G = Germaniawerft, S = Schichau, V = Vulcan. British destroyers from the L class onward all had names beginning with the class letter, but the M class were so numerous that the letters N, O and P had to be used as well as M.

The British lost eight destroyers in the battle; *Ardent, Fortune, Nestor, Nomad, Shark, Sparrowhawk, Tipperary* (destroyer leader) and *Turbulent*. German losses were five, *S35, V4, V27, V29, and V48*.

Destroyers were not armoured. They could not survive a torpedo strike and would be terribly damaged by a hit from a heavy shell. Fortunately for them, armour-piercing shells frequently would go right through the hull without exploding. *G86* for example, was either hit or very closely missed by a 13.5-inch shell from *Iron Duke* and survived. Casualties in British destroyers sunk were very heavy, totalling 727 killed, wounded or taken prisoner. *Tipperary* suffered the most, losing 197 men, 185 killed, 4 wounded and 8 prisoners. She was destroyed by the 6-inch secondary battery of *Westfalen*. The Germans attributed the heavy losses in British destroyers partly to the fact that they were oil burners, oil being much more combustible than coal. Also, the heavy secondary armament of German battleships proved very effective against torpedo attack by small ships.

Appendix V

Order of Battle: Jutland

	Calibre Ins	No Of Guns	Projectile Wt Lbs	Total Wt Lbs
Grand Fleet				
2nd Battle Squadron – Vice-Admiral Sir M Jerram				
King George V	13.5	10	1400	14000
Ajax	13.5	10	1400	14000
Centurion	13.5	10	1400	14000
Erin	13.5	10	1400	14000
Orion	13.5	10	1250	12500
Monarch	13.5	10	1250	12500
Conqueror	13.5	10	1250	12500
Thunderer	13.5	10	1250	12500
4th Battle Squadron – Admiral Sir J Jellicoe				
Iron Duke	13.5	10	1400	14000
Royal Oak	15	8	1920	15360
Superb	12	10	850	8500
Canada	14	10	1586	15860
Benbow	13.5	10	1400	14000
Bellerophon	12	10	850	8500
Temeraire	12	10	850	8500
Vanguard	12	10	850	8500

	Calibre Ins	No Of Guns	Projectile Wt Lbs	Total Wt Lbs
1st Battle Squadron – Vice–Admiral Sir C Burney				
Marlborough	13.5	10	1400	14000
Revenge	15	8	1920	15360
Hercules	12	10	850	8500
Agincourt	12	14	850	11900
Colossus	12	10	850	8500
Collingwood	12	10	850	8500
Neptune	12	10	850	8500
St Vincent	12	10	850	8500
Total of Battleships:				**282980**
3rd Battle Cruiser Squadron – Rear–Admiral Sir H Hood				
Invincible	12	8	850	6800
Inflexible	12	8	850	6800
Indomitable	12	8	850	6800
Total Grand Fleet Battle Cruisers:				**20400**
Total Grand Fleet:				**303380**

1st Cruiser Squadron – Rear–Admiral Sir R Arbuthnot
Defence, Warrior, Duke of Edinburgh, Black Prince

2nd Cruiser Squadron – Rear–Admiral H L Heath
Minotaur, Hampshire, Cochrane, Shannon

4th Light Cruiser Squadron – Commodore C E Le Mesurier
Calliope, Constance, Caroline, Royalist, Comus

Attached Cruisers
Active, Bellona, Blanche, Boadicea, Canterbury, Chester.

4th Destroyer Flotilla – (Capt C J Wintour)
Tipperary (Destroyer Leader)
19 Destroyers

11th Destroyer Flotilla – (Commodore J R P Hawksley)
Castor (Light Cruiser)
15 Destroyers

!2th Destroyer Flotilla – (Captain A J B Stirling)
Faulknor (Destroyer Leader)
15 Destroyers

Attached ships
Abdeil (Minelayer) Oak (Destroyer tender)

Battle Cruiser Force

1st Battle Cruiser Squadron – (Vice-Admiral Sir D Beatty)

Lion	13.5	8	1250	10000
Princess Royal (Rear-Admiral O deB Brock)	13.5	8	1250	10000
Queen Mary	13.5	8	1400	11200
Tiger	13.5	8	1400	11200

2nd Battle Cruiser Squadron – (Rear Admiral W C Pakenham)

New Zealand	12	8	850	6800
Indefatigable	12	8	850	6800
Total of Battle Cruisers of Battle Cruiser Force:				**56000**

	Calibre Ins	No Of Guns	Projectile Wt Lbs	Total Wt Lbs
5th Battle Squadron – (Rear-Admiral H Evan-Thomas)				
Barham	15	8	1920	15360
Valiant	15	8	1920	15360
Warspite	15	8	1920	15360
Malaya	15	8	1920	15360
Total of 5th Battle Squadron:				61440
Total of Battle Cruiser Fleet:				117440
Total British Heavy Guns at Jutland:				420820

1st Light Cruiser Squadron – (Commodore E S Alexander-Sinclair)
Galatea, Phaeton, Inconstant, Cordelia

2nd Light Cruiser Squadron – (Commodore W E Goodenough)
Southampton, Birmingham, Nottingham, Dublin

3rd Light Cruiser Squadron – (Rear Admiral T D W Napier)
Falmouth, Yarmouth, Birkenhead, Gloucester

1st Destroyer Flotilla – (Captain D C Roper)
Fearless (Light Cruiser)
9 Destroyers

9/10th Destroyer Flotilla – (Commander M L Goldsmith)
Lydiard + 7 destroyers

13th Destroyer Flotills – (Captain J U Farie)
Champion (Light Cruiser)
10 Destroyers

Attached Ship
Engadine (Seaplane Carrier)

High Seas Fleet
3rd Battle Squadron

5th Division – (Rear-Admiral P Behnke)

Konig	12	10	893	8930
Grosser Kurfust	12	10	893	8930
Kronprinz	12	10	893	8930
Markgraf	12	10	893	8930

6th Division – (Rear Admiral H Nordmann)

Kaiser	12	10	893	8930
Kaiserin	12	10	893	8930
Prinzregent Luitpold	12	10	893	8930
Friedrich der Grosse	12	10	893	8930

1st Battle Squadron – (Vice-Admiral V Schmidt)
1st Division

Ostfriesland	12	12	893	10716
Thuringen	11	12	666	7992
Helgoland	11	12	666	7992
Oldenburg	11	12	666	7992

	Calibre Ins	No Of Guns	Projectile Wt Lbs	Total Wt Lbs
2nd Division – (Rear-Admiral W Engelhardt)				
Posen	11	10	666	6660
Rheinland	11	10	666	6660
Nassau	11	10	666	6660
Westfalen	11	10	666	6660
2nd Battle Squadron – (Rear-Admiral F Mauve)				
3rd Division				
Deutschland	11	4	529	2116
Hessen	11	4	529	2116
Pommern	11	4	529	2116
4th Division – (Rear-Admiral Freiherr von Dalwigk zu Lichtenfels)				
Hannover	11	4	529	2116
Schlesien	11	4	529	2116
Schleswig Holstein	11	4	529	2116
Total High Seas Fleet Battleships:				**145468**

4th Scouting Group (Light Cruisers) – (Commodore L von Reuter)

Stettin, Munchen, Hamburg, Frauenlob, Stuttgart

Destroyer Flotillas (Commodore E Michelsen)

Rostock (Light Cruiser) 32 Destroyers

Battle Cruiser Force

1st Scouting Group (Vice-Admiral F Hipper)

Lutzow	12	8	7144
Derfflinger	12	8	7144
Seydlitz	11	10	6660
Moltke	11	10	6660
Von der Tann	11	8	5328
Total Battle cruisers:			**32936**
Total German Heavy Guns at Jutland:			**178404**

2nd Scouting Group (Light Cruisers) – (Rear Admiral F Boedicker)

Frankfurt, Wiesbaden, Pillau, Elbing

Destroyer Flotillas – (Commodore P Heinrich)

Regensburg (Light Cruiser) 30 Destroyers

Charts

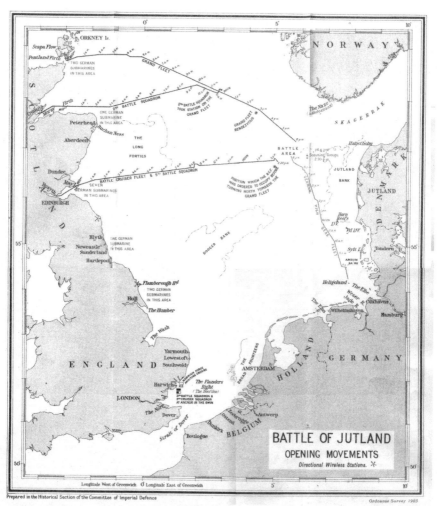

Chart 1: The chart shows the movements of the two fleets leading up to the battle. The High Seas Fleet steamed towards the Scagerak to try to intercept British ships enforcing the blockade in the northern North Sea and provoke the British battle cruisers to intervene. They followed a course taking them outside the Amrum Bank with Hipper's battle cruisers some 50 miles ahead of the battleships. The British sailed at a leisurely pace to intercept them, having been misinformed as to their time of departure. Beatty, with the Battle Cruiser Force was to scout ahead of the Grand Fleet and if he found nothing, to rendezvous with Jellicoe's battleships as shown. It was just as he was turning towards this rendezvous that the enemy was sighted.

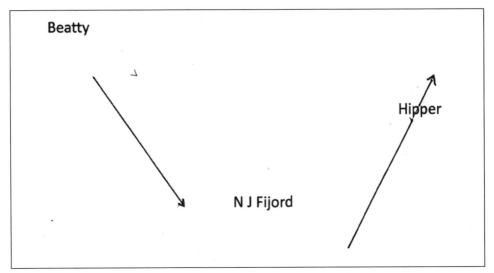

Chart 2: Had it not been for the neutral *N J Fijord*, Hipper would have slipped ahead of Beatty without either side being aware of the other's presence. The two fleets might then never have met. *N J Fijord* was intercepted by German light forces and as she stopped she let off steam, drawing British light cruisers to the scene. Fire was exchanged and the rival battle cruiser fleets clashed.

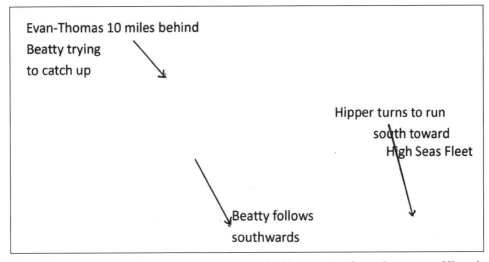

Chart 3: Beatty chases Hipper south eastwards, both sides opening fire at long range. Hipper's object is to bring the British battle cruisers under the guns of the High Seas Fleet battleships. The German battle cruisers sink *Indefatigable* and *Queen Mary* during the chase. Evan Thomas's fast battleships eventually manage to catch up with the battle just as the High Seas Fleet battleships come within range of Beatty's battle cruisers.

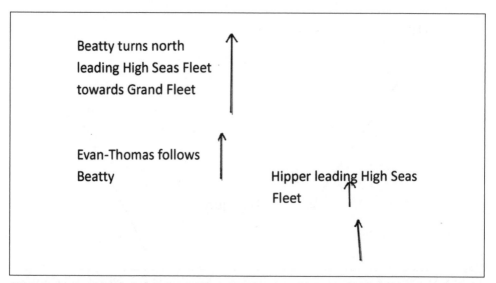

Chart 4: As soon as Beatty realises that the High Seas Fleet is at sea he turns north to lead them towards the Grand Fleet approaching from the north west. The British fast battleships bring up the rear, suffering heavy punishment from Hipper's ships and from the battleships of the High Seas Fleet. They themselves inflict serious damage on the German battlecruisers and on the battleships.

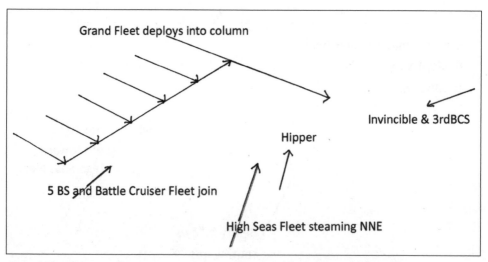

Chart 5: Beatty successfully leads the High Seas Fleet towards Jellicoe. Although he is unsure as to the exact position of the High Seas Fleet, Jellicoe deploys to port so as to get between it and its route home. The Battle Cruiser Force falls in astern of Jellicoe's battleships before pulling ahead in line with *Invincible*, which is re-joining the fleet from the east. Until this point Scheer has been unaware that the Grand Fleet is at sea.

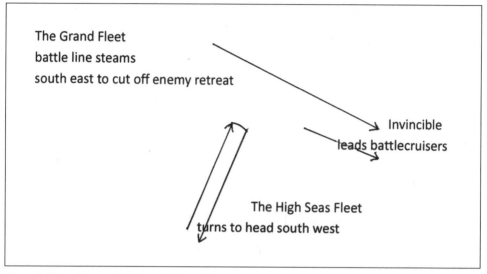

Chart 6: When he sees the Grand Fleet, Scheer turns round. The actual process of turning involves the rear ship of the column to turn first through 180 degrees and the rest of the fleet then turns in succession. During this time the leading ships of the High Seas Fleet are severely hammered. *Invincible* finds herself under fire from the enemy battle cruisers and is destroyed.

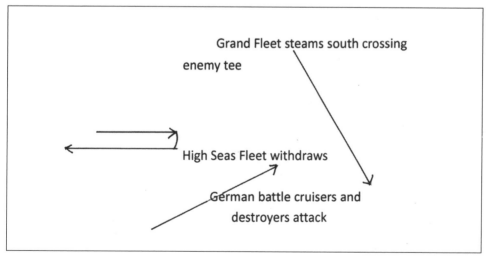

Chart 7: Scheer attempts to slip astern of the Grand Fleet and make for the Horn Reefs. Jellicoe is made aware of his new course by Goodenough. Faced by overwhelming fire the High Seas Fleet turns round once again. Its headlong retreat is covered by the battle cruiser's "death ride" and an attack by destroyers firing torpedoes and dropping protective smoke floats.

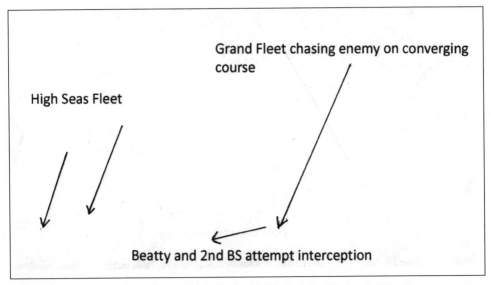

Chart 8: Both fleets are on a generally southerly course. Beatty, supported by light forces and by the Second Battle Squadron, attempts to cut across the bows of the High Seas Fleet, but poor visibility and uncertainty about the enemy's location frustrate this.

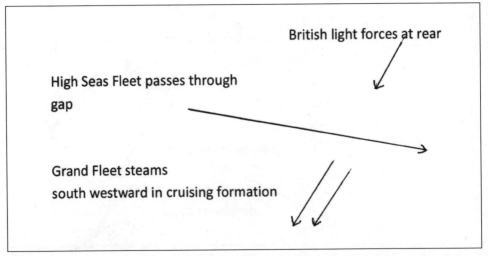

Chart 9: The Grand Fleet remains on a southerly course in night cruising formation. Light forces are disposed astern of it with a gap of about four miles. The High Seas Fleet locates and passes through this gap. There are sporadic fierce encounters with British light forces, but Scheer pushes relentlessly on towards the Horn Reefs.

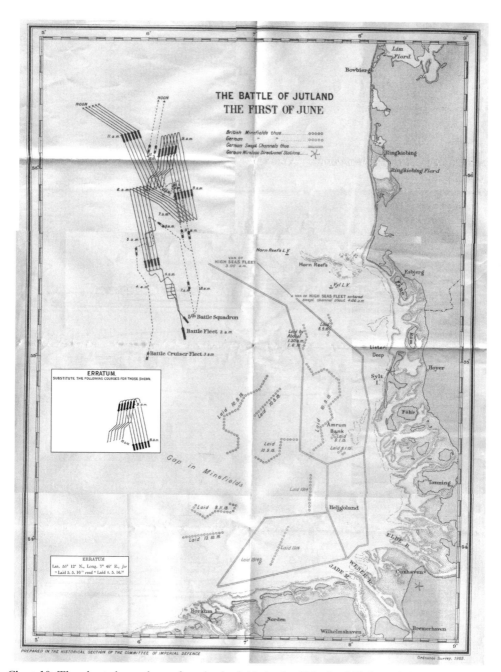

Chart 10: The chart shows the reefs and minefields in the Helgoland Bight and the disposition of the two fleets on 1 June. Note the extent of the various minefields. The High Seas Fleet followed the easternmost of the swept channels except for the damaged *Ostfriesland* which passed outside the Amrun Bank.

Appendix VII

Plans

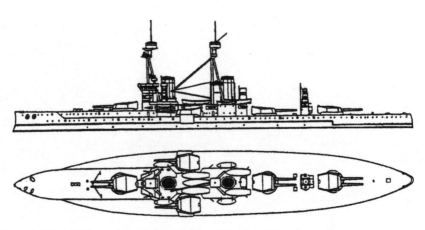

Plan 1. Bellerophon

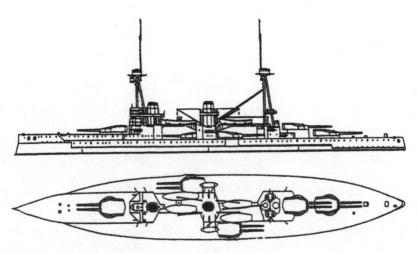

Plan 2. Neptune

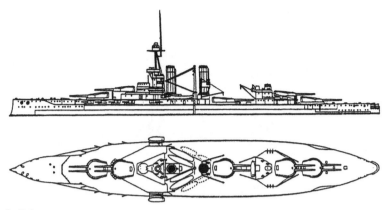

Plan 3. Orion

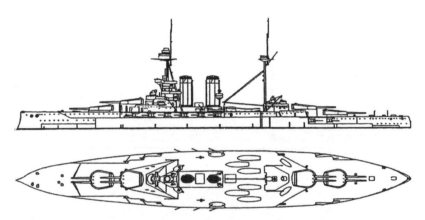

Plan 4. Queen Elizabeth

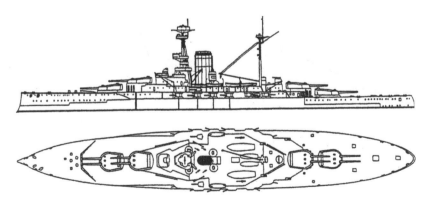

Plan 5. Royal Oak

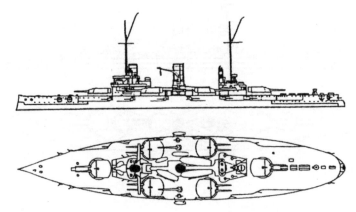

Plan 6. Nassau

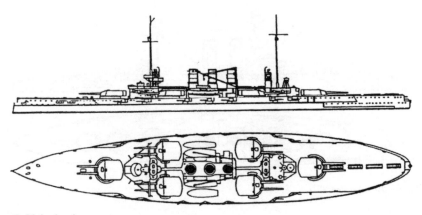

Plan 7. Helgoland

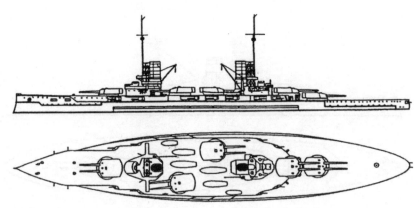

Plan 8. Kaiser

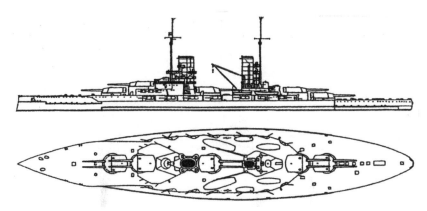

Plan 9. Konig

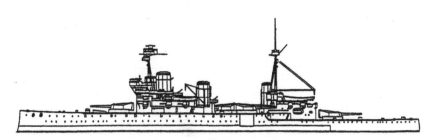

Plan 10. Invincible

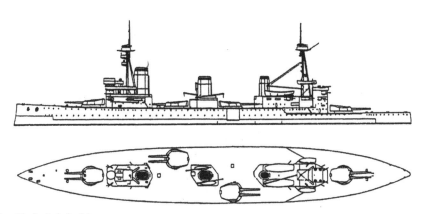

Plan 11. Indefatigable

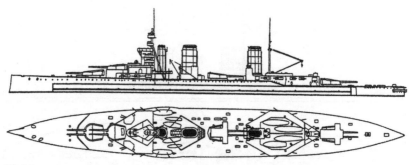

Plan 12. Lion

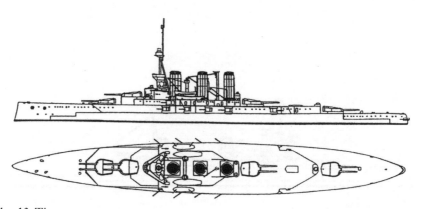

Plan 13. Tiger

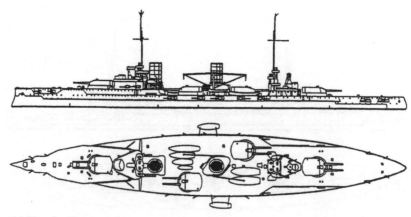

Plan 14. Von der Tann

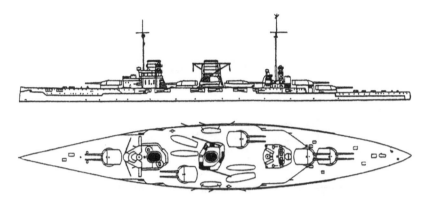

Plan 15. Moltke

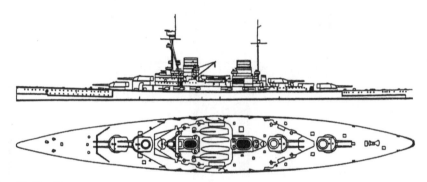

Plan 16. Derflinger

Appendix VIII

Drawings

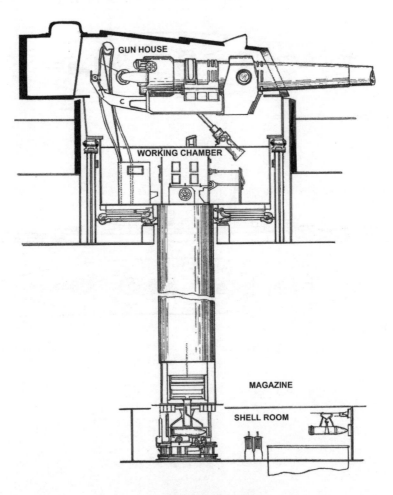

GUN HOUSE

WORKING CHAMBER

MAGAZINE

SHELL ROOM

15 - INCH GUN TURRET

A 15-inch gun turret as fitted to *Queen Elizabeth* and *Royal Sovereign* class battleships. This was an extremely efficient and reliable turret. Although slightly different to the turrets fitted to the ill-fated battle cruisers the principle is the same. In 1916 far too much cordite and too many shells were held in the working chamber and in the gun house itself, and trails of gunpowder spilt from the cordite bags onto the gun house floor. It is easy to see how these could explode and flash back down the trunk of the main cage lift into the magazines and cause a devastating explosion.

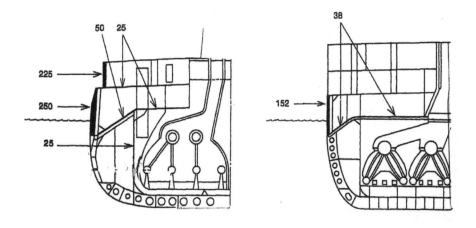

Von der Tann   **Invincible**

A comparison of the cross sections of *Invincible* and *Von der Tann*. Note the extra beam of the German ship giving much more space for underwater protection and the heavy side armour.

Letters

Remembering Daddy.

I wish Eva so much I could come and see you all tucked up in bed tonight and give you a good night kiss, but it must wait a little. I hope you are all very happy and I know you are all very good. Good night darlings. Ever so many kisses from

your loving Daddy

Lucy   Myrtle   Norah   Prudence

A busy man makes time for family. A letter sent by Jellicoe to his four daughters a few weeks before the battle. A kind and thoughtful family man, Jellicoe was inclined to overwork himself and at this point could only find time to write one letter to the four little girls at home.

Friends in the end. A most moving letter sent by the Kaiser, in exile in Holland, to Lady Jellicoe on the death of her husband. He had at one point commanded a German landing party in the China wars. The letter reads as follows:

"Madam,

It is with deep emotion I read your kind letter I received from Fritzie yesterday. How very kind of you to take this trouble on a day full of so many mournful duties and impressions and I beg to be allowed to thank you for this kind thought. I am glad that my dear grandson was enabled to represent me at Lord Jellicoe's funeral and in my name as Chief of my old Imperial Navy and of the officers and men still alive who once belonged to it, present our last respects to the illustrious Admiral, whose sterling qualities, as a gallant leader, splendid sailor, chivalrous antagonist and British gentleman will ever be treasured in our hearts.

I shall always gratefully remember the command given by the admiral to Capt. von (illegible), leader of the detachment of German sailors who had the honour of being placed under his orders during the Chinese campaign "Germans to the front". – Your appreciation of Fritzie's work for the better understanding between our two countries has given me deepest satisfaction, indeed it is high time the "two great nations" as British naval officers often say, should close in mutual friendship to save the peace of the world. Believe me Madam, with deep respect.

William"

Acknowledgements

There are a number of excellent recent books covering the Battle of Jutland or specific aspects of it among them:

Jutland: An analysis of the Fighting by John Campbell.

Castles of Steel by Robert Massie.

Flawed Victory by Keith Yates.

Jutland The German Perspective by V E Tarrant.

The Battle of Jutland by Geoffrey Bennett.

The Rules of the Game by Andrew Gordon.

Room 40 by Patrick Beesley.

British Battle cruisers 1914-18 by Laurence Burr.

German Battle cruisers 1914-18 by Gary Staff.

The British Naval Staff in the First World War by Nicholas Black.

Sources more contemporary with the battle include:

The Fighting at Jutland – A collection of survivor's memories is a fascinating read. Another eyewitness account is "Jutland: an Eye Witness Account of a Great Battle" assembled by Stuart Legg.

Naval Operations – Corbett is the official history of the war at sea, including charts.

Also interesting are:

The Grand Fleet, its creation, development and work. Admiral the Viscount Jellicoe.

The Truth about Jutland. Rear Admiral J E T Harper.

The Jutland Scandal. Admiral Sir Richard Bacon.

Fear God and Dread Naught. The correspondence of Admiral of the Fleet Lord Fisher edited by Arthur Marder.

Records. Admiral of the Fleet Lord Fisher.

The Life and Times of Admiral Lord Beatty. Rear Admiral W S Chalmers.

A Rough Record. Admiral W E Goodenough.

The First Destroyers. David Lyon

Destroyers of the Royal Navy. Maurice Cocker

A Naval Digression. "GF"

Note – All photographs by courtesy of the Imperial War Museum

Index